MW00667232

YES, Mary! (Cut out this order

Please send me:

☐ *The Collard Patch* (newly released story/cookbook)

☐ *Flavored with Love, Mary Lou's Family and Friends Can Cook, Third Edition*

(revised and expanded story/cookbook)

Name: (First)_____ (Last)_____

Mailing address:(Street)_____

(City)_____ (State)_____ (Zip)_____

Phone Number (if needed to check order):_____

I am enclosing:

☐ a check

☐ a money order

(To pay with a credit card, go to http://www.CollardLovers.com or http://www.FlavoredWithLove.com and make your purchase.)

Send the cookbook to:

☐ the address listed above (We promise not to share your personal information with anyone.)

OR (for gifts) to ☐ Name:

(First)_____ (Last)_____

Mailing address:(Street)_____

(City)_____ (State)_____ (Zip)_____

Here's my e-mail address so I can receive future special offers and announcements:_____

Order several! They make GREAT GIFTS
for friends, relatives, and special occasions!

The Collard Patch	$22.97	X __ (number of books)	$
Flavored with Love, Third Edition	$22.97	X __ (number of books)	$
U. S. Shipping and Handling	4.00	X __ (number of books)	$
Gift Wrapping + Gift Card	4.00	X __ (number of books)	$
Sales Tax (Louisiana Residents 8.5%)	1.95	X __ (number of books)	$
TOTAL	XX	XXXXX	$ _____

Mail order to: Blue Moon Books—Louisiana
207 N. Service Rd. E. #213
Ruston, LA 71270 Call us at 318-548-1716, if you have any questions.

For a special free gift visit us at: http://www.FlavoredWithLove.com/cpgift and http://www.CollardLovers.com/cpgift

Super Bargain!

Buy any 2 cookbooks for only $35.00 plus shipping and handling of $8.00 (and Louisiana tax, if you live in Louisiana).

This is a savings of $14.94!

—*The Collard Patch* (newly released story/cookbook) is all about collard greens—growing, cooking, and eating—and stories about growing up in Collard Country. **If you think you don't like collards, you haven't tasted *our* collards!**

—*Flavored with Love, Mary Lou's Family and Friends Can Cook, Third Edition* (revised and expanded story/cookbook) is a wonderful experience with recipes for some of the best food you'll ever put in your mouth and wonderful stories of life in the South. Imagine the delightful aromas wafting through your house as you enjoy the stories. **The earlier editions are completely sold out, and this one has many more recipes and wonderful stories!**

Order several! They make GREAT GIFTS
for friends, relatives, and special occasions!

☐ Mary, I can hardly wait for the delicious food and delightful stories! My check for $43.00 ($46.66 for Louisiana residents) is enclosed. **Please rush my order!**
BE SURE to put your address on the other side of this page.

Any Special Instructions?

For a **special free gift** visit us at: http://www.FlavoredWithLove.com/cpgift   and
http://www.CollardLovers.com/cpgift
(Give your friends a copy of this form.)

The Collard Patch

The Best Collard Cookbook In the World™

Collard Country Cookbook and Reader

Collards And Cornbread Y'all Will Love

By

Mary Lou Cheatham and Paul Elliott

2006

Blue Moon Books

Louisiana

The Collard Greens Experience

Read *The Collard Patch*.

You will be . . .
- Blessed by the memories of a callow youth in Collard Country
- Informed about the process of growing, gathering, cooking, and eating collards
- Enlightened by intriguing ways to cook cornbread

The Collard Patch is full of the gastronomic joy of Louisiana and Texas. Everywhere we go, people are trying to duplicate the pleasurable tastes we cook here. We are sharing *La Cuisine Texianne*™ with you in this book.

Cook these recipes.

You will enjoy your accomplishment. If you are not accustomed to eating collards, you will soon discover that you have missed incredibly tasty flavor. You will find yourself looking for collards every time you go to the grocery store.

Good luck shopping! The shelves labeled "collards" in the frozen food section are often empty. Try some of the lovely prepackaged fresh collards. If your store does not have these, demand them!

Eat this food—one of the world's healthiest vegetables!

You will be satisfied by the work of your hands. Your body will benefit from vitamins A, B, and C; calcium; beta-carotene; and fiber in a marvelous natural food free of fat and low in carbohydrates. Collards and olive oil (so healthy!) are a blissful match.

Share your pleasure.

We are simultaneously publishing two cookbook readers:
- *The Collard Patch*
- *Flavored with Love, Third Edition*

Buy several of each. Keep some on hand to give as wedding gifts, holidays that slip up on you, and times when you simply want to say, "I love you."

Write us with your recipes!

Send us your recipes, stories, and suggestions. You may be our guest in a future edition. Be sure to e-mail us and select your free gift. You will love what we have for you.

Collard green cuisine—experience it!

If you think you don't like collards, you haven't tasted *our* collards!

Copyright

The Collard Patch, Copyright 2006 by Mary Lou Cheatham and Paul Elliott

First Edition

Cover Design

Cover design by Austin Jones, Austin's Graphics, http://www.austinsgraphics.com. Photographs by Paul Elliott

Disclaimer

The stories in *The Collard Patch* are not intended to offend the sensibilities of the readers. This cookbook is meant to give some fresh ideas about preparing collards and cornbread and to give us something to make us smile while we cook.

All the recipes are real ones that work, and they are original in the earnest opinion of the cooks. Unless other authors are listed, the recipes are original recipes developed and tested by Mary and Paul. The authors and the publisher do not accept any responsibility for making people sick or overweight if they eat too much delicious food or food with ingredients not recommended by their doctors or dietitians. If there is any doubt about whether you should eat any ingredients in any of the materials herein, consult your physician or dietitian. Use your discretion as you apply spices to foods you prepare.

Trademarks, copyrights, and patents are the property of their respective holders. No brands are endorsed. They are merely the brands we customarily use when we prepare the recipes, and we have listed them in order to maintain consistent results.

About *The Collard Patch*

ISBN: 0-9741912-3-X
PUBLISHED BY BLUE MOON BOOKS—LOUISIANA, 207 N. Service Rd. E. #213, Ruston, LA 71270

The Collard Patch is a collard country cookbook and reader. Y'all will love our collards and cornbread. We want you to enjoy the stories, which will enrich your life. Here is a book of great eating and good living.

If you think you don't like collards, you have not tried *our* collards. Collards are a cool weather crop that can be grown almost anywhere. Their distinctive taste makes them suited for many types of recipes. Their nutritional value is supreme.

If you are a collards newbie, try the recipe on page 174 first! If you like soup, you'll love Collard Stew.

Acknowledgements

Mary Lou is thankful to Paul for his contributions to *The Collard Patch*. The idea was his, and he has given his help. After researching the market, he had a vision of writing an entire book devoted to cooking collards, a popular food included in many online recipes but neglected in cookbooks. Mary Lou embraced the idea, but she required a cornbread section to complement the collard greens.

When Paul told Mary Lou the poignant and hilarious stories of his childhood, she recognized their value and demanded that he write them to be published. He has shared these stories with candor in *The Collard Patch* in a section called "Growing Up in Collard Country," even when they made him look bad.

Also he has contributed extensive factual information about collards. With his experience as a printer, he has helped produce the book.

Furthermore, he has helped in all aspects of the business of this cookbook. Most importantly he has offered his opinions about the tastes of the recipes. If a dish is supposed to contain 20 ingredients and the cook omits one, Paul, the Spicemouth™, will know by the time the food hits the back of his tongue.

Paul thanks Mary Lou for making his vision of a cookbook about collards, a versatile food long popular and emerging as a favorite dark leafy green, a reality. Not only is her inventive performance in the kitchen unsurpassed as she deftly concocts the most delicious dishes from scratch; she is able to write her stories with equal innovation and precision. Dedicated eaters and readers the world over will forever be indebted to her.

Those who have shared their recipes, stories, and comments have honored the authors and enhanced *The Collard Patch*. Special appreciation is due our guest contributors:

- Felder Rushing, the master of Southern gardening, Felder Rushing, Jackson, Mississippi, http://www.felderrushing.com
- Beth Jacks; author of *Snippet*s and syndicated columns; http://www.USADeepSouth.com; Cleveland, Mississippi
- Melinda Ridge; fabulous cook and delightful person; veteran traveler; North Carolina
- Ruth Ishee; prize-winning cook; Mary Lou's sister; Laurel, Mississippi
- Bill Ishee; collard grower; Ruth's husband; Laurel, Mississippi
- Wiley Hilburn; journalist and professor at Louisiana Tech University, Ruston, Louisiana; popular columnist
- Willie Crawford; best-selling cookbook author and internationally prominent Internet marketer; http://www.WillieCrawford.com; Navarre, Florida
- Lisa Foster; nurse; great cook; radiant Christian; Simsboro, Louisiana
- Paul Urso, PhD; talented cook of authentic Sicilian food; author; scientist; retired medical school professor; Conyers, Georgia
- Martha White; retired insurance professional; Farmerville, Louisiana
- Cheryl Sowers; authority on down-home Southern cooking; high-quality human being; Ruston, Louisiana

- Margaret Scott; retired hospital telemetry technician; classy lady; Ruston, Louisiana
- Sandra Winzer; hospital telemetry technician; outstanding cook; Ruston, Louisiana
- Rosemary Ficklin, exceptionally efficient employee in hospital central services longtime friend, missionary, Ruston, Louisiana
- Carolyn Forche`; noted author, editor, writing coach; Houston, Texas
- Dorothy Reinhold; Supervisor of Cut `n Clean Greens® Test Kitchen; prize winning chef; food columnist; authority on cooking greens; http://www.cutncleangreens.com; Malibu, California
- Terry Chrisman; renowned cook; hairdresser; antique collector; Farmerville, Louisiana
- Yvette Freeman; famous actress; Nurse Haleh Adams on NBC's *E R;* expert about dietary management; National Advocacy Ambassador for the Diabetes Association; film director; speaker in demand; lover of collard greens; Los Angeles, California
- John Manikowski; chef; author of *Fish: Grilled & Smoked;* restaurateur in Massachusetts and New York*;* interior designer; former art teacher at Harvard
- Jim Rooker; chef at Armand's, Grammercy, Louisiana; formerly apprenticed to John Martin Terranova
- John Martin Terranova, deceased; former executive chef of the Castle, an exquisite restaurant located in the old stables of historic Dunleith Plantation, Natchez, Mississippi
- Tim Ellis; colorful character; exotic cook; wild story teller; somewhere in the Big Piney country of East Texas
- Vincent Fields; versatile cook who has run a catering business; son of the former chef for the governor of Kentucky; collector of antiques; husband of Mary Lou's niece, Judi; retired Army helicopter pilot and instructor; Dallas, Texas
- Lynn Salter; health food authority; home school educator; vivacious person; http://www.Whole-Food-and-Healing.com; Monticello, Florida
- Mary Vaughn; retired teacher; Mary Lou's cousin;, Mississippi
- Jane Galay; Marketing Consultant; home school educator; artist; Tennessee; http://www.NetworkingEveryWoman.com; Jane@NetworkingEveryWoman.com/PratersMill
- Patricia Squires; developer of superior cornbread recipes; early childhood educator; Simsboro, Louisiana
- Marie Null; cute lady who says she never cooks; one with the gift of greeting card ministry; Ruston, Louisiana
- Melody Burch, student at University of Louisiana at Monroe, employee at McDonald's, cheerful young lady with a sweet face and unique cooking knowledge, Spearsville, Louisiana
- Paula Howell; registered nurse (CCRN); expert cornbread cooker, cake baker, flower arranger; artistic person; Bienville, Louisiana
- Cathy George; pharmacist; talented cook in the Cajun style; former resident of Cajun country; Simsboro, Louisiana

Thanks to the helpful taste testers:

- ChristieStanley, PhD; and Mike Stanley, DVM; Campbellsport, Wisconsin
- Members, First Baptist Church of Simsboro, Louisiana
- Danon Roberts; Peachtree Dental Clinic; http://www.PeachTreeDental.com; Ruston, Louisiana
- Patti Hancock, RN, Monroe, Louisiana
- Mary B. Cheatham, Madison, Mississippi
- Cheryl Sowers, Ruston, Louisiana
- Terry Chrisman, Farmerville, Louisiana
- Apala Miller, Plano, Texas
- Jon Miller, College Station, Texas
- Danielle Miller, Plano, Texas
- Elizabeth Elliott, Plano, Texas
- John Elliott, Allen, Texas
- Stephanie Williams, Plano, Texas
- Andrew Gore, Waco, Texas
- Ken Bradford, Plano, Texas
- Dan Swanson, Dallas, Texas
- KTVE Television Station Staff, West Monroe, Louisiana
- Aaron Conley, Ruston, Louisiana

Thanks to:

- Willie Crawford, author of *Soul Food Recipes,* for his encouragement and helpful advice
- Rachel Goad, Melissa Jones, and Laura Monserrate, KTVE Television News Staff, for their enthusiasm and for publicizing our books
- Paula Howell for her support and her clever suggestions. She has a genius way with words
- Cheryl Sowers for helping cook in the test kitchen
- Patti Hancock for listening and encouraging
- Jo Baker for her advice on artistic matters
- Ruth and Bill Ishee for sharing collards from their amazing collard patch
- Jane Galay for suggesting several of her favorite Bible verses, for sharing her ideas about marketing, and for cheering near the finish line
- Carolyn Forche` for setting a beautiful example as a sister writer and for her lovely spirit
- Wilton Wall D.Min., Pastor, First Baptist Church of Simsboro, Louisiana, for being a shepherd
- Ray Denson, Customer Service Representative, Rose Printing; http://www.RosePrinting.com; Tallahassee, Florida; for help with printing our books
- Christie Stanley, Mary Lou's daughter, for her daily encouragement

To

Elizabeth and Andrew

Stephanie and John

Christie and Mike

Them Collards

Many of us in the South have learned to appreciate collard greens in our youth. They are a delightfully delicious dish prepared in the traditional way with such additions as ham hock, salt pork, onions, okra, or garlic.

When a family member urged some on us from about a ¼ acre garden, we harvested collard leaves with enthusiasm that faded only as we realized we had two large plastic leaf bags full. The back seat of the car was so full the 'possum dog, Delilah, could scarcely get in for the ride. Poor thing!

This bumper harvest filling a deep freeze prompted thinking about various ways to prepare the luscious leaf to complement the traditional recipes. Our odyssey has been richly rewarding and all the recipes included are "eater tested" by us or by the contributors. To our pleasant surprise, we learned that many others worldwide share the same appreciation of the delectable greens and have been inspired by the new recipes, the "collard collection," we have developed.

This book is an ongoing, or living project. We urge you to enjoy it and urge you to send your comments and recipes. We will be including some in future books and offer a free e-book copy to any person whose recipe we use. Of course, proper attribution will always be included.

Too, many people have said they don't like collards. What a shame: They suffer such a loss.

You don't have to be hungry to eat and love these!

If you think you don't like collards, you haven't tasted *our* collards! ™

And the Other Stuff
To go with a rich selection of collard recipes you will enjoy:
*   Seasoning mixes
*   Pepper sauce
*   Cornbread recipes
*   Collard facts
*   Captivating stories

Cinderella
When you see a collard leaf, think of it as the Cinderella of the vegetable world. It is beautiful and good unadorned; but when it is dressed, it is splendid!

(Idea from *Conran Cook*book by Terence and Caroline Conran)

Fear thou not; for I am with thee: be not dismayed: for I am thy God: I will strengthen thee, yea I will uphold thee with the right hand of my righteousness. Isaiah 41:10 KJV

Collard Essentials
The Nuts and Bolts Of Collards

The unsigned articles in this section are contributed by Paul Elliott.

Chapter One
Ah, Collards

When you start appreciating collard greens, aka collards and smooth-leaf kale among other things, you will find there are subtypes in the general category. Collards are not to be confused with spinach, mustard greens, turnip greens, kale, etc. While excellent greens, each in its own right, none matches collards. Collards have been referred to as "headless cabbage," and the leaves of each are very similar in appearance.

Collard leaves have all the best qualities. They can be durable when necessary, such as the covering for stuffed collard rolls like the Mediterranean tradition of grape leaves, or as tender as spinach in collard manicotti. However, the taste is the most important quality.

The delicious flavor of raw collards is a mildly pungent, slightly peppery quality that is moderated by cooking. The taste of collards is unique among the greens. Its taste quality is rich and distinctive when prepared in the traditional "mess 'o collards" way, yet compliments and enhances other flavors when mixed in more nontraditional ways, such as collard cake.

Collards can be considered a seasoning ingredient in their own right. Their unique flavor rounds out and mellows the flavors of other seasonings, giving food richness in color and taste. Keep a bag of chopped collards in your freezer at all times. Sauté ½ cup of frozen collards in 2-3 teaspoons of olive oil. They blend well with celery, green onion tops, garlic, and bell pepper. They cause an explosion of flavor! Ordinary dishes become exquisite gourmet experiences delightful to the most discriminating palates.

If you think you don't like the taste or texture of collards you can turn them into spinach, almost. When substituting collards for spinach, cook the collards first. Collards are firmer, whereas spinach is tender. Season the collards with your favorite spices and stir-fry them (or sauté them) five minutes at the highest heat possible. If they are tough, toss in ⅛ teaspoon baking soda and use them as spinach. They will be tenderer, and their flavor mellower. Only the most discerning gourmets, aficionados, and sons-in-law will be able to tell the difference.

Chapter Two
Collard Culture

True collard lovers often consider raising their own in whatever plots of soil there are available to them. This is understandable and quite natural.

The mature plants grow to about 2 feet across and about 2 feet high. This means they can be grown in flowerbeds and containers on driveways or patios. Of course, they have to have plenty of sunlight, water, and fertilizer. Some growers convert some of their yard space to flower beds for collard production. The plants need to be about 10-12 inches apart in rows about 2 feet apart.

The plants can be started in the early spring from seeds planted in potting soil in the small containers made for seedlings. Protect them from freezing. They will emerge with a primary set of leaves. Then they get their secondary set of leaves, at which point they can be transplanted into your garden, provided the danger of frost is passed in your area of the country.

Collard sets are also available from nurseries and Wal-Mart®, at least in some sections of the country, that can be transplanted into gardens, flowerbeds, or containers. The collard leaves can be harvested as early as 6-8 weeks, depending on conditions. Begin with the bottom-most leaves, which are the largest. A single plant will produce leaves regularly for 90 days or more.

Water regularly and fertilize the plants about every 2 weeks, for the best leaf production.

More plants can be started from spring through late summer in most areas of the United States. Collards can tolerate frost quite well, and it is reported that light frost makes the leaf texture tenderer. A hard freeze below 15 degrees Fahrenheit will kill the plants and end your collard season. When that happens, harvest all the remaining leaves on the plant and prepare or freeze them.

If such a freeze doesn't occur in your area, you can grow and harvest collards all winter. Harvest the leaves from the bottom up. If the bottom leaves are already too tough when you begin, move to the middle growth. Wash the leaves thoroughly to remove dirt and any insects. Some have reported putting a large number of leaves in their washing machines, setting them to rinse in cold water, and retrieving the collards after the spin cycle. Please do not use soap, bleach, or fabric softener! <weak sigh>

Since freezing tenderizes the collard leaves somewhat, you can plan to freeze some of the lower, tougher leaves.

Cleaned whole leaves can be stored for no more than four days in a container in the refrigerator. After collards have been prepared, they should be used within two days or frozen for later use.

Preparing the leaves begins with cutting or stripping the center stems from the leaves. The stems are usually too tough to be included and should be discarded. The leaves can be left whole without the stems for use in wraps, rolls, etc., or chopped. The leaves, now without stems, can be rolled from one side to the other forming a tight roll that is the easiest way to chop collards. Begin by slicing the roll in half lengthwise. Then, the halves can be chopped from one end to the other with good results.

When thou passest through the waters, I will be with thee; and through the rivers, they shall not overflow thee; when thou walkest through the fire, thou shalt not be burned; neither shall the flame kindle upon thee. Isaiah 43:2

Chapter Three
Others Like Collards, Too

A variety of other folks love collards, too—and who can blame 'em! For the most part they have six or more legs, wings, or no legs at all. For the collard lover growing his or her own crop, they are seldom a serious problem, providing careful attention is paid to the crop. When the first teeth marks show up carefully inspect all your plants for poachers. Most daytime culprits are caterpillars, aphids, and grasshoppers. Depending on the size of your collard operation and the strength of your infestation, you may be able to simply manually remove the caterpillars and grasshoppers.

Careful manual removal of the offenders is usually adequate for smaller numbers of plants. If you have a larger number of plants than would be practical to manually salvage from the mouths of useless eaters, you may want to consider other pest controls suggested by your garden center advisors.

Aphids may be controlled by putting a capful of dishwashing liquid in a gallon of water and spraying this solution on the beasts. You may have to lift the leaves to get good coverage on the under surfaces where they are feeding on your precious collards. This mild detergent solution will kill the tiny, soft-bodied suckers, but is harmless to the plants or people. It certainly is not strong enough to remind you of times when you had your mouth washed out with soap!

Another method is to put ¼ cup of hydrogen peroxide in a gallon of water and spray the crop.

A very natural and environmentally sound solution to many collard pests is Bacillus thuringiensis (Bt), a naturally occurring bacterial disease of insects. Insecticides have been manufactured that contain this bacterium as the active ingredient. Bt insecticides are most commonly used against certain collard-leaf-feeding caterpillars, such as cabbage "worms" (cabbage looper, imported cabbage worm, diamondback moth, etc.).

Bt is considered safe to human beings and non-target species, such as pets and wildlife. Some formulations can be used on essentially all food crops including collards.

Since Bt does not cause a rapid kill, users may incorrectly assume that it is ineffective a day or two after treatment, if the little rascals are still kicking. This, however, is merely a perceptual problem, because Bt-affected insects eat little or nothing before they die.

Since Bt insecticides do not have a broad spectrum of activity (as do most insecticides), beneficial insects are not killed by applications of Bt. This includes the natural enemies of insects (predators and parasites), as well as beneficial pollinators, such as honeybees.

Grasshoppers are a different problem. Sevin® dust or liquid, powdered or sprayed on the collard leaves, works. Follow the labeled instruction for application and time from application to safe harvest.

Some growers prefer to use a bait for the grasshoppers. One grasshopper bait mix is as follows: 25 pounds of wheat bran, one quart of molasses, one quart of water, two pounds of 50% mixture of Sevin® dust or 25 ounces of powered pyrethrum. Mix together and roll into tiny balls while still moist and place around the collard plants. Reduce the amounts for smaller plots.

Chapter Four
Slugfest or Don't Drink and Eat—Part I

When you begin growing your own collards, you'll find the sets develop tiny holes in the leaves in the dark of the night, an hour at which any self-respecting predator should be asleep. That's right—never a tooth showed itself in my collard patch during daylight.

Sometimes it was serious loss of leaf space early in their growth when the plants needed it most. Who were the useless eaters?

Obviously, an intelligence operation was in order! Creeping around under cover of darkness with a red-lensed flashlight à la TV series, *Alias,* I located the monsters! Slugs! . . . and a few snails.

The slimy little rascals were quietly but very effectively gnawing on my collard sets. I never knew their squirming slimy soft bodies had *teeth!* But there they were stuffing great chunks of my precious little collard leaves in their slimy faces. The nerve!

Once again, the Internet came to the rescue of this erstwhile collard culturist. The solution? Beer! No pun intended.

That's right, beer! I first located this recommendation on a site from foggy England. Feeling the writer may have merely used that as a cover for his excessive ale consumption, I explored further. Next I located similar advice on a site in the good old US of A. Perhaps they were a bit tipsy, too.

I rattled off an e-mail to the master of Southern gardening, Felder Rushing <http://www.FelderRushing.com>. I had recently met him and knew him to be stone sober . . . at least at the time of his lecture. Felder replied that, indeed, beer was an attractant due to its yeast odor. I used small open containers, such as the bottom of aluminum disposable muffin tins cut apart with scissors or drink cans cut to a 1.5 inch depth, placed three feet apart, emptied and recharged daily with about ½ inch of beer.

Felder suggested an alternative would be to take a small container with a lid, such as a butter tub or a coffee can, bore a hole in the lid making it big enough to accommodate snails, too, bury it close to the collard plants flush with the ground, and bait it with a small amount of beer. The slugs and snails can crawl through its hole and drown without being able to escape. Every several days the gardener can dispose of the slimy contents over the fence without having to look at the mess, then re-beer and re-bury the traps. Talk about all natural organic methods!

It serves them drunken little sots right!

Chapter Five
Slugfest or Don't Drink and Eat–Part II

any who resist the wholly natural beer solution to slugs and snails, or who care to avoid purchasing alcohol for others to drink, Felder Rushing <http://www.FelderRushing.com>, the master Southern gardener, also suggested the use of day-old banana peels. It seems that slugs and snails love said peels, but you must mix commercial slug bait on and around some small pieces of the banana peel; otherwise you simply offer them a more varied menu producing more slug and snail reproduction.

After all, you do intend to eradicate them rather than simply fattening them up, don't you?

Create a "slug haven," such as a small board raised an inch or two off the ground, where birds and dogs can't get to the bait.

Another organic solution is to use diatomaceous earth or well-rinsed shells from hard-boiled eggs finely crushed. Sprinkle the items on the soil around the collard plants. These materials are very sharp and cut the fragile bodies of snails and slugs as they crawl over the materials causing them to dry out and die.

One could also sprinkle these materials around pieces of banana peel simply to draw the snails and slugs away to something they prefer to eat.

Chapter Six
Slugfest—Part III

Here is what the Oregon State University Extension Service has to say about slug and snail baits at <http://eesc.orst.edu/agcomwebfile/garden/pestsandpesticides/slugbait.html> Slug bait—What's the scoop on slug bait formulations?

CORVALLIS - Two chemicals are currently licensed and formulated into slug and snail baits for use on home gardens and on food and seed crops in Oregon - metaldehyde and iron phosphate.

Metaldehyde has been an active ingredient in slug and snail baits since the 1930's. Products containing varying concentrations of metaldehyde include: "Cory's Slug and Snail Death®," "Deadline®," and "Slug-Tox®." These products are sold as granules, sprays, dusts, pelleted grain or bait and typically applied to the ground around plants or crops to attract and kill slugs and snails.

"They work by destroying the mucus-producing system unique to slugs, which severely reduces mobility and digestion," explained Glenn Fisher, Oregon State University entomologist who has researched slugs as agricultural pests for many years.

Metaldehyde is classified by the U.S. Environmental Protection Agency as a "slightly toxic compound that may be fatal to dogs or other pets if eaten." The deaths of birds feeding in metaldehyde-treated areas have been reported in the scientific literature. These deaths were from the birds eating the slug bait, not dead slugs. The 4 percent pelleted metaldehyde bait, a concentration commonly sold to home gardeners is reported to be toxic to wildlife, according to the U.S. EPA.

"Sometimes pesticide manufacturers add insecticides such as carbaryl to a metaldehyde bait to provide additional control of certain pest insects such as cutworms, army worms, pillbugs and earwigs," said Fisher. But then earthworms, harvestmen ("Daddy Long Legs") and beetle predators of slugs that feed on these dual-purpose baits are killed as well.

Iron phosphate slug and snail baits, originally used in Europe, have been registered in the United States since 1997. Products containing iron phosphate include: "Sluggo®," "Escar-Go!®" and "Worry Free®" slug and snail bait. These are sold as pelleted bait, typically applied to the ground around plants or crops. Iron phosphate baits have proven to be relatively non-toxic around children and pets than those baits containing metaldehyde.

According to Fisher, scientists do not yet completely understand how iron phosphate kills snails and slugs. According to the U.S. EPA's Office of Pesticide Programs, iron phosphate has "no unreasonable adverse effects to human health," and there is a "known lack of toxicity of iron phosphate to birds, fish and non-target insects."

A third chemical, called methiocarb (sold in products such as "Mesurol®") has been available for limited use on ornamentals as a repellent spray, but cannot be used on food crops in the United States.

In recent trials, OSU entomologists found the metaldehyde bait more effective at killing gray garden slugs in the field than baits containing iron phosphates. But they also determined that iron phosphate baits are much better at killing slugs than using no bait at all.

Carol Savonen,
SOURCE: Glenn Fisher

Collards grow as high as four feet. In the Deep South they can last through the winter if the freezes are not too hard.

Chapter Seven
History of Collards–Part I

What is a collard? What is its history? Who are its relatives?

The word *collard* is an alteration of *colewort,* which is a stalked smooth-leaved kale. Collards are member of the cole family. The etymology of *cole* stems from a Greek word, *kaulos,* which means stem. The technical name of the family is *Brassica.* Some other members of the cole family are broccoli, kale, Brussels sprouts, cabbage, cauliflower, and kohlrabi. What an illustrious, palatable group!

Collard greens have the distinction of being some of the oldest members of the cole family. According to botanists, the collard plant has barely changed during the last 2000 years. Before the birth of Christ, the Greeks and Romans were eating collards. Also there are rumors that collards were growing wild in Asia Minor (Turkey) during the same period. Maybe the Romans took them to Britain, Germany, and France; or perhaps the Celts spread them around that area before the Romans arrived. There is a record of people growing collards in the British Isles in the fourth century B.C.

Also collards have Oriental cousins dating back to ancient times. Confucius wrote about members of the cole family. The Asian coles include Napa cabbage, Chinese broccoli, and bok choy.

Collards have spread all around the world:
- When the explorers arrived in the West Indies at Hispañola located between Cuba and Puerto Rico in 1565, they found people cultivating collards.
- There are conflicting reports about whether the Africans brought collards with them to America on the slave ships in the 1600's or whether they found them already growing in the South.
- Also, when the British colonists settled the East Coast, they brought collards to the New World.

The South began its love affair with collards back in the times when the slaves had a limited selection of foods to sustain themselves. They developed ways to cook collards and make them good—really delicious. A well-kept secret was that the tasty greens of the South were not only delicious: they were loaded with food value.

With our emergent awareness of beneficial nutrition and with the development of sophisticated taste buds throughout the world, collards have gained an enormous popularity. In the supermarkets, shoppers queue up with long plastic bags to buy the fresh collards; the shelves designated for the frozen ones are often empty; and the washed bagged ones are difficult to find. The health food stores take pride in the collards they sell. Collard plants—attractive, hardy, and easily cultivated—are popping up in yards and gardens. Fresh air markets and collard farms are flourishing.

People are enjoying collards prepared in the basic Southern ways; also they are experimenting with all sorts of fascinating dishes containing collards. Mary Lou

Chapter Eight
History of Collards–Part II

Thanks to Cut 'n Clean Greens for allowing us to share the following information:

History of Greens

Collard greens date back to prehistoric times and are one of the oldest members of the cabbage family. Collards are also known as tree cabbage or non-heading cabbage, are a cool-season vegetable, and are extremely nutritious – rich in vitamins and minerals that help prevent and fight disease.

Greens originated in the eastern Mediterranean, but it wasn't until the first Africans arrived in Jamestown, Virginia, in the early 1600's that America got its first taste of the dark green leafy vegetable. Greens were just one of a few select vegetables African-Americans were allowed to grow and harvest for themselves and their families throughout times of slavery, and so over the years cooked greens developed into a traditional food. Even after the Africans were emancipated in the late 1800's, their love of greens continued, and they kept handing down their well-developed repertoire of greens recipes from one generation to the next.

Though greens did not originate in Africa, the habit of eating greens that have been cooked down into a low gravy and drinking the juices from the greens (known as "pot likker") is of African origin. Pot likker is quite nutritious and delicious, and contributes to the comfort-food aspects of the dish.

Today, many varieties of greens—collards, mustard, turnips, chard, spinach, kale—continue to be a traditional offering at potlucks, picnics, parties, and family dinners and are a staple in African-American culture.

And these days chefs of many ethnicities have also discovered greens and have eagerly added them to a variety of trendy restaurant dishes, garnering interest from diners who might not have been exposed to cooked greens before. Home cooks are buying an increasing amount of greens, as well, as they attempt to combine good flavor with the nutrition they know their families need.

Quoted with permission from http://www.cutncleangreens.com/history/

"Try not to become a man of success but rather a man of value." Albert Einstein

Chapter Nine
Health with Collards—Part I

Collards are a very healthy food, and we'll get into that a little later. But what about ticks! If ticks like to grow where your collards do, that can be a problem.

You should avoid getting tick bitten, when possible. Ticks can't jump or fly and have to snag a ride on you with their outstretched arms from wherever they reside. They detect your body heat and the carbon dioxide from your breath. When they sense either or both, they stretch their front legs out hoping to snag your skin, hair, or clothing.

As always, avoidance of ticks is the best policy.

Ticks are most active from April through October in most areas of the country; so exercise additional caution when venturing into tick country during that time period. Tuck pants cuffs into boots or socks, and wear long sleeves and light-colored clothing to make it easier to spot ticks.

Use just enough repellent to cover exposed skin and/or clothing. Heavy application and saturation is generally unnecessary for effectiveness; if biting insects do not respond to a thin film of repellent, then apply a bit more.

Inspect yourself and your children for clinging ticks after leaving an infested area. Ticks are sometimes hard to see—nymphs, the immature stage, are dot sized like a pinhead; adults can be smaller than a sesame seed.

After returning indoors, bathe or wash treated skin with soap and water. This is particularly important when repellents are used repeatedly in a day or on consecutive days. Also, wash treated clothing before wearing it again.

If you suspect that you or your children are reacting to an insect repellent, discontinue use, wash treated skin, and then call your local poison control center. If/when you go to a doctor, take the repellent with you.

If you discover a tick feeding, do not panic. Studies indicate that an infected tick does not usually transmit the Lyme organism during the first 24 hours.

If you suspect Lyme disease or its symptoms, contact your doctor immediately.

Repellents

When in a tick-infested area, an insect repellent is good prevention; however, consider using a product designed to be applied to clothing rather than skin.

The best insect repellent, without equal, is DEET. The more DEET there is in the product the better it works with less amount and the longer an application lasts. Strengths vary and can be from about 2% to 100%. You can get products with 100% DEET usually at sporting goods stores.

The most common brand of DEET is Off®, but I have never seen preparations of more than about 30% in the Off® brand. I have seen 100% DEET in the Muskol® and Repel® brands among others.

Liquid preparations are better than sprays or wipes, because there is a lot of loss with the latter two. If you have the 100% liquid, 1-3 drops in your palm is all that is required. Rub your hands together and then brush your skin and clothing lightly with your hands' palmar surfaces. It is not necessary to get your clothing or skin the least bit greasy.

If you are not going to be in brushy areas or around trees, you only need to apply the DEET to your shoes, ankles, and legs or pant legs. Otherwise, apply it to your head (avoid the eyes), arms, and trunk as well. To be repelled, the bug needs to touch the chemical with its feet.

CAUTION: Any brand of DEET in any strength will dissolve some plastics, such as some plastic camera bodies, glasses frames and lenses, and some synthetic fibers. If your clothing contains a synthetic fiber, first test a small area of the material that doesn't show.

Travelers should be advised that permethrin-containing repellents (e.g., Permanone® or deltamethrin) are recommended for use on clothing, shoes, bed nets, and camping gear. Permethrin is highly effective as an insecticide and as a repellent. Permethrin-treated clothing repels and kills ticks, mosquitoes, and other arthropods and retains this effect after repeated laundering. There appears to be little potential for toxicity from permethrin-treated clothing. The insecticide should be reapplied after every five washings.

Most authorities recommend repellents containing N,N-diethylmetatoluamide (DEET) as an active ingredient. DEET repels mosquitoes, ticks, and other arthropods when applied to the skin or clothing. In general, the more DEET a repellent contains, the longer time it can protect against mosquito bites. However, there appears to be no added benefit of concentrations greater than 50%. A microencapsulated, sustained-release formulation can have a longer period of activity than liquid formulations at the same concentrations. Length of protection also varies with ambient temperature, amount of perspiration, any water exposure, abrasive removal, and other factors.

No definitive studies have been published about what concentration of DEET is safe for children. No serious illness has arisen from use of DEET according the manufacturer's recommendations. DEET formulations as high as 50% are recommended for both adults and children >2 months of age. Lower concentrations are not as long lasting, offering short-term protection only and necessitating more frequent reapplication. Repellent products that do not contain DEET are not likely to offer the same degree of protection from mosquito bites as products containing DEET. Non-DEET repellents have not necessarily been as thoroughly studied as DEET and may not be safer for use on children. Parents should choose the type and concentration of repellent to be used by taking into account the amount of time that a child will be outdoors, exposure to mosquitoes, and the risk of mosquito-transmitted disease in the area. The recommendations for DEET use in pregnant women do not differ from those for nonpregnant adults.

DEET is toxic when ingested and may cause skin irritation in sensitive persons. High concentrations applied to skin can cause blistering. However, because DEET is so widely used, a great deal of testing has been done, and over the long history of DEET use, very few confirmed incidents of toxic reactions to DEET have occurred when the product is used properly.

For more information, go to: <http://www.cdc.gov/travel/bugs.htm>.

Duranon® Tick Repellent (0.5% Permethrin) for clothing, lasts up to 2 weeks.

Permanone® or Repel® (0.5% Permethrin) for clothing. Active ingredients bond with fabric and last a minimum of two weeks; formula also holds up to repeated washing. Effective against ticks, mosquitoes, chiggers and mites. 6-oz. aerosol.

This is intended for use on clothing and should not be applied to your skin as it quickly breaks down on the skin and becomes ineffective. When your clothing is sprayed as directed, an active ingredient actually binds to the fabric being treated providing residual protection which lasts a minimum of two weeks and holds up through several machine washings. Permanone® repels and kills ticks which may carry Lyme Disease and Rocky Mountain Spotted Fever and is also effective against mosquitoes and mites. It has been granted full EPA approval in all states.

If you want to know more about tick-borne diseases, go to <http://www.afraidtoask.com/lyme/index.html>

Chapter Ten
Health with Collards—Part II

What do collard greens contain?
> Beta carotene and vitamin C—this chapter is starting to read like the label on your antioxidant bottle, right? The more intense the green color, the more beta carotene is present.

> Calcium—our bones need us to eat collards.
> Fiber—most of us are aware of the healthy amount of fiber in greens; most of us need more fiber.

> Carotenoids—like their cousins, cabbage, kale, and broccoli, collards are considered good for cancer prevention.

What are the food components that are scarce in greens?
> Fat, cholesterol, and calories—few of us need more of those.

Are collards old-fashioned?
> No—you don't have to cook them the old-fashioned way, but if you wish, go ahead. Invite us over to enjoy them with you. If you prefer, eat them raw, or stir-fry them.

Will eating collards make me look younger?

Possibly—they contain vitamin A, zinc, selenium, and vitamin E. These nutritional components are being sold over the counter as additives to cosmetics. While it is true that you won't send a large amount nutritional benefit to your skin by eating foods containing the good things, a portion of them will go to help your skin.

Niacin and vitamin E—these are excellent circulation enhancers.

Improving your overall nutritional state with a great vegetable such as collards will make you feel better and improve your overall health.

As a tasty, low-calorie food loaded with nutrients, collards may be included in weight loss programs. Also, collards are filling. Slim is young.

Will eating collards improve my eyesight?

Macular degeneration—it is believed that lutein and vitamin C can help prevent this type of blindness. Collards are an excellent source of lutein and vitamin C.

Can eating collards prevent breast cancer?

Research studies have concluded that eating dark green leaf vegetables can help prevent breast cancer.

Mary Lou

Collard greens are an excellent component of any diet with many health benefits. They are ideal for anyone but especially for those who dislike cabbage, kale, or broccoli. They have the benefit over spinach of a better taste and greater versatility.

If you think you don't like collards, you haven't tried *our* collards!

For by grace are ye saved through faith; and that not of yourselves: it is the gift of God: Not of works, lest any man should boast. Ephesians 2:8-9

Chapter Eleven

To reassure you that it is all right to eat a little dirt not washed from your collards, we have included the following essay by Beth Jacks. She will explain that we all eat dirt and plenty of it.

Dirt Eating
All the Facts You Never Wanted to Know

"If a lump of soot falls into the soup and you cannot conveniently get it out, stir it in well and it will give the soup a French taste.—Jonathan Swift

I'm going to get down and dirty in this column, so don't keep reading if you're averse to such things. I also recommend your not continuing to read if you're snacking, especially while chewing on something straight from the garden.

And why?

Because the latest info from the American Dietetic Association tells us that, like it or not, each of us probably eats several pounds of dirt from birth to death, and no matter how well we wash those turnip greens or carrots we're still going to be putting down some reechy matter.

Since it's time to start hauling in veggies from our gardens, I thought I ought to alert everybody to this new information, although the old saying "You've got to eat a peck of dirt before you die" has been around for generations. Anybody with a baby has quoted that one.

The U. S. Food and Drug Administration says it's really impossible to get all the dirt and foreign objects (insects, rodent hairs, worms, maggots!) off our food, fresh and processed, but for the most part, the USFDA states, this unappetizing stuff won't kill us or even make us sick. That's good to know.

I still have fond childhood memories of pulling radishes straight from the garden, washing those suckers off with the hose, and eating 'em like candy. Makes my mouth water to think about it. Little did I know I was digesting a palatable portion of grit and grime also, no matter how long I washed those radishes.

And as little bitties, sister Kathy and I had the most adorable playhouse where we spent hours making mudpies and cinnamon "coffee" in dusty bowls and cups. We never partook of our gourmet offerings but fed them instead to baby cousins and dogs. Must not have adversely affected them because they're still around. (Not the dogs—but the cousins seem all right.)

Then there are folks who eat dirt on purpose. You read that right. They're called geophages (from the Greek "geo"—earth and "phagein"—eat).

Trying to explain the attraction of soil gobbling, scientists and sociologists have come up with a bunch of explanations ranging from hunger to cravings to heredity. But when they ask geophages why they eat dirt the main response is that dirt tastes good.

Well . . . I guess so.

One dirt eater in an article written by Associated Press writer Kathy Eyre compared her habit to using a pinch of chewing tobacco every day. I'll say "Amen" to that.

Another lady claims she eats a cupful every afternoon while she watches TV and works her crossword puzzle. I can hear the conversation now: "Hey, honey, while you're up would you get me a cup of dirt?"

Dr. Kevin Grigsby, a social worker and professor of psychiatry and health behavior at Medical College of Georgia explains that geophagia exists all over the world and has for centuries, but is especially prevalent in the American South. That's a lot of dirt excavating. No wonder we need kudzu for soil conservation.

Anyway, I was telling hubby G-Man about all this dirt eating research I was doing and he said he didn't eat much dirt as a child, but did enjoy munching on chicken feed, the closest thing to junk food his mama kept around the house. He swears the little chicken feed pellets were tasty. (And this is a man who won't eat English peas.)

But listen, I've always maintained "to each his own." I'm not one to get all up into peoples' business. They can just proceed if they want to devour stuff like chicken feed and dirt (which, by the way, comes from the Old Norse word "drit," meaning excrement).

Not me. I'll dish the dirt, but there will be nary a time I'll intentionally eat it.

Quoted from *Snippets,* 2004, by Beth Boswell Jacks

Beth Jacks

Beth is a weekly essay/humorist columnist for a number of Southern newspapers. Her verse is published frequently in children's magazines, and she is the editor of http://www.USADeepSouth.com. The epitome of Southern ladiness, she lives in the Mississippi Delta with her husband, G-Man.

We love Beth and the way she writes. When we requested her favorite collards or cornbread recipe, she said, "Greens? The only greens I ever tried to cook were a ruined mash of slimy green. I cooked them all night long, thinking that was what my mama had always done. Where did I get that? And cornbread. I love it, but I always use a box mix."

Neither is there salvation in any other; for there is none other name under heaven given among men, whereby we must be saved. Acts 4:12

Chapter Twelve
Washing Collards

Since collards grow well in sandy soil, farmers often grow them there. Dirt and insects cling tenaciously to the big clinging leaves. Consequently collards require vigorous washing.

Innovative cooks have developed solutions to the problem:
* Some people soak their collards in their bathtubs.
* Some people give them a spin in the washing machine.
* Others bargain with their children: "If you'll wash the collard leaves in 10 rinses, you won't be grounded anymore."
* Then there are the women who try to excuse the dirt and insects in the collards. ("It's just a little sand, dearest. I heard that people eat about five pounds of dirt in a lifetime. See? It won't kill you. The bugs? Extra protein. Nice flavor.")

Melinda Ridge, a dear girl who really knows quite a bit about how to cook collards says:
* You never know how much those greens will cook down; so I just wash, and wash and when I get tired of tearing leaves, say that is enough. (A guesstimate)
* Also, we have a friend (I would never try this) who actually washed her greens in the washing machine all the time. I never fully understood, but I think she put them in the strainer of the washing machine. YUK! But it would be interesting to know if others do that!

My sister Ruth gives the following advice:
* Before washing collards, soak them in salt water to release the insects and dirt.

Bill Ishee, Ruth's husband, advises:
* If you don't want to spend all your time and energy washing collards, cut them loose from the stalks. That way you can grow some more collards.
* Don't go pulling them up, wasting the plants and toting dirt into the house.

Sometimes I coerce Paul into washing collards in the test kitchen and freezing them. Usually I don't like to spend a large amount of time washing collards.
* I choose fresh collards that have been partially pre-washed or frozen chopped collards. (The frozen ones are almost always tender and tasty as well as clean.)
* Lately I have found some delicious, inexpensive, tender collards, already washed and chopped—ready to stuff into the pan.

Mary Lou

Although the fig tree shall not blossom, neither shall fruit be in the vines; the labour of the olives shall fail, and the fields shall yield no meat; the flock shall be cut off from the fold, and there shall be no herd in the stalls: Yet I will rejoice in the Lord, I will joy in the God of my salvation. The Lord is my strength, and he will make my feet like hinds' feet to walk upon mine high places. Habakkuk 3:17-19

Chapter Thirteen
Lasting Magic of Collards
Pot Likker Sustains Us Still

With Wiley Hilburn's permission, we are sharing his story about collards, which was posted on December 15, 2003, in The Shreveport Times

Another gubernatorial race has come and gone. Indian summer has established itself as a separate and independent season. But the first hard frost has fallen on North Louisiana.

It's now the politics of pot likker in the Deep South, where greens - especially collard greens - are a historically unique foundation of the food chain.

And it may be rural legend, but collards taste better after that first frost - more tender, more fragrant.

The pot likker, of course, is the vitamin-concentrate soup that comes from a prolonged boil of the greens. Pot likker is the real fuel for the soul. Sop your corn bread in that tasty broth.

Collards transcend politics. But the Huddle House crew is going to chew on something - even collards.

"They (collards) smell like sulfur and taste like iron," said Murray Van Hooser of Ruston. Murray has been abroad too much in his retirement. He's eaten in too many foreign restaurants.

Collards have what could be called a loud smell, I concede. But to me, it's a smoky, ham-based aroma.

In North Louisiana, a sufficient quantity of greens to feed a family or a particular appetite is called "a mess." Yankees never have understood the term "mess," but it applies.

Collards should be cooked for hours—the longer the better. Ham hocks or fatback complete the recipe. No garlic for me in collards. But leave the stems in the brew.

Collards are healthy eating - no fat or cholesterol, low in sodium and a good source of vitamins A and C as well as iron. The ham hocks can't subtract that much from the healthy aspect of the greens.

The best collards I ever have eaten were cooked by Gwen Riser of Ruston. Mrs. Riser boiled her collards in a pressure cooker at red-alert heat for hours. I could smell the collards in the driveway. Ambrosia.

The best collard luncheon ever was put together by my grandmother Peg Hilburn on Alabama Street in Ruston.

She served collards purchased off a truck, pork chops, and mealed potatoes (potatoes mealed in thin circles and fried). What I would give for some mealed potatoes, by the way.

The Deep South is full of mystery, and the lasting magic of collards and pot likker is something that in a changing world sustains us still.   Wiley Hilburn

Wiley Hilburn

Wiley Hilburn has spent most of his life living in and writing about the people and places of the piney woods of North Louisiana. For more than 37 years, he has headed the Journalism Department at Louisiana Tech University in Ruston, Louisiana. His former students can be found working in almost every major publication in the United States at one time or another.

For more than 25 years, Wiley Hilburn has written a popular weekly column in *The Times* (of Shreveport), and in the last few years, in both *The Times* and *The Monroe News-Star*. He has also served on the editorial staff of *The Times* and continues to contribute editorials. He is one of only two journalists who have been inducted into the Louisiana Political Hall of Fame. Hilburn lives with his wife, Kate, a photographer, in Choudrant, Louisiana, along with their three dogs—Jack, Girlfriend, and Boo Radley.

New Seasons is a new collection of Wiley Hilburn's columns written for *The Monroe News-Star* and *The Times* (of Shreveport) over the last fifteen years. Hilburn's first book from his weekly column, "Fragments," introduced us to the North Louisiana of our childhood, took us down country lanes, and conjured up the seasons and lost time. Copies of his now sold-out book found their way to bedside tables, Christmas stockings, and the floorboard of many a North Louisiana pickup truck.

In this new book, he continues to delight us with his wry humor and keen insight into North Louisiana life, love, stray dogs, weather and the social order at the Huddle House.

Unsigned recipes throughout the book are contributed by Mary Lou.

Chapter Fourteen
Cooking Perfect Collards

Collards that taste perfect are not difficult to attain.

Collards naturally have a tart taste, which you will want to enjoy. To enjoy it completely, you will need to embellish it. Collard cooks usually add something sour to balance the tartness and make it more interesting. You may want to add sour fruit juice, such as lemon juice or lime juice. Perhaps you will prefer vinegar. Different types of vinegar go well in various dishes. Be careful not to select vinegar that has added sodium. Here are some types to try:

- Pear
- Apple cider (which is a strong vinegar taste)
- Rice (without added sodium)
- Red wine
- Balsamic

Mixing different flavors will enhance the flavor of a dish. Blending juice and vinegar can boost the tart collard flavor. You may want to use hot pepper sauce, which is liquid poured off peppers that have been bottled and covered with heated vinegar. Also you may like to try pickle juice or the liquid from pickled jalapeño peppers.

The most important principal in adding vinegar is not to be afraid to do so.

A small amount of sweetness is essential to make tart collards taste perfect. You don't want an overly sweet taste; however, a slightly sweet flavor enables your palate to appreciate the tartness and the sourness that good greens should have. Traditionally Southern cooks have added a tiny spoon of cane sugar to greens. You may want to try a sweetener that will not add calories. The best low-calorie sweetener we have found to use in collards is Splenda®. In many of our recipes, we use it simply because we like the taste of it. To sweeten the collards and add some interesting other flavors try one of these:

- Apple juice
- Pineapple juice
- Wine
- Maraschino cherry juice
- Grape jelly
- Apricot preserves
- Orange marmalade

We love orange marmalade in collards.

All my life I have thought that "mess o' greens" was a Southernism, but in my research I discovered that New Englanders use the expression too! Mary Lou

Also, collards need a little salt. We like to use salt substitute. Let us remind you that you should check with your physician, registered dietician, or registered nurse before using salt substitute. Make sure that you can tolerate the added potassium in your diet.

Traditionally collard lovers have enjoyed some heat with their collards. You may like pepper sauce or jalapeños with collards. Almost any source of red pepper or black pepper will suffice. Be careful to read the labels on hot sauces. Most of them are loaded with sodium.

Collards and garlic complement each other. Their compatible flavors blend in culinary bliss. Also both are excellent selections of nutritional food. It is impossible to eat too many collards or too much garlic!

Often, collards are slightly chewy. They should be tender enough that you don't have to work your gums too much—the way you do when you eat salt-water taffy or peanut brittle. We once thought that we had to boil them until they became very tender, but we learned that they would be mushy and tasteless by the time they were tender. There are certain techniques for tenderizing collards to make them perfect to the palate without making them mushy or bland. As a matter of fact, these procedures release the delightful flavor of collards.

First, select the tenderest collards available. Collards kissed by frost are best. Many experienced cooks, including Ruth and Cheryl, have said that freezing collards will tenderize them. Frozen chopped collards purchased from the grocery store are usually tender. Often frozen collards are unavailable. The empty shelves labeled *collards* tell us that collards are some of the most popular frozen vegetables in our area.

If you are preparing fresh collards, be sure to chop the collards to fine ribbons. Cut out the toughest stems and roll the leaves like cigars. Chop them with a sharp knife or cut them with kitchen scissors or an inexpensive pair of sewing scissors designated for kitchen use. Cut them in narrow strips like linguine.

Sauté the collards over high heat for a few minutes. Some collards will not require further cooking. If you are preparing collards grown in the Deep South in the summer or if you are cooking collards that have been chopped coarsely, you may need to add some water and cook them more. Add ½ to 1 cup of water each time and check the collards when the water is absorbed. Cook them over very high heat.

Save yourself some grief: purchase a cooking pot with a see-through lid so will be able to observe the rate of water absorption without finding it necessary to lift the lid. If you must, add more water and simmer them a few minutes.

(Unless you are preparing soup or gumbo, don't allow collards to swim in "pot likker", the vegetable-cooking liquid that we Southerners like to sop our cornbread and biscuits in. Cook collards in minimal water. Instead, cook some turnip greens or field peas if you want pot likker.)

There is one magical ingredient that will tenderize the toughest of collards. First, before I tell you about it, let me say that the lemon juice and/or vinegar will help while they make the collards taste wonderful. Our grandmothers and great grandmothers knew that collards require a pinch of baking soda. This ingredient has earned a bad reputation because of overuse. All you need is a tiny pinch. One-eighth teaspoon will tenderize a stockpot full of collards. Excessive use of baking soda raises the sodium level of collards.

Following all these methods will produce collards of delectable texture. There are a few more points we need to discuss about seasoning collard greens. Let's start with the sautéing procedure. Olive oil and canola oil are excellent choices. Some people who are watching fat intake closely sauté collards in a well-cured thick pan coated with a thick coat of cooking spray.

Traditional oils that Southern cooks have rendered to cook greens are salt meat and bacon fat. Although these are delicious, we can readily see that we cannot afford to eat them often. Collards, with their richness of flavor and nutritional value, can benefit and sustain us if we prepare them in a variety of ways.

Southern Collard Meals

Collards go well with many other foods. Most Southern people eat collards with some kind of cornbread. A good old-fashioned Southern feast could also include some of the following: field peas, black-eyed peas, sweet potatoes, fresh green onions, beets, creamed corn, sliced tomatoes, peppers, and squash.

Although you may want to add fried chicken or stuffed eggs on Sunday, the vegetables are enough to bring joy to your man's heart and music to his belly.

Don't forget the tea—usually sweet, and for dessert we suggest banana pudding or blackberry cobbler.

Mary Lou

The Blue Light

March 9, 2006: One of our dearest friends told us yesterday that she is planning to move away. She may move to Fort Worth, Texas, Lafayette, Indiana, or Seattle, Washington. She does not know yet. She called me and said, "I'm not sure when I'll see you and Paul again. Let me take you to the Blue Light." Her offer was one we could not refuse.

The Blue Light Café has national fame. It's an old house south of Louisiana Tech in Ruston, Louisiana. As you might expect, it is painted bright blue, and it has some of the best soul food in the United States.

Louisiana Tech and Grambling alumni come back to Ruston to eat at the Blue Light. When guest celebrities visit Lincoln Parish, they know what to say: "Take me to the Blue Light."

The pork chops are too big to fit on our big plates; the hot water cornbread disappears as soon as we can open our mouths. And the collards—they are the good old-fashioned kind, chopped and loaded with the taste of pork. We always order their collards.

Essential Collards
Lip-Smacking Messes O' Greens

Awesome Collard Greens

Willie Crawford is sharing the following, which is the world's most famous written collards recipe. For years it has been appearing on the Internet search as the most researched recipe for cooking collard greens. Here is his recipe with a comment:

Collard greens are a very nutritious and inexpensive treat. When I was growing up, my grandmother would buy about 50 cents worth of collard seeds and this would grow enough collard greens to feed us for the entire year. That 50 cents worth of seeds would produce hundreds of collard plants in our North Carolina backyard garden.

Ingredients

2-3 medium smoked ham hocks or 2 pounds smoked pork neck bones
5 pounds of collards or several large bunches (If you can't get them fresh, frozen will do.)
2 teaspoon of salt

My favorite way to cook collard greens is very simple. I take 2 or 3 smoked ham hocks and put them in a large (6 quart) pot of water. Bring the water to a rolling boil and let it boil for about 1½ hours. Add more water as it boils down. The idea is to boil the ham hocks until they begin to fall apart. You should always cook pork very thoroughly and use proper food handling techniques. You want the ham hocks to be falling apart before you add the collard greens.

Take the collard greens and separate the leaves (if fresh). Now rinse each leaf individually under cold running water. After you rinse the collard greens thoroughly, stack several leaves on top of each other. Roll these leaves together. Then slice the leaves into thin strips using a cutting board and large knife. Rolling them together speeds up the process as you are slicing through several leaves at once.

Next, add your collard greens to the pot. Since this is a lot of collards, you will need to add them until the pot is full. Then allow them to wilt as they cook—then add more. Add your salt, cover, and cook for thirty minutes on medium heat. Stir every few minutes to distribute the smoked meat taste evenly. Taste to confirm they are the tenderness you prefer. Serve with your favorite meat dish such as chitterlings. Eat the ham hocks or neck bones right along with the collards.

If you used frozen collards, simply pour them—frozen—right from the package to the pot.

If you use smoked neck bones, they usually don't take as long to cook as ham hocks.

People in my neck of the woods usually sprinkle lots of hot sauce on their collards. I like them that way. Give it a try.

Since this is a large pot full, just save the extras in the refrigerator. They should keep for a long time and actually get better as the juices settle in.

Willie Crawford

Willie Crawford

Willie Crawford, president of Willie Crawford, Incorporated, is a veritable rags-to-riches story. Growing up on a tobacco farm so poor that he once had to wear his grandmother's shoes to school, he decided at an early age that he would not be trapped by the cycle-of-poverty that permeated his world.

After high school, Willie worked his way through North Carolina State University. He earned a business degree and an Air Force commission on the same day. After serving more than 20 years in the Air Force, Willie decided it was time to start living his dream.

In 1996, while still in the Air Force, Willie ventured onto the Internet and started building the business he planned to be his full-time occupation after his military retirement. With hard work and a good business plan, Willie's big break came when he decided to share some of his favorite recipes with website visitors. Willie built the website http://www.Chitterlings.com, which proved to be a commercial success right from the start.

After being prompted to write a cookbook full of his recipes, Willie wrote *Soul Food Recipes Learned On A North Carolina Tobacco Farm*. This book has also been a huge commercial success.

Willie enjoys teaching others how to build successful on-line businesses. Frequently featured in radio, magazine and newspaper articles, and interviews, Willie teaches the average guy what the top marketers are doing but seldom talking about. He relaxes by going deep-sea fishing in the Gulf of Mexico, reading, and practicing karate, which he has studied since 1979.

And don't forget to ask him and his wife Nancy about their granddaughter.

When you get your copy of *Soul Food Recipes*, be sure to try the tasty collard soup recipe Willie has included in his cookbook. For more information about Willie Crawford's book, go to http://www.FlavoredWithLove.com.

Lisa's Collards

Although Lisa is busy working as a home-health nurse, she manages to cook special food for special occasions. Her husband Robert and his coworkers love her collards.

- Wash the collards and chop them fine.
- Fill the Crock-Pot® with greens.
- Cover them with water.
- Add smoked meat and other seasonings as desired. Cook on low heat overnight.

Lisa Foster

All have sinned and come short of the glory of God. Romans 3:23

♥ *Heart Health Cuisine*

Perfect Collard Greens

Foolproof—Perfect Collard Greens require the cook to mix only 5 ingredients together (if the Perfect Collard Seasoning Blend™ —see the next recipe after this one—has been prepared in advance). No elaborate preparations are required.

As a matter of fact, preparation time is less than a minute, and cooking time is 10 minutes. The taste is perfect, and the preparation is ultra simple.

The nutritional value is unsurpassed. There are only 80 calories in a large satisfying serving. Collards are an excellent source of fiber, as well as energy and protein.

Try some pepper sauce with these.

Ingredients

2 tablespoons olive oil
5 cups (1 pound) frozen chopped
  collards
⅛ teaspoon baking soda
3 tablespoons lemon juice
Perfect Collard Seasoning Blend™ to
taste

Preparation

* In a large heavy pan or Dutch oven, sauté the collards in the olive oil. 5 minutes. Stir often.
* Add the baking soda, ½ cup water, the lemon juice, and Seasoning Blend to taste.
* Cover and cook 5 minutes.

Equipment/Utensils

Large heavy pan or Dutch oven with lid, preferably a see-through lid

Nutrition Facts

Perfect Collard Greens
Per Serving
Makes 4 servings

Amount per serving	
Calories	80
Calories from fat	34

	% Daily Value *
Total Fat 3.8g	6%
Saturated Fat 0.5g	2%
Cholesterol 0 mg	0%
Sodium 93 mg	4%
Total Carbohydrate 8.3g	3%
Dietary Fiber 4.1g	16%
Protein 3.1g	

Percent values are based on a 2,000-calorie per day diet. Your daily values may differ.

Additional Information

42.7% of calories from Fat
41.7% from Carbohydrates
15.6% from Protein

♥ *Heart Health Cuisine*

Perfect Collard Seasoning Blend™

Here is our special seasoning for cooking greens—Perfect Collard Seasoning Blend™. Sprinkle it on collards as you sauté them in olive oil. You will have everything you need to make them delicious. Add a pinch of baking soda if you need it and some tart juice or vinegar. Perfect! Also if you wish, provide this mix at the table as an add-on. It has no significant calories. Be aware that we use potassium chloride in this mixture.

Use Perfect Collard Seasoning Blend™ as you would use salt for cooking collards. Omit all other seasonings except baking soda. Also use it to season other greens. It is delicious on yellow crookneck squash! Give your collards pizzazz by simply shaking on them the amount of seasoning that you like.

Ingredients

3⅛ ounces salt substitute (potassium chloride)
¼ cup Splenda®
1 tablespoon dried parsley
1 tablespoon gumbo filé
2 teaspoons ground red pepper
2 teaspoons ground black pepper
2 teaspoons basil
2 teaspoons paprika
2 teaspoons Adams® chili powder (or other brand without sodium)
2 teaspoons garlic powder
1 teaspoon onion powder
1 teaspoon oregano
½ teaspoon thyme
2 teaspoons rosemary
1 teaspoon sage
2 teaspoons crushed dried mint leaves
¼ teaspoon nutmeg
½ teaspoon cinnamon
½ teaspoon ground ginger
1 teaspoon cumin

Preparation

- Measure the ingredients carefully.
- Grind them in the blender until they are almost uniform.
- Store the mixture in an airtight container.
- Shake before using.

Equipment/Utensils

Measuring cups and spoons • Blender • Airtight container

♥ *Heart Health Cuisine*
Simply Delicious Collards

This recipe is a basic, trouble-free nutritionally sound method to prepare really tasty collards with consistent results.

Ingredients

1½ cups water
2 tablespoons olive oil
5 cups (1 pound) frozen chopped
   collards
2 tablespoons chopped garlic
¼ cup balsamic vinegar
1 teaspoon basil leaves
2 tablespoons Splenda®
⅛ teaspoon baking soda
Salt substitute to taste
Ground red pepper to taste
Freshly ground black pepper to taste

Preparation

- In a large heavy pan or Dutch oven, heat ½ cup water with the oil until it is very hot.
- Add the greens and garlic. Cover and cook 5 minutes.
- Add the remaining ingredients and cook until almost all the liquid has evaporated.

Nutrition Facts	
Simply Delicious Collards, Per serving Makes 4 servings	
Amount per serving	
Calories	113
Calories from fat	65
	% Daily Value *
Total Fat 7.2g	11%
Saturated Fat 0.9g	4%
Cholesterol 0 mg	0%
Sodium 94 mg	4%
Total Carbohydrate 8.7g	3%
Dietary Fiber 4.2g	17%
Protein 3.4g	
Percent values are based on a 2,000-calorie per day diet. Your daily values may differ.	
Additional Information 57.3% of calories from Fat 30.7% from Carbohydrates 12% from Protein	

Equipment/Utensils

Large heavy pan or Dutch oven with lid, preferably a see-through lid

Odor

When you cook collards, wear pretty cologne. The way our grandmothers and great grandmothers could make the entire house smell like an outhouse when they cooked collards was amazing. I don't know to this day how they did it. My hypothesis is that collards acquired the obnoxious odor by overcooking them.

If you follow the methods explained in these recipes, such as sautéing them quickly or including lemon juice or vinegar, you will not have the problem. The purpose of the cologne is not to cover cooking aromas (most collard recipes in this book smell yummy): instead, the cologne is to make you feel happy inside your sweet, special self.

"Like what you do. If you don't like it, do something else." Paul Harvey

♥ *Heart Health Cuisine*

The Simplest Way to Cook Tasty Collards

What could be simpler?

- Pour about a tablespoon of olive oil into a Dutch oven.
- Toss in a bag of frozen chopped collards.
- Put the lid on and let them cook on high a couple of minutes.
- Add a half cup of water, a pinch of baking soda, and about a tablespoon of lemon juice.
- Stir that, put the lid back on, and let the collards cook about 5 more minutes.

Nutritional Value
Frozen Raw Chopped Collards
For your information, the food value of uncooked collards is provided.

Notes to Cooks and Readers
We have included some vegetables and food combinations that many people don't usually eat. We'd like for you to try them because there are many wonderful tastes that we have the privilege of enjoying. Also, the nutritional value of eating a variety of vegetables cannot be overly emphasized.

Attempts have been made to include nutritional information about some of our recipes.

If you would like to obtain nutritional information about any recipe, please feel free to write the authors. We'd love to hear from you.

Nutrition Facts	
Frozen Raw Chopped collards Per serving Serving size: 4 ounces, About 1¼ cup	
Amount per serving	
Calories	46
Calories from fat	4
	% Daily Value *
Total Fat 0.4g	1%
Saturated Fat 0g	0%
Cholesterol 0 mg	0%
Sodium 54 mg	2%
Total Carbohydrate 7.3g	2%
Dietary Fiber 4.1g	16%
Protein 3.1g	
Percent values are based on a 2,000-calorie per day diet. Your daily values may differ.	
Additional Information 8.8% of calories from Fat 64% from Carbohydrates 27.2% from Protein	

Writers about nutrition believed a few years back that the food eaten by Southerners—especially poor rural Southerners—was not nutritious. Some nutritionists have taken a second look at Southern nutrition. Few foods are more nutritious than Southern greens.

♥ *Heart Health Cuisine*

Collards for Mike

Mike, my wonderful intelligent son-in-law, does not like some types of vegetables. Spinach has always been the only green leafy vegetable he would consider. While developing collard recipes, I have fed him dips, casseroles, enchiladas, and lasagna without telling him he was eating collards. Finally he became suspicious.

When I was visiting Christie and Mike, I cooked collards—straight, unadorned collards—by the recipe below for Christie, who savors most vegetables. That night she placed the food on the plates before calling people to dinner. She served Mike these collards, and with a countenance of contentment he ate them!

It's amazing that something this simple to fix is so delicious. And I can remember when I thought I didn't like collards.

Ingredients

3 tablespoons olive oil
5 cups (1 pound) frozen
   chopped collards
12 ounces frozen seasoning blend
⅛ teaspoon baking soda
1 tablespoon Splenda®
⅓ cup vinegar
Salt substitute to taste

Preparation

- Sauté the collards and seasoning.
- Blend in the olive oil.
- Add the baking soda, Splenda®, vinegar, and salt substitute. Cover and cook until the vinegar is absorbed.

Equipment/Utensils

Deep pan, preferably with transparent lid

Note

That's all! And Mike liked them.

Nutrition Facts	
Collards for Mike, per serving Makes 5 servings	
Amount per serving	
Calories	125
Calories from fat	76
% Daily Value *	
Total Fat 8.5g	13%
Saturated Fat 1.1g	6%
Cholesterol 0 mg	0%
Sodium 43 mg	2%
Total Carbohydrate 9.2g	3%
Dietary Fiber 19.3g	77%
Protein 3g	
Percent values are based on a 2,000-calorie per day diet. Your daily values may differ.	
Additional Information 60.9% of calories from Fat 29.5% from Carbohydrates 9.6% from Protein	

Microwave Collard Greens

Cook finely chopped collards in a small amount of chicken broth in the microwave. Cover them in a vented dish or with clear plastic wrap that has some holes in it. You don't need to cook them long—maybe 2 minutes. Then let them stand a couple more minutes. Season them with some lemon juice and some of your favorite seasonings.

♥ *Heart Health Cuisine*

Sicilian Greens

Collard greens, turnip greens, greens of the daisy flower—these are all delicious Italian dishes, and they did not originate in the South. Italians (Sicilians) used them in the Middle Ages, or even before.

But none of this, a cup of that an ounce of this, etc. They were cooked, and BOY are they good!

All you do is boil them in water with olive oil and garlic (don't forget to cut the garlic into small pieces if you can stand it).

Fry some garlic cloves in olive oil with oregano.

After the leaves get tender, put them into the frying pan with the garlic and oregano, and a little bit of salt.

Stir well; then pass through a colander.

Add some hot Italian pepper flakes, olive oil, a little more garlic, and oregano.

Stir and serve. *Delicioso* (that means delicious)!   Paul Urso

Paul Urso

Now this is the TRUTH! My father brought the whole family to the U.S. from Sicily in the spring of 1931 (yes we were ALL born in Sicily). I was five years old and couldn't speak a word of English, but I spoke Italian (Sicilian) extremely well!

We settled in a tenement in Brooklyn, NY, by the East River. That area of Brooklyn was over-run by mobsters, but my Dad had nothing to do with them, even though he was out of work (the depression you know), and they had those big fancy, white-walled black cars (bullet proof I might add).

We lived in a one LARGE room cold flat and off to the sides there were three SMALL bedrooms. In order to keep warm on cold winter nights, my Dad used to heat bricks on the wood (sometimes coal when we could get it) stove and place them in the beds. We had lots of bricks! I had to learn English right away (the neighborhood kids called it American); otherwise the kids would beat me over the head or kick me in the rear while they screamed, "WOP, DAGO, GREASEBALL!" The funny thing, they were of Italian descent also!

I was in World War II (Signal Corps), went to St Francis College in Brooklyn, NY, on the G.I. Bill, and received a scholarship for Graduate Study at Marquette University, Milwaukee, Wisconsin. After receiving the Ph.D. degree from The University of Tennessee in Immunology and Zoology, I researched in immunology and taught in medical schools.   God bless, Paul

The Way Mama Cooked Greens

Mama always mixed collards with other greens, such as turnips and mustard. She required her children to wash them a hundred times it seemed. Into the pot she would throw a big ham bone and some chunks of ham.

She seemed to think that adding seasonings was cheating. When she thought no one was watching, she added a dash of vinegar, a pinch of baking soda, plenty of salt, and a bit of black pepper. She always slipped a spoonful of sugar, to keep the greens from being bitter—turnips are usually bitter.

Daddy had a horror of eating onions, but Mama loved them. She would place a whole onion in the pot and cook it with the greens. Then she would discretely remove it and dispose of it.

She would stuff them into a big pot and cover them with water. Then she would cook them a couple of hours. By then, the collards would be mushy, but the turnips would still be chewy.

She always made wonderful cornbread to go with the greens. When she had fresh corn, she would cut the corn off the cob. She would barely nick the corn, and then she would scrape that inimitable juice from the corn. All that unforgettable freshness of corn would be included in her cornbread.   Myrtle's recipe as told by Mary Lou

Martha White's Greens

Martha said:
Greens are cold weather food. If I get to feeling puny, give me turnip green soup.

This is my basic recipe for any kind of greens—turnip greens, mustard, collards— whatever.

When I cook collards, I toss in some other greens to go with it. I like to mix it all up. Kale is like a weak collard green; I like to add some of that.

I put any kind of pork in there. (In the background her friend Elizabeth commented that cooking some greens with leftover grilled pork chops yields laudable results.) If I'm watching my weight, I substitute a vegetable cube for the pork.

Take the stems out. While I'm picking and washing greens I begin taking the stems out. I don't like that big stemmy piece. I chop greens ahead of time. By the time I start cooking them in the pot, they are already chopped.

I chop up some green onions. Also, I like just a little jalapeño chopped in there.

I'm a soupy person. I like all that pot likker for my cornbread. So I add plenty of water and cook the till they are tender.
                                                                                        Martha White

Cheryl's Collards

Cheryl cooks collards at least once a week. Although she makes them taste delicious, she does not have a complicated recipe. This is it:

Cook collards with smoked neck bones or ham hock, salt, and black pepper. Also add 1 onion, finely chopped.

"I have to have my black pepper."

Cheryl Sowers

Thoughts about Cooking Collards

- Collards grown in cool weather are tender, especially after they have been kissed by a couple of frosts.
- Summer collards tend to be tough. To tenderize summer collards place them in the freezer for a few hours before cooking. Freezer frost is almost as good as natural frost.
- Adding a pinch of baking soda to the water will also tenderize tough collards.
- Butter or bacon fat may be used to season collards.

Ruth Ishee

Seasoning Meat for Collards

Side meat, salt pork, smoked pork neck bones, bacon, sliced ham, tasso, ham hocks, crawfish, oysters, sausage, fatback, chicken, turkey—several meats taste good with collards.

Tasso, a heavily spiced and smoked cured ham made from pork shoulder, is delicious with or without collards. It is a Creole and Cajun specialty popular in Louisiana.

Because oysters and crawfish require little cooking, they should be added toward the end of the process. Pork, on the other hand, should be precooked before adding the collards.

Collard Accompaniments

- Cornbread is an essential.
- Thinly sliced tomatoes and red (called red, but actually purple) onion rings layered over collards are pretty and flavorful.
- In south Mississippi piney hill country, fresh green onions are essential with collards.
- Jalapeño peppers spread over collards taste great.
- Crushed pepper sprinkled over greens will make a forehead break out in sweat, but what a way to go!

Cooking Hint

Using a deep pan prevents spills on the stove.

Collard Greens, Charleston Style

Ingredients

½ pound ham hock
¼ teaspoon salt
¼ teaspoon pepper
½ teaspoon garlic powder
1 tablespoon Texas Pete® or Louisiana Hot Sauce®
3 quarts water
1 stick butter
Fresh collards (See notes below.)

Preparation

- Cook ham hock, salt, pepper, garlic powder, seasoned salt, and hot sauce in 3 quarts water for 1 hour.
- Add collards and butter.
- Cook for 1 hour or until tender.
- Reduce cooking time if using frozen greens.

Melinda's Notes

Sorry I did not include [the amount of collards], you know how we cooks never measure; a pinch here, a handful there, a sip in the bowl and 2 sips for me. I would say the yield for this recipe should be 6 servings. Of course then, our serving might be a bowlful *versus* Dr. Atkins' 2 tablespoons full.

I have also used this on bagged greens when I have been in a hurry. But I feel like we would be safe in saying 4-6 servings. You never know how much those greens will cook down; so I just wash and wash, and when I get tired of tearing leaves, say that is enough. (A guesstimate)

Also, we have a friend (I would never try this) who actually washed her greens in the washing machine all the time. I never fully understood, but I think she put them in the strainer of the washing machine. YUK! But it would be interesting to know if others do that!   Melinda Ridge

Equipment/Utensils

Big cooking pot

Ham Hocks

Ham hocks, which are pieces of lower pork legs, contain bone, lean meat, fat, and rind. They may be purchased fresh, but usually they are smoked and salted. Southern cooks use them to add flavor and enrich the texture of greens.

Beautiful presentation says, "I love you."

Two Sisters' Collards

Ruth said, "The way a vegetable is cut has a lot to do with the way it tastes. I roll collards like cigars and shred them as thin as possible with a very sharp knife. In fact, I shred them so thin they look like green spaghetti. This way they are crunchy, crispy, bright green, and collard-like."

Ruth gave me this recipe, but I meddled with it.

Ingredients

2 tablespoons chopped bacon
½ finely chopped onion (½ cup)
1½ cups warm water
1 gallon-sized bag finely chopped winter
   collards
2 teaspoons Tone's® spicy spaghetti
   seasoning mix
1 teaspoon dried basil

Preparation

- In a Dutch oven or other thick, deep, and heavy cooking pan, sauté the onion with the bacon.
- Add the warm water. Turn the heat as high as possible.
- When the water reaches a rolling boil, add the greens and spices.
- Cook at high heat until the water has evaporated—about 5-7 minutes.

Equipment/Utensils

Heavy pot

Nutrition Facts	
Two Sisters' Collards, per serving Makes 6 servings	
Amount per serving	
Calories	95
Calories from fat	53
	% Daily Value *
Total Fat 5.8g	9%
Saturated Fat 2.1g	10%
Cholesterol 6 mg	2%
Sodium 171 mg	7%
Total Carbohydrate 7g	2%
Dietary Fiber 3.7g	15%
Protein 3.4g	
Percent values are based on a 2,000-calorie per day diet. Your daily values may differ.	
Additional Information 56% of calories from Fat 29.6% from Carbohydrates 14.4% from Protein	

Notes

- I could not resist the urge to embellish Ruth's recipe. When she cooks collards, she adds a small amount of bacon drippings and salt.
- I add bits of bacon, chopped onion, Italian seasoning, and basil leaves as listed in the recipe. Don't tell her I changed her recipe.
- Ruth says she uses only *fresh* winter collards. Our staff discovered that the winter collards from her collard patch could be *frozen* and prepared satisfactorily. As a matter of fact, they are tasty and tender.
- If the greens are bitter—Ruth's greens are never bitter—I add a tiny pinch of sugar. Ruth doesn't use sugar.   Ruth and Mary Lou

❤ *Heart Health Cuisine*
Hot Pepper Sauce

An absolute essential item where collards are served and always served with any piece collard Ruth has ever thought about cooking...

Wash a mixture of red, green, and yellow peppers—hot skinny peppers. Pack them into a jar and fill the jar with boiling vinegar. Seal the jars. The pepper sauce can be canned in a cold pack cooker for 10 minutes. Food color can be added for pepper sauce placed in fancy bottles. By following these instructions you will be using the cold pack method of canning.

Ruth Ishee

What to Serve with Collards

- Contrasting flavors, colors, and textures add to the pleasure of eating greens, which complement many different foods.
- Sliced sweetened strawberries over collards—try it!
- Also fresh, sweet peaches enhance the taste of collards.
- For a gastronomic event you will remember with fondness forever, heat some boudin (rice and meat in sausage casing) to complete your meal. Heat it in the iron skillet.
- Red radishes beautify the plate and add additional tartness.
- Pickled beets, okra, cucumbers—anything pickled will go well.
- Rice—especially basmati—served underneath collards will catch all the rich flavor that goes to the bottom of the plate.

More Suggestions

Try these toppings:
- Lemon wedges
- Lime slices
- Avocado wedges
- Fresh cucumber slices
- Carrot sticks
- Bacon bits
- Sliced raw turnips
- Parsley
- Cilantro
- Olives
- French fried onion rings
- Canned French fried onions
- Tiny new potatoes
- Cantaloupe
- Relishes

Although well-prepared collards are tasty enough to be enjoyed day after day without garnishes, sauces, and relishes, intriguing presentation increases dining pleasure. Serving delicious food with pretty garnishes is a little way to show you care.

Paul's Collards

- Pick the collards by breaking the leaves off. (There is no need to pull up the roots. (Ruth and Bill Ishee have an excellent collard patch this year. If you stop by their house, they will be glad to share a mess with you.)
- Wash the dirt and insects off the leaves.
- Cut the leaves in strips.
- Remove the stalks.
- Fill a cooking pot about two-thirds full and add seasonings. (Select from the list below.)
- Add water. (Don't add too much, because the collards will cook down fast.)
- Bring to a boil.
- Lower heat and simmer 15-20 minutes. (If you want to make the collards irresistible, add some fried and crumbled bacon.) Paul

Note

This recipe was acquired by unobtrusively observing Paul prepare collard greens on multiple occasions.

Cooking Them Collards

It's time to eat more vegetables. Greens: mustard greens, turnip greens, collards. They will help you stay slim and beautiful if you limit the amount of hog fat. Collards have broad, slick leaves that easily give up the coat of sandy dirt often found on greens. Also they reach a state of doneness in 15-20 minutes. (Mustard and turnip greens must be cooked forever to reach doneness, as defined by Southern palates.)

To cook delicious collards without excessive calories, one needs a creative urge coupled with a wide assortment of condiments that can be employed at various times in various ways, as the cook desires. Here are some seasoning suggestions:

Paul's Collard Seasoning List

- Cubes of Oven Roasted Turkey Spam®
- Leftover precooked lean pork
- Andouille sausage
- Chicken broth
- Olive oil
- Tabasco® sauce
- Cumin
- Maraschino cherry juice
- Sweet pickle juice
- Salt
- Black pepper, red pepper
- Onion flakes
- Sautéed fresh onions
- Garlic powder
- Pear vinegar
- Balsamic vinegar
- Lemon juice
- Basil
- Liquid smoke

One must develop his own concoction, which will vary on different occasions.

Lemon, Butter, and Garlic Collards

When they are available, we use baby collards instead of frozen chopped collards. If you use fresh collards, be sure that they are very tender. Fresh garlic is essential in this recipe.

Ingredients

2 lemons
1 tablespoon extra virgin olive oil
16 ounces (5 cups) frozen chopped collards
2 garlic bulbs, minced
⅛ teaspoon baking soda
2 tablespoons Splenda®
Salt substitute to taste
Freshly ground black pepper to taste
Ground red pepper to taste
½ cup water
2 tablespoons unsalted butter

Preparation

- Squeeze a lemon and remove the seeds from the juice. Cut the second lemon in wedges.
- Sauté the garlic in the olive oil 2 minutes; add the collards; continue to sauté 3-5 minutes or until the collards are tender (but not mushy).
- Add the baking soda, Splenda®, salt substitute, peppers and water.
- Cover and cook at high heat 3 more minutes.
- Sprinkle the lemon juice over the collards and cook them until the liquid is reduced.
- Transfer the collards to a serving bowl.
- Dot the butter over the hot collards and garnish them with the lemon wedges.
- Serve immediately.

Equipment/Utensils

Heavy pot or Dutch oven with tight lid, preferably see-through. • Garlic press • Knife • Cutting board • Serving bowl

About Garlic

A garlic bulb is composed of approximately 12 cloves, often called "toes." We have never tasted anything with too much garlic; therefore, I have concluded that the situation does not exist.

If you don't have a garlic press, simply whop the garlic with a knife handle. You may need to chop it more if you don't strike it hard enough.

We are guilty of using minced garlic from a jar. In Baton Rouge there is an open-air market that sells peeled garlic in jars. We use that too when it is available.

Collards are precious. Never waste a collard leaf.

Collard Greens with Ham Hocks And Garlic

Ingredients

2 large smoked ham hocks, about 2 pounds
1 tablespoon olive oil
1 cup onions, thinly sliced
2 garlic bulbs, minced
5 cups (16 ounces) frozen chopped collards
2 quarts chicken stock
¼ cup red wine vinegar
2 tablespoons Splenda®
⅛ teaspoon baking soda
Perfect Collard Seasoning Blend™ to taste

Preparaton

- Cover the ham hocks in the chicken stock, bring them to a boil, and simmer 30 minutes.
- Sauté the onions and garlic in the Dutch oven.
- Add the collard greens, vinegar, and Splenda®.
- Remove the meat from the ham hock bones and add the meat to the collards.
- Add the stock, baking soda, and seasoning blend to taste. Simmer until the collards are tender.

Equipment/Utensils

Large saucepan • Dutch oven • Knife • Cutting board

Topping Suggestion

- Chop some hard-boiled eggs and serve over collards.

Margaret's Classical Collards

Margaret Scott, who is a very classy lady, and I stopped in a grocery store to chat. Since we had chatted in another grocery store the day before, I explained to her, "I am writing a cookbook about collards. What's your excuse?"

Eventually, she told me how she cooks collards. She said, "I fix them the classical way." Here is what she told me:

- I just fry some salt pork until it's crisp. Then I add a little water and steam it.
- I make sure the collards are washed well.
- I put the collards in with the salt pork and cook them until they are tender.

Margaret Scott

"Goals are dreams we convert to plans and take action to fulfill." Zig Ziglar

Bacon Seasoned Collard Greens

The seasonings allow the truly delicious collard flavor to emerge.

Ingredients

8 ounces thick-sliced bacon, cut into ½ inch pieces
1 large yellow onion (approximately 1½ cups) thinly sliced
3 pounds fresh collard greens, finely chopped
Salt substitute to taste
⅛ teaspoon baking soda
1 tablespoon Splenda®
⅓ cup vinegar
Generous shakes of black pepper
Crushed red pepper as desired
3 tablespoons minced garlic

Nutrition Facts	
Bacon Seasoned Collard Greens per serving Makes 6 servings	
Amount per serving	
Calories	386
Calories from fat	272
	% Daily Value *
Total Fat 30.3g	47%
Saturated Fat 10.9g	54%
Cholesterol 33 mg	11%
Sodium 418 mg	17%
Total Carbohydrate 17.8g	6%
Dietary Fiber 9g	36%
Protein 10.8g	
Percent values are based on a 2,000-calorie per day diet. Your daily values may differ.	
Additional Information 70.4% of calories from Fat 18.4% from Carbohydrates 11.2% from Protein	

Preparation

- Fry the bacon until it is crisp in a large heavy pot. Remove the bacon and set it aside.
- Sauté the onion in the bacon drippings until it is translucent.
- Add the collard greens, salt substitute, baking soda, black pepper, and red pepper to the onions; sauté for 10 minutes or until they are tender.
- Add the vinegar and sweetener.
- If the collards need more tenderization, add water in small increments and continue to cook.
- Immediately before serving, crumble the bacon and stir it into the collards.

Equipment/Utensils

Cutting board • Knife • Scissors • Heavy pot

Notes

- For an old-fashioned Southern flavor, substitute salt pork for the bacon.
- If you wish, add some hot pepper sauce to these greens; spicemouths™ have been observed, however, eating them with nothing added.
- Jalapeño peppers, banana peppers, and slices of red onions go well with Bacon Seasoned Collards, also.

♥ *Heart Health Cuisine*

Collard Greens

This simple, but delicious collard greens recipe has diabetic exchanges included in the nutrition facts.

Ingredients

1 large bunch of collard greens (64 ounces, cut and washed)
3 cup low-sodium chicken broth or homemade chicken stock without meat
2 medium onions, chopped
3 whole garlic cloves, crushed
1 teaspoon red pepper flakes
1 teaspoon black pepper

Preparation

- Wash and cut greens.
- Mix greens in large stock pot together with the remaining ingredients.
- Cook until tender. (Allow flavors to blend by preparing the dish early in the day. The longer it blends the better it tastes!)

Exchanges:

2 vegetables

Additional Nutrition Facts

Serving Size is ⅛th recipe
Servings Per Recipe 8
Amount Per Serving
Calories 61
Calories from Fat 4
Total fat 0g (1% Daily Value)
Saturated fat 0g (0% Daily Value)
Cholesterol 0mg (0% Daily Value)
Sodium 29mg (1% Daily Value)
Total Carbohydrate 14g (4% Daily Value)
Dietary Fiber 5g (21% Daily Value)
Sugars 3g
Protein 3g (5% Daily Value)
Vitamin A 30%
Vitamin C 37%
Calcium 5%
Iron 2%
Percent Daily Values are based on a 2,000-calorie diet. Your daily values may be higher or lower depending on your calorie needs.

Recipe courtesy of the American Diabetes Association

Sandra's Greens

We are sharing this recipe from <u>Flavored with Love</u> because it has a unique approach.

You can start with collards or mustard or turnips. For this recipe we are going to use a mixture of turnip greens and mustard greens.

Wash them thoroughly to remove any residual dirt or sand. Peel and slice the turnip roots. Place all that in a large pot. Almost fill the pot. The greens will cook down. Add a teaspoon of sugar when you are cooking turnips because they may be bitter without it. Add salt, black pepper, cayenne pepper, and ham hock. Add water not quite to the top of the greens.

Cook slowly–about 2 or 3 hours–until the greens are almost done. Don't scorch them.

Add several pods of okra on top and continue to cook just until the okra is done.

Note: After the okra is added, don't be stirring the greens and don't overcook the okra.

Sandra Winzer

Sandra Winzer

Sandra is a beautiful young woman, who is a telemetry technician in hospital cardiac units. As the years go by, Sandra never ages. Her face is adorned with an infectious smile, and she usually has something funny or witty to say. She is often able to laugh at herself.

Rosemary's Collards

Rosemary insists that there is only one way to cook collards, and here it is. She said she cannot wait to get her hands on this cookbook and discover other ways. Here is her recipe in her own words as she dictated it to me one night before church:

- Wash and look the greens. That means look at them and check them over for bugs. Take off the stems.
- What I do first: I take my smoked neck bones and put just a little water, enough to cover them.
- I cut me up a big ole onion to put in there. If I've got green onions, I put them instead of the regular onions—about a cup.
- Bring that to a boil, and boil it for about 20 minutes. Add fresh collards—a pot full—3 bunches!
- Salt and pepper to taste—not too much salt because the neck bones are salty.
- Cover and boil for about 45 minutes.

Rosemary Ficklin

Read more about Rosemary in "Angels and Saints," which begins on page 203

Embellished Collards
Enhanced Cuisine

Sweet Tomato Collards

This unusual recipe is guaranteed to convert anyone into a collard lover. One taster said, "Prepare to have your tongue get so excited it'll start slapping you in the face vigorously!" The sweet tomato sauce is also good on boiled cabbage, black-eyed peas, field peas, pinto beans, October beans or kidney beans, should you wish to branch out and experiment beyond collards.

Source: Cut 'n Clean Greens® (http://www.cutncleangreens.com)

Ingredients

4 quarts water
1 tablespoon salt
1 (2-pound) bag Cut 'n Clean® Collard Greens
½ cup (1 stick) butter
½ cup granulated sugar
2 (14.5-ounce) cans Italian-style sliced stewed tomatoes
¼ teaspoon crushed red pepper flakes (or more if you like things spicy)
Freshly ground black pepper
1 tablespoon cider vinegar
2-3 cloves garlic, chopped

Preparation

In a large stockpot, bring water and salt to a boil; add collards and stir to submerge. Boil, uncovered, for 20 minutes, stirring occasionally so greens cook evenly.

While greens are cooking, put butter, sugar, tomatoes, red pepper, a few grindings of black pepper, vinegar and garlic in a saucepan and bring to a boil. Boil gently, uncovered, while greens are cooking, stirring occasionally. Near the end of the cooking time, use a knife or the edge of a spoon to break up any large chunks of tomato. Tomato mixture will reduce slightly from evaporation during cooking.

When greens are done, drain well in a colander and return them to the stockpot. Add the tomato mixture and stir well to combine.

Serves 6-8.

Dorothy Reinhold

Reprinted with permission from Cut 'n Clean Greens® (http://www.cutncleangreens.com)

Dorothy Reinhold

Dorothy Reinhold runs the test kitchen for Cut 'n Clean Greens® and develops recipes starring their healthy greens varieties. She writes a bi-weekly food and recipe column that is published in the San Gabriel Valley Newspaper Group. Her recipes have won contests and have been featured in *Sunset Magazine* and other food publications and Web sites.

About her employer, Dorothy said, "Cut 'n Clean Greens® is a great company, and the people who run it are just very fine human beings, as well."

The Cut `n Clean Greens® Story

Cut `n Clean Greens®—America's original and leading brand of fresh-cut cooking greens—are grown and processed year-round by San Miguel Produce Inc. in the coastal plains of Oxnard, California, where the temperate climate is ideal for growing the highest quality greens. The company's focus on freshness and quality continues from out in the field to inside on the production line. In fact, San Miguel Produce developed specialized equipment and methods for cutting and washing cooking greens so the greens make it from the field to the bag and on their way to the store the same day, with all of nature's goodness intact.

All Cut `n Clean Greens® are grown exclusively 365 days a year and are harvested fresh every morning to fulfill the orders that will be processed and shipped out that same day. This unmatched quality and freshness has established Cut `n Clean Greens as the nation's leading brand of bagged greens. San Miguel Produce is committed to providing consistent supplies of the freshest greens with the largest selection of single and mixed varieties year-round, throughout North America. Cut `n Clean Greens® offers 12 varieties, including: Collards, Kale, Mustard (flat and curly), Chard (red, green and rainbow), Spinach, Turnip, Beet and Euro Greens (Swiss chard, mustard, turnip and kale) and Country Greens (collard, mustard, turnip).

Cut `n Clean Greens® is not only the originator of bagged cooking greens, but continues to provide online consumer help on its Web site (http://www.cutncleangreens.com). The site contains more than 100 nutritious recipes and is packed with nutritional information about the health benefits of greens.

Collard Information

Quoted from http://www.cutncleangreens.com/products/collard:
With a texture similar to cabbage, and a mildly bitter flavor collard greens have become a staple vegetable of the Southern United States. Often thought of as a soul food, collards are being consumed by an increasing number of people trying to incorporate healthy foods into their diet….

Distinctively broad flat leaves blue-green in color are distinguishing characteristics of this healthy vegetable. Collards greens are a non-heading member of the Brassica family, which includes such vegetables as broccoli and cauliflower.

Collard greens pair well with other vegetables and with meats such as smoked turkey or salt pork. Collards can also be added to soups and stews, or slow-cooked in their own juices for a completely satisfying side dish.

Collard greens have a high concentration of several key nutrients including vitamin C, vitamin E, and beta-carotene—antioxidants that reduce harmful free radicals. Because they reduce free radicals, collards may help to fight the onset or progression of certain diseases.

"Get your vitamins in their original package!" Cut `n Clean Greens®

Terry's Collards and Tomatoes

Ingredients

4 slices bacon

2 pounds collards

2 tablespoons Italian seasoning (basil, rosemary, oregano)

1 teaspoon minced garlic

1 hand full (approximately) onion and bell pepper mix

1 can sliced tomatoes (Drain and save liquid.)

Preparation

- Place the bacon in a skillet or large pot.
- Add the garlic, onion, and bell pepper.
- Add chopped cleaned collards. Cook down. Add Italian season mix and drained tomatoes.
- Cook 5 minutes. Add juice. Heat 5 to 6 minutes. Serve with cornbread.

Equipment/Utensils

- Skillet or large pot

Nutrition Facts	
Terry's Collards and Tomatoes per serving makes 4 servings	
Amount per serving	
Calories	222
Calories from fat	108
	% Daily Value *
Total Fat 12.1g	19%
Saturated Fat 4.1g	20%
Cholesterol 12 mg	4%
Sodium 206 mg	9%
Total Carbohydrate 20g	7%
Dietary Fiber 16.1g	64%
Protein 8.6g	

Percent values are based on a 2,000-calorie per day diet. Your daily values may differ.

Additional Information
48.6% of calories from Fat
36% from Carbohydrates
15.5% from Protein

Terry Chrisman

Terry Chrisman

Terry was inspired to cook after she bought a 107-year-old house, and she can't seem to get enough new recipes. She is a great cook who loves to share her recipes at the Collard Patch blog and to share her food with hungry people who like to eat Louisiana style.

During an ice storm, she and her husband boarded six members of the Louisiana Tech University football team in their home for several days. The smallest one weighed 280 pounds. One of their favorite dishes was Taco Soup. Visit the Collard Patch Blog (http://collardpatch.blogspot.com) for the recipe the football players loved. (A blog is a weblog, often a diary of a person's interesting events. The Collard Patch Blog is loaded with recipes. Go there to see what we have added lately.)

When Terry is not cooking, she spends her time working in her lovely yard, where she has beautiful morning glories, antique roses, hydrangeas, and hollyhocks. She is planning to place a bottle tree in her yard. In their spare time, she and her husband are constructing a Cajun cook shack, where they will house their crawfish boiler pot, a barbecue pit, and a fish fryer.

Collards Risotto

Arborio is a pearly, round fat Italian rice, which forms the foundation of Risotto, a creamy Italian rice dish cooked with broth and sprinkled or tossed with cheese.

Serve the rice with collards on top. Add one of these: crab meat warmed and tossed with lemon juice and butter; shrimp cooked, seasoned, and peeled; chicken cooked, seasoned, and chopped; sautéed mushrooms. Shape leftovers in balls, roll in breadcrumbs, and deep fry.

Collards

Ingredients

3 tablespoons olive oil
5 cups (16 ounces) frozen chopped collards
12 ounces frozen seasoning blend
⅛ teaspoon baking soda
1 tablespoon Splenda®
⅓ cup vinegar
Crushed red pepper, ground black pepper, and salt to taste
1 can (10 ¾ ounces) cream of chicken soup

Preparation

- Sauté the collards and seasoning blend in the olive oil.
- Add the baking soda, Splenda®, vinegar, red pepper, black pepper, and salt. Cover and cook until the vinegar is absorbed.
- Add the chicken soup, heat thoroughly, remove from heat, and set aside.

Risotto

Ingredients

3 tablespoons olive oil
12 ounces frozen seasoning blend
2 tablespoons minced garlic
1½ cups Arborio rice
3½ cups chicken broth
1 tablespoon I Can't Believe It's Not Butter® Spray
1 cup Kraft® shredded Parmesan, Romano, and Asiago cheeses (or Parmesan)

Preparation

- Sauté the seasoning blend and garlic in the olive oil.
- Stir in the rice. Sauté 1 minute.
- Add 1 cup of the broth and simmer. Stir frequently. Cook until the liquid is absorbed.
- Add the remaining broth and cook covered until the liquid is absorbed.
- Remove from heat. Stir in the cheese and butter spray.

Equipment/Utensils

2 large pots, preferably with see-through lids

Aegean Collard-Rice Casserole

Collards with a Middle Eastern flair!

Ingredients

Non-stick cooking spray
1 cup basmati rice (uncooked)
2 cups water
2 tablespoons olive oil
16 ounces (5 cups) frozen chopped
　　collards
¼ cup minced onions
2 tablespoons minced garlic
⅛ teaspoon baking soda
2 tablespoons Splenda®
3 tablespoons rice vinegar
2 tablespoons A-1® steak sauce
1 teaspoon basil
½ teaspoon ginger
¼ to ½ teaspoon ground red pepper
Salt substitute to taste
1½ cups Fat Free Half & Half®
4 ounces Athenos® crumbled feta
　　cheese with garlic and herb
3 eggs, beaten
1 cup golden raisins
½ cup breadcrumbs
2 tablespoons butter

Nutrition Facts	
Aegean Collard-Rice Casserole per serving makes 15 servings	
Amount per serving	
Calories	195
Calories from fat	57
	% Daily Value *
Total Fat 6.5g	10%
Saturated Fat 2.7g	14%
Cholesterol 53 mg	018%
Sodium 198 mg	8%
Total Carbohydrate 28.4g	9%
Dietary Fiber 1.7g	7%
Protein 6.1g	

Percent values are based on a 2,000-calorie per day diet. Your daily values may differ.

Additional Information
29.2% of calories from Fat
58.3% from Carbohydrates
12.5% from Protein

Preparation

- Spray a baking dish with cooking spray.
- Place the rice and water in a 3-quart saucepan; bring to a boil; stir once.
- Simmer the rice covered with a tight-fitting, see-through lid 15 minutes or until the water absorbs.
- Sauté the collards, onions, and garlic with the olive oil in the large pot 5 minutes and turn off the heat. Add the baking soda, Splenda® vinegar, steak sauce, basil, ginger, red pepper, and salt substitute.
- As soon as the collards cool, stir in the cream, cheese, and eggs. Stir well. Toss the raisins into the mixture.
- Transfer the mix to the casserole; top it with breadcrumbs and dots of butter.
- Bake at 350° 30 minutes or until the dish bubbles.

Equipment/Utensils

3-quart (13"X 9 X 2") Pyrex® baking dish • 3-quart saucepan• Dutch oven

Creamed Collards

Here is one of those recipes designed to take to a covered dish meal because it is scrumptious.

Ingredients

1 package (1 pound) frozen chopped
    collard greens
1 tablespoon olive oil
⅛ teaspoon baking soda
3 tablespoons rice vinegar (with no
    added salt)
3 thick slices bacon
1 cup chopped onions
3 tablespoons minced garlic
2 cups Fat Free Half & Half®
3 tablespoons flour
¼ teaspoon red pepper
½ teaspoon black pepper
¼ teaspoon nutmeg
1 teaspoon rosemary
Salt substitute to taste
2 tablespoons Splenda®

Nutrition Facts	
Creamed Collards per serving, approximately 1 cup Makes 8 servings	
Amount per serving	
Calories	171
Calories from fat	91
% Daily Value *	
Total Fat 10.1g	16%
Saturated Fat 3.2g	16%
Cholesterol 9 mg	3%
Sodium 213 mg	9%
Total Carbohydrate 14.7g	5%
Dietary Fiber 2.6g	10%
Protein 5.4g	

Percent values are based on a 2,000-calorie per day diet. Your daily values may differ.

Additional Information
53.1% of calories from Fat
34.3% from Carbohydrates
12.6% from Protein

Preparation

- Sauté the collards and baking soda in the olive oil 3 minutes.
- Add the vinegar and 1 cup water. Cover and cook at high heat until the water is absorbed to make the greens very tender.
- Cut the bacon into small pieces. Grind the bacon, onions, and garlic in the blender with 1 cup water.
- Sauté the bacon, mixture in a deep saucepan until the water is absorbed.
- Without taking time to wash the blender, pour the Half & Half® into it. Add the flour and the seasonings, including the Splenda®. Mix thoroughly.
- Stir the cream mixture into the bacon mixture and cook over low heat until the sauce is smooth and creamy.
- Add the sauce to the collards. Stir and heat slowly until the mixture reaches a desired consistency.

Equipment/Utensils

Stockpot, deep soup pan, or Dutch oven with lid, preferably see-through •
Blender

"There are no gains without pains." Benjamin Franklin

Collard Mayonnaise Soufflé

This soufflé is easy to assemble, the taste is incredibly delicious, and the nutritional analysis is excellent.

Ingredients

2 tablespoons olive oil
5 cups (1 pound) frozen
    chopped collards
12 ounces frozen seasoning blend
⅛ teaspoon baking soda
2 tablespoons Splenda®
⅓ cup vinegar
Salt substitute to taste
½ teaspoon cinnamon
½ teaspoon ginger
1 can cream of mushroom soup
2 eggs, beaten
1 cup light mayonnaise
1 cup (4 ounces) grated sharp cheddar
    cheese
1-2 teaspoons Tony Chachere's or
    Swampy Land Seasoning (p. 182)

Nutrition Facts	
Collard Mayonnaise Soufflé Per serving Makes 15 servings	
Amount per serving	
Calories	**195**
Calories from fat	57
	% Daily Value *
Total Fat 6.5g	10%
Saturated Fat 2.7g	14%
Cholesterol 53 mg	18%
Sodium 198 mg	8%
Total Carbohydrate 28.4g	9%
Dietary Fiber 1.7g	7%
Protein 6.1g	

Percent values are based on a 2,000-calorie per day diet. Your daily values may differ.

Additional Information
29.2% of calories from Fat
58.3% from Carbohydrates
12.5% from Protein

Preparation

- Sauté the collards, seasoning blend, and seasonings in the olive oil 5 minutes or until tender.
- Allow the collards to cool.
- Preheat oven to 375°
- Combine the collards, soup, eggs, mayonnaise, and cheese. Mix thoroughly.
- Spoon into the baking dish.
- Bake approximately 45 minutes or until a knife inserted into the center comes out almost clean.

Equipment/Utensils

Deep saucepan, preferably with transparent lid • 8X 11½" baking pan or casserole dish

Don't be too shy to make the plates look pretty with garnishes. While you are cooking, save a few ingredients and place them on the individual plates or serving platters.

A few pieces of grated cheese, some raw vegetables, a strawberry, or a tomato—look around and use your imagination.

Make the food pretty. Enjoy food; enjoy life.

Collard Crock-Pot® Casserole Weapon

Every widower knows that a casserole is a devious weapon that available women use to attack poor helpless eligible men. This casserole is a dangerous example because it is loaded with flavor and yummy richness. You can dump the ingredients into the Crock-Pot® and leave it. If you wish, you can dress it up.

Ingredients

16 ounces (5 cups) frozen chopped
    collard greens
2 tablespoons olive oil
2 tablespoons balsamic vinegar
1 teaspoon salt substitute
2 teaspoons Splenda®
1 can (10 ½ ounces) cream of mushroom
    soup
1 can (10 ½ ounces) cream of chicken
    soup
1 can french-fried onions

Preparation

- Place all ingredients except the onions in the Crock-Pot®.
- Turn on the heat. Use low if you are going to work or shop.
- Use high if it's 2-3 hours until dinner.
- Cook the mixture until the greens are tender and the liquid has thickened.
- Layer the onions over the top of the mixture 10 minutes before serving.

Nutrition Facts	
Collard Crock-Pot® Casserole Weapon per serving makes 8 servings	
Amount per serving	
Calories	352
Calories from fat	229
	% Daily Value *
Total Fat 25.5g	39%
Saturated Fat 8g	40%
Cholesterol 3 mg	1%
Sodium 789 mg	33%
Total Carbohydrate 27.6g	9%
Dietary Fiber 2.2g	9%
Protein 3.1g	
Percent values are based on a 2,000-calorie per day diet. Your daily values may differ.	
Additional Information 65.1% of calories from Fat 31.4% from Carbohydrates 3.5% from Protein	

Equipment/Utensils

Small Crock-Pot®

Suggestion for Pot-Luck Supper

Prepare 2 batches in a medium-sized Crock-Pot®. After it cooks until the collards are tender, transfer it to a large casserole or baking dish (2 quarts). Top it with 1 cup (4 ounces) grated sharp cheddar cheese, 1 cup toasted pecan pieces, and then the onions.

But these are written, that ye might believe that Jesus is the Christ, the Son of God: and that believing ye might have life through His name. John 20:31

♥ Heart Health Cuisine

Carrots and Collards

Three outstanding characteristics of Carrots and Collards are as follows:
- *Explosion of satisfying, dramatic taste—spicy Southern flavor with a kick*
- *Ease of preparation—pre-washed, pre-chopped carrots and collards*
- *Satiety with excellent nutritional value—ample fiber but low caloric and low fat intake*

Ingredients

8 ounces turkey sausage
1 pound baby cut carrots
1 package (12 ounces) frozen seasoning blend
1 package (16 ounces) fresh, chopped collards
1 can (28 ounces) crushed red tomatoes in puree
2 tablespoons lemon juice
¼ cup (or less) pepper sauce
1 teaspoon oregano
1 tablespoon (or less) crushed red pepper
⅛ teaspoon baking soda
2 cups water
4 tablespoons Splenda®

Preparation

- Break the sausage into small pieces.
- Place all the ingredients together in a deep pot.
- Cook over medium heat until the collards are tender—45 minutes.

Nutrition Facts	
Carrots, and Collards	
Per serving (approximately ½ cup)	
Makes 16 servings	
Amount per serving	
Calories	69
Calories from fat	15
% Daily Value *	
Total Fat 1.8g	3%
Saturated Fat 0.4g	2%
Cholesterol 9 mg	3%
Sodium 229 mg	10%
Total Carbohydrate 9.6g	3%
Dietary Fiber 7.4g	30%
Protein 4g	

Percent values are based on a 2,000-calorie per day diet. Your daily values may differ.

Additional Information
21.6% of calories from Fat
55.3% from Carbohydrates
23.1% from Protein

Equipment/Utensils

Deep cooking pot with lid

Filling a Pot with Fresh Collards

If you cannot add all the collards at once, fill the pot, allow them to cook down, and add the rest.

"For there is one God, and one mediator between God and men, the man Christ Jesus."
I Timothy 2:5

Glorious Collards

Every Christmas and on special occasions, we enjoy Frankie's Glorious Choux (cabbage), which is found in Flavored with Love *and which is the inspiration for Glorious Collards. Family members who think they dislike cabbage and collards eat second helpings of the glorious versions.*

Ingredients

6 tablespoons butter
1 pound chopped frozen collards
1 cup chopped onions
1 large onion, chopped fine
1 tablespoon minced garlic
Pinch of baking soda
1 tablespoon brown sugar
1 tablespoon lemon juice
2 tablespoons red wine vinegar
1 cup water
½ pound light Velveeta® cheese food, cubed
1 can (11 ounces) cream of mushroom soup
1¼ cup fine dry breadcrumbs, divided
Salt or salt substitute to taste
Ground red pepper to taste

Preparation

- Preheat the oven to 350°.
- In a deep pot, melt the butter. Add the collards, onions, and garlic. Sauté the mixture until the onions are translucent. Be careful not to burn the butter. Add the baking soda, sugar, lemon juice, vinegar and water. Simmer on low heat several minutes until the greens are tender and the water is absorbed.
- Lower the heat to warm. Add the cheese and stir until the cheese is absorbed. Stir frequently. Stir the soup into the mixture. Add about 1 cup breadcrumbs to make the mixture fairly thick. Mix thoroughly. Season with salt and red pepper and remove from heat.
- Transfer the mixture to an ungreased 2-quart casserole, sprinkle with ¼ cup breadcrumbs, and bake uncovered until bubbly and hot, 20-30 minutes. Serve immediately. 12-16 servings.

Equipment/Utensils

Deep cooking pot with lid • 2-quart casserole

Collards and Cancer Research

Quoted from http://www.cutncleangreens.com/products/collard:
Collard greens and other members of the Brassica family have been the subject of much anti-cancer research. The early findings show reductions in the occurrence of many types of cancer.

Collards and Rice Casserole

Ingredients

Cooking spray
1 cup sliced fresh mushrooms
2½ cups collards, precooked and drained
1 cup chopped onions
1 package chicken flavored rice and vermicelli
4 tablespoons butter (2 to cook rice and vermicelli, 2 to mix with bread crumbs for topping)
1 can (11 ounces) cream of mushroom soup
8 ounces processed cheese, cubed
⅛ teaspoon ground red pepper
½ teaspoon sodium-free Creole seasoning
1 teaspoon Splenda®
½ cup seasoned breadcrumbs

Preparation

- Spray a 9 x 13" baking dish. Preheat the oven to 350°.
- In a Dutch oven sauté the collards, onions, and mushrooms in cooking spray. Remove them and set them aside.
- In the same pan cook the vermicelli and rice with 2 tablespoons butter according to package directions.
- Combine the collards, onions, mushrooms, rice, undiluted soup, and cheese, in the same pan. Mix.
- Taste it and adjust the seasoning. You may like a little more heat. Stir thoroughly after adding seasonings.
- Spoon the mixture into a baking dish. Sprinkle the breadcrumbs on top and dot with small slices of butter.
- Bake 20 minutes or until the rice dish is heated throughout.

Yield: 8 servings

Equipment/Utensils

2 Dutch ovens with lid or other big pots • 9 x 13" baking dish

About Cutting Boards

- Always clean cutting boards with soap and water after using them.
- Use a separate cutting board for raw meats or fish. I like to wash my cutting board in the dishwasher after cutting meat or fish on it. Then I feel sure that it is really clean.
- When you are preparing a recipe that requires a number of different fruits and vegetables or when you are cutting fresh raw collards from the bunches, you need a huge cutting board that will allow you to spread everything out and make little piles of the different ingredients. Also using a big board will prevent spills.

"Never, never, never quit." Winston Churchill

Terry's Collards and Potatoes

Terry's neighbor gave her some fine messes of collards and some unique recipes, which she reworked and made even more delicious than her neighbor's.

Ingredients

4 to 5 medium red potatoes
4 tablespoons bacon drippings or butter
8 ounces sliced fresh mushrooms
½ onion chopped
Salt, pepper, Tony Chachere's®, red
    pepper to taste
Garlic (if you like it)
1 pound fresh collards, washed and
    chopped

Preparation

- Boil potatoes to just tender. (Do not cook them until they are completely done.) Cool, peel, and slice. Place them inside the skillet.
- Add the bacon drippings.
- Add the onions and mushrooms. Cook until the mushrooms are tender and the potatoes are hot.
- Add the chopped collards and other ingredients.Cook the mixture until the collards are wilted.
- Continue to cook the mixture about 4 to 5 minutes. Serve hot.

Nutrition Facts	
Terry's Collards and Potatoes per serving makes 4 servings	
Prepared with butter and 1 teaspoon salt	
Amount per serving	
Calories	286
Calories from fat	111
	% Daily Value *
Total Fat 12.3g	19%
Saturated Fat 7.3g	37%
Cholesterol 31 mg	10%
Sodium 623 mg	26%
Total Carbohydrate 37.1g	12%
Dietary Fiber 7g	28%
Protein 6.7g	
Percent values are based on a 2,000-calorie per day diet. Your daily values may differ.	
Additional Information 38.8% of calories from Fat 51.9% from Carbohydrates 9.4% from Protein	

Serving Suggestion

Terry's friend who gives her collards serves Collards and Potatoes with pickled beets.

Note

We Southerners love bacon drippings. Since collards are flavorful and Terry has included some tasty sesaonings, collard and potatoes would be tasty with olive oil instead of bacon drippings or butter.

Equipment/Utensils

Very large skillet

Terry Chrisman

Curried Collards and Potatoes

With one of the cornbread dishes containing protein, Curried Collards and Potatoes can be served as a satisfying meal. Also, it would be an excellent complement for roast beef or lamb. This distinctive flavor is one to be enjoyed.

This dish is easy to prepare, although the explanation is involved.

Ingredients

4 medium red skinned potatoes cut in large cubes
¼ cup unsalted butter
¼ cup olive oil
Salt or salt substitute to taste
Plenty of freshly ground black pepper
Crushed red pepper to taste
Dash savory
Dash mint
Dash parsley
1 pound (5 cups) frozen chopped collards
12 ounces Creole frozen seasoning blend
⅛ teaspoon baking soda
2 tablespoons lemon juice
2 tablespoons Splenda®
2 tablespoons Madras curry

Preparation

- Preheat the oven to 400°.
- Gently heat the butter and oil together in a Dutch oven or deep sauté pan.
- Add the potatoes and cook them slowly a couple of minutes to warm them and to coat them with the butter and oil. Save the pan with the oil and butter in it for cooking the greens.
- Dip the potatoes from the fat into a baking dish. Salt them and grind generous amounts of black pepper over them.
- Place them in the oven and cook them while you prepare the collards.
- Check them occasionally. Carefully slide an egg-turning spatula underneath them and turn them after about 20 minutes.
- The potatoes should be tender after cooking 20 more minutes. Sprinkle crushed red pepper, savory, mint, and parsley. Toss the potatoes gently.
- Meanwhile sauté the seasoning blend, collards, baking soda, Splenda®, and curry in the same pan where you cooked the potatoes until the liquid is absorbed.
- Add ½ cup water. Cover and simmer slowly until all the water is absorbed and the collards are tender.
- When the collards are ready and the potatoes are crisp and golden, remove the potatoes from the cooking pan. Spread the collards into the pan and top them with the potatoes.

Equipment/Utensils
• Dutch oven or sauté pan with lid • Cutting board • Knife • 9 X 13 X 2" cooking pan

Comments
- This dish is delightful! Curry is a taste that some people have to develop before they enjoy it. Besides the distinctive taste, there is another reason to learn to enjoy curry. The people of India eat curry every day, and they almost never develop Alzheimer's. Whether there is a connection is unknown—we can only guess.
- The curry in the collards has a subtle taste that does not overpower the other flavors.
- The potatoes are crisp and spicy.
- Curried Collards and Potatoes—a pretty dish with a variety of colors, textures, and flavors—is a guest-worthy dish.

♥ *Heart Health Cuisine*
Collard Corn

A high-fiber side dish with a spicy kick—

Ingredients
1 medium onion
1 garlic bulb
1 tablespoon extra virgin olive oil
2 cups frozen chopped collards
2 cups frozen whole kernel corn
⅛ teaspoon baking soda
1 tablespoon Splenda®
¼ cup lemon juice
1 tablespoon chili powder

Preparation
- Peel and chop the onion.
- Cut the end off the garlic bulb, microwave it 30 seconds on high, and push the toes out onto the cutting board.
- Slice them. Sauté the onions and garlic in the olive oil (3 minutes).
- Toss the other ingredients into the pan and sauté until the collards are tender and the lemon juice is absorbed (5 minutes).

Equipment/Utensils
Deep saucepan • Cutting board • Sharp knife

Nutrition Facts	
Collard Corn per serving makes 4 servings	
Amount per serving	
Calories	165
Calories from fat	41
	% Daily Value *
Total Fat 4.5g	7%
Saturated Fat 0.7g	3%
Cholesterol 0 mg	0%
Sodium 66 mg	3%
Total Carbohydrate 26.7g	9%
Dietary Fiber 4.2g	17%
Protein 4.2g	

Percent values are based on a 2,000-calorie per day diet. Your daily values may differ.

Additional Information
24.9% of calories from Fat
64.9% from Carbohydrates
10.2% from Protein

Collard Greens Collage

Here's a huge pot of greens seasoned deliciously by Carolyn A. Forche`, author. She describes her cooking methods in detail. Read this recipe to gain some new insights into cooking collards. In this recipe you will read not only the process but also the reasons behind the process.

Carolyn has developed a recipe that is an artistic collage for the eyes and a medley of aromas and tastes for the nose and the palate.

Ingredients

2 Fresh Bunches Each:
Collard greens
Turnip greens
Mustard greens
Kale
Only 1 bunch spinach
Small head cabbage
1 large can chicken stock

2 large smoked turkey legs
1½ pounds of smoked turkey or pork necks
2 large white onions
6 to 8 large cloves garlic
1 whole bulb of shallots
1 small tomato (balances flavor, tenderizes collards)
Morton's® seasoned salt to taste—or 2 tablespoons
1 level teaspoon red pepper flakes
1 teaspoon Tony Chachere's® Creole Seasoning

Preparation

- In a very large pot, completely cover split, smoked turkey legs and neck bones with water.
- Add large can or box of non-fat chicken stock to the water (To keep flavor of meat from becoming too watery). Cook on high heat till boiling, lower to medium heat, and watch carefully, to add water a little at a time to keep from boiling dry. Cover. Let simmer for 45 minutes to an hour, to get as much substance from the meat and bones as possible.
- Add chopped onions, garlic, and shallots after heat is turned to medium.
- Meanwhile, trim large stems and wash the collards first and separate. Then trim and wash turnip greens, mustard greens, and kale. Separate washed spinach. Do not trim.
- Rinse the cabbage and score into medium sized shreds, separate to go into pot later.
- When the meat is fully cooked, remove excess bones into a large pot or bowl to cool. When cool, pull off the meat—discarding the skin and fat and bones from meat. Add the meat to the greens when they are all cooking together.
- Cut the collards into large pieces and put into the pot of turkey and chicken stock Add the small tomato, quartered, and cover.
- Stir to turn over leaves to cook well. When the collards are half tender, put in cut up leaves of the kale, turnip and mustard greens. Let the collards remain on the bottom of the pot till completely tender. Press down on the greens to make sure they get saturated in the stock. When the turnip and mustard greens are beginning to get tender, about 20-25 minutes, add the cabbage greens. Now add the meat

that you pulled from the bones. Begin completely stirring all the greens from bottom to top to mix well. When the greens are completely cooked, add the 1 bunch of spinach and stir well into the mixture. Add the spices and mix well, turning the greens well to blend all spices well. If greens need a little more liquid, add chicken stock. Water may dilute the flavor of the meat stock. Taste the stock to see if more seasoning is needed. Cover and simmer on low heat or turn heat off and let the heat in the pot finish the cooking.

- Do not overcook. The greens should be tender, but not mushy. Turn heat off and cover to prevent over-cooking.

Serves 10-12 people

Serve with Fresh Corn-Cornbread (p. 226) and a side of sliced, ripe tomatoes and green onions.

Carolyn Forche`

Carolyn Forche`

Carolyn discusses her writing and cooking:

I have two passions—writing and cooking. Does that seem a bit strange to you? Think about it. Both are creative passions, and when you hear about my collard greens, which I have appropriately named Collard Greens Collage, you may deduce that I have taken license with creativity; but then, that's how some of the great recipes we enjoy were created, starting with the simple sandwich begun by John Montagu (1718-92), the 4th Earl of Sandwich, a town in southeast England. It seems he had such a passion for table games, in order to keep from having to leave his games for meals, he squeezed his food between two slices of bread and chomped away. I shudder to think what his very proper English colleagues thought of such a sight; but he also took license with creativity that has become a world famous, palate-pleasing pastime, with every culture having its own variation of "The Sandwich." But I digress; I'm here to talk about collard greens and Fresh Corn-Cornbread.

As I share my Collard Greens Collage and Fresh Corn-Cornbread with you, let me tell you a little bit about myself, and how these twin passions came to be. My mother was an incredible cook, and I loved watching and helping her prepare foods. It was always fascinating to watch the magical transition at her hands of raw products like flour, eggs, yeast, milk, butter, cream and fruit and see them segue into perfectly shaped cakes, rolls, pies, cobblers, donuts and unforgettable, home-made ice cream. Ummm! We took turns as kids, churning the ice and rock salt around the cold canister, containing the fresh fruit-filled ice cream in the making. And I will never forget those wondrous aromas wafting from the tall pots of her mouth-watering delicacies of homemade soups, gumbo, stews, pastas and baked dishes, or the golden brown fried chicken, cooked in those big, black iron skillets.

I am so grateful that I am young enough to enjoy the modern conveniences of today's mixes and "just add water" concoctions, yet old enough to know the savoring difference of her not-to-be-compared-with "from scratch" recipes. I soon began writing about my childhood experiences, the things I learned from my parents and family life growing up in Chicago. Somehow writing became a creative extension of the culinary art form I learned in my mother's kitchen. Cooking, in many ways, is much like writing. Real cooking, that is. You start from scratch with raw facts and knead them into a finished product with your hands and your creative thinking. Likewise, with cooking and writing, there are basic rules to be learned and followed as you put your personal touches into the mix.

Little did I know that my growing fascination with writing would one day usher me into a prestigious position as a cabinet level speechwriter during the administration of President Jimmy Carter. And little less did I know that painful experiences encountered by my beautiful brown princess, my granddaughter, would inspire me to write a book to her, *Colors Come From God ... Just Like Me!*—which won the Gilded Quill Award by The Manuscriptor's Guild, was later published by Abingdon Press, and is now a continuing bestseller. Today, I am an editorial consultant, (http://www.CarolynsQuill.com), and keep very busy editing manuscripts and writing my own books as well. In my limited leisure time, I am fully engaged in my second passion, cooking great meals. It is a joy to hear the Ummm! sounds emanating from my family and friends as they feast on my sometimes gourmet, and other times simply Forche` fare. But the greatest joy for me is in the serving.     Carolyn Forche`

Melody's Cooking Suggestions

Melody Burch, the author of Melody's Oven Bread, suggested:

- The best collard greens are the ones cooked with smoked neck bones. Don't use bones that are not smoked and try to season them yourself because they won't taste as good.
- You can cook collards with turnip roots in them just like with turnip greens.

More Thoughts about Turnip Roots

When I was a child, I hated the taste of cooked turnip roots, but considered raw roots a special treat. I still enjoy them with low-fat ranch dressing for a dip.

To cook turnip roots, wash them well, peel them and slice them. Add the roots when the greens—turnip greens or collard greens—are almost cooked. That way they will remain crisp. I still dislike squishy roots.   Mary Lou

Then the LORD answered me and said, "Write the vision, and make it plain upon tablets, that he may run who reads it." Habakkuk 2:2 NKJV.

Spinach and Collards

Serve the spinach and collards promptly after you cook them. Top them with Peach Salsa prepared in advance. (See the recipe on the next page.)

Peach salsa is warm with flavor. The spinach and collards will make your tongue tingle with a hint of slightly bitter mystifying flavor. When the chilled salsa kisses the hot spinach and collards—oh, what a sensuous delight to the taste buds!

Ingredients

3 tablespoons olive oil
¼ cup minced garlic
10 ounces fresh collards
10 ounces fresh spinach
⅛ teaspoon baking soda
½ cup water
¼ cup lemon juice
Dash salt or salt substitute
1 teaspoon Creole seasoning (low sodium)
1 teaspoon rosemary
1 teaspoon crushed mint leaves

Preparation

- Chop the collards to fine slivers.
- Chop the spinach to coarse pieces.
- In a Dutch oven heat the oil over medium heat and sauté the garlic for a few seconds. Do not let it burn. Increase the heat to medium-high and add a large handful of the collards to the pan.
- Toss the collards until they wilt. Continue adding large handfuls of collards to the pan and toss until they are wilted.
- Add the baking soda.
- Add the spinach and wilt it.
- Place the water and lemon juice in the blender with the seasonings. Blend them a few seconds to make sure the rosemary and mint are chopped to fine pieces. Also, blending the spices helps to release their flavors.
- Add the liquid to the greens, cover, and simmer 5 minutes—no longer.
- Serve immediately with chilled Peach Salsa (next page)

Equipment/Utensils

Cutting board • Sharp knife • Large sauté pan

Serving Suggestion

Collards and Spinach with Peach Salsa would be good enough to satisfy your appetite and make you sing with delight. If you want to have even more gastronomic pleasure, which may be too much to handle in one meal, we suggest that you find some smoked boudin (Cajun sausage) and heat it in a skillet.

Peach Salsa

This recipe is a companion to the preceding one. Prepare and chill the salsa 1 or 2 hours before you cook the greens. Paul likes the salsa on vanilla bean ice cream!

Ingredients

1½ pounds firm ripe peaches (or 1 pound frozen peaches)
2 tablespoons chopped fresh cilantro
Non-stick cooking spray
½ cup finely chopped red onion
1 tablespoon finely chopped pickled jalapeños
¼ cup sweet roasted red bell peppers, finely chopped
3 tablespoons fresh lime juice
Dash salt substitute
1 teaspoon ground ginger
1 teaspoon Madras curry
⅛ teaspoon ground cloves
⅛ teaspoon ground red pepper
3 tablespoons white sugar

Preparation

If you are using fresh peaches:
* Drop a few of the peaches at a time into a large pot of simmering water for about 30 seconds. Remove with a slotted spoon, and slip the skins off. Remove the pits and finely dice the peaches. You will need about 3 cups.

If fresh peaches are unavailable:
* Finely dice 1 pound frozen peaches.
* Place the peaches and cilantro into the bowl you will use for serving.
* *Lightly* mist a skillet with non-stick cooking spray.
* Sauté the onion about 30 seconds. Do not brown it. Add the jalapeños and bell peppers. Turn off the heat.
* In a small saucepan mix the lime juice and the remaining seasonings and sugar. Warm the mixture on low heat. Do not let it come to a boil. Instead, heat it enough to blend nicely and release the flavors.
* Add the lime juice mixture to the onion mixture. Allow all that to cool thoroughly.
* Pour the cooled mixture on top of the peaches and cilantro. Be sure to scrape the sides of the pans with a spatula to keep all the delicious flavors in the mix. Toss the ingredients together. Toss it again immediately before serving.
* Cover and refrigerate 1 to 2 hours. Spread the cool salsa on top of the greens on the individual plates.

Equipment/Utensils

Cutting board • Sharp knife • Optional food processor • Skillet • Medium serving bowl with cover (plastic wrap)

Collards-Asparagus Casserole I

We couldn't help eating too much of this!

Ingredients

4 eggs
Non-stick cooking spray
16 ounces (5 cups) frozen chopped
   collards
1 tablespoon canola oil
2 tablespoons red wine vinegar
1 tablespoon orange marmalade
½ teaspoon ground red pepper (more or
   less)
½ teaspoon ground black pepper
1 large can cream of mushroom soup
2 cans (14½ ounces each) cut asparagus
   spears, drained
6 ounces grated Swiss cheese
1 large can (6 ounces) french fried
   onions

Nutrition Facts	
Collards-Asparagus Casserole Per serving Makes 10 servings	
Amount per serving	
Calories	304
Calories from fat	178
	% Daily Value *
Total Fat 19.7g	30%
Saturated Fat 7.4g	37%
Cholesterol 102 mg	34%
Sodium 836 mg	35%
Total Carbohydrate 20.2g	7%
Dietary Fiber 3.1g	12%
Protein 11.3g	
Percent values are based on a 2,000-calorie per day diet. Your daily values may differ.	
Additional Information 58.6% of calories from Fat 26.6% from Carbohydrates 14.9% from Protein	

Preparation

- Boil the eggs.
- Spray a large casserole with non-stick cooking spray. In a deep saucepan heat the oil. Add the collards.
- Stirring them, continue to cook at high heat for 2 minutes.
- Stir in the vinegar, marmalade, peppers, and soup. Heat until the mixture bubbles.
- Spread the mixture into the casserole dish.
- Drain the asparagus and layer it over the collards. Grate the eggs and spread them over the asparagus. Place the grated cheese on top of the eggs.
- Finish the dish by spreading the entire can of onions over the top.
- Bake at 350° until the casserole bubbles, the onions turn a shade browner, the cheese melts, and the entire dish smells wonderful.

Equipment/Utensils

1-quart sauce pan • 3-quart deep saucepan • 3-quart (13 X 9 X 2") Pyrex® baking dish • Grater

Collards-Asparagus Casserole II

Ingredients

Non-stick cooking spray

1 cup cooked and seasoned collards, drained

1 can (14½ ounces) cut asparagus spears, drained

2 cans cream of mushroom soup (10¾ ounces each)

4 eggs, boiled and chopped

¼ package low sodium saltine crackers, crumbled

4 ounces sharp cheddar cheese, grated

4 tablespoons unsalted butter

½ cup milk (2%)

Preparation

- Preheat the oven to 350º.
- Spray the bottom of the casserole.
- Layer the ingredients in this order: collards, asparagus, undiluted soup, eggs, cheese, crackers, dots of butter.
- Spoon the milk over the top to soften the crackers.
- Bake until the casserole bubbles.

Nutrition Facts

Collards-Asparagus Casserole II,
Per serving
Makes 8 servings

Amount per serving	
Calories	230
Calories from fat	144

	% Daily Value *
Total Fat 16.1g	25%
Saturated Fat 8.1g	41%
Cholesterol 32 mg	11%
Sodium 511 mg	21%
Total Carbohydrate 15g	5%
Dietary Fiber 1.2g	5%
Protein 6.5g	

Percent values are based on a 2,000-calorie per day diet. Your daily values may differ.

Additional Information
62.6% of calories from Fat
26.1% from Carbohydrates
11.3% from Protein

Equipment/Utensils

1-quart sauce pan • 3-quart deep saucepan • 2-quart (13"X 9" X 2") Pyrex® baking dish or casserole • Grater

Cooking collards is an old skill handed down from former generations. Currently people are cooking collards in new ways.

We have invented various new methods to cook an ancient food, recognized by our ancestors for its pleasurable taste and outstanding nutritional value. Our new food styles are a transformation for the taste buds.

Eggplant Parmigiana

Tomato Sauce

Ingredients

¼ cup dry onion flakes
¼ cup hot water
2 teaspoons olive oil
½ cup frozen chopped collards
¼ cup chopped celery
1 tablespoon minced garlic
1 teaspoon basil
1 teaspoon oregano
½ teaspoon cumin
3 tablespoons pineapple preserves (or other fruit preserves)
1 can (28 ounces) crushed tomatoes in puree

Nutrition Facts	
Eggplant Parmigiana per serving makes 8 servings	
Amount per serving	
Calories	281
Calories from fat	128
	% Daily Value *
Total Fat 14.2g	22%
Saturated Fat 4.5g	22%
Cholesterol 43 mg	14%
Sodium 481 mg	20%
Total Carbohydrate 25.8g	9%
Dietary Fiber 3.6g	14%
Protein 12.4g	
Percent values are based on a 2,000-calorie per day diet. Your daily values may differ.	
Additional Information 45.6% of calories from Fat 36.8% from Carbohydrates 17.7% from Protein	

Preparation

* Place the onion flakes in the hot water to soften them.
* Stir-fry the collards and celery in the olive oil 5 minutes at high heat.
* Add the remaining ingredients and simmer 30 minutes.

(You don't really have to time it. Just cook it while you prepare the eggplant.)

The Eggplants

Ingredients

2 medium egg plants, peeled and cut crosswise in ½" slices
1 egg
½ cup fat-free Half & Half®
¾ cup self-rising flour
1 cup vegetable oil
½ cup grated Parmesan cheese
6 ounces mozzarella cheese, cut in thin slices

Preparation

* Beat egg and Half & Half® together.
* Dip eggplant into egg mixture and then into flour.
* Sauté eggplant in hot oil until golden brown.
* Drain the slices on a paper towel.

The Final Preparation—Assembling

- Layer the dish by placing ½ the eggplant in a single layer, followed by ½ the Parmesan cheese and ½ the mozzarella cheese, and half the tomato sauce.
- Then add the remaining eggplant, Parmesan cheese, and tomato sauce in layers.
- Top it off with the remaining mozzarella cheese.
- Bake uncovered at 400°F 20 minutes or until it bubbles.

Equipment/Utensils

Skillet • 9 X 9 X 2" baking dish

Note

To calculate the nutritional value, a measurement of ¼ cup oil and ½ cup flour were used because not all these ingredients are absorbed.

About Eggplants

Eggplants, also known as *garden eggs* and *egg apples,* are spongy, bland-tasting vegetables. Because they have a mild, slightly bitter flavor, they require generous amounts of seasoning to amplify their taste potential. With their meaty texture, eggplants can make dishes seem rich, even though they are low in calories.

Eggplants can be baked with stuffing, grilled with marinade, sautéed with a crust, or simmered in pasta sauces. Use your imagination, but don't try to eat them raw.

Along with their many cousins, including tobacco, potatoes, tomatoes, and belladonna, eggplants belong to the nightshade family. There are many different varieties of eggplants, such as Japanese, Italian, Sicilian, and Thai.

When recipes include eggplants, usually American cookbook authors are referring to American eggplants, which are large, rich purple, pear-shaped vegetables.

Collards with their distinctive taste combine well with eggplants. In this recipe, collards are used in a way similar to parsley. Also mushrooms, with their similar texture, combine tastefully with eggplants. Italian recipes for eggplant dishes are tasty and popular.

Cutting the Mustard

Cooking Tip from Ruth: Our mother washed mustard greens and then dropped them into boiling water to blanch them. Then she drained them in a colander and cut them into shreds. Next she returned them to the pot and cooked them with seasonings until they were tender.

Blanching greens intensifies the color but washes the nutrients down the drain.

Mary Lou

But the fruit of the Spirit is love, joy, peace, longsuffering, gentleness, goodness, faith, meekness, temperance: against such there is no law. Galatians 5:22

Steamed Collards with Fruit, Nut, And Cheese Topping

Collards

Ingredients

5 cups (1 pound) frozen chopped
    collards
1 tablespoon lemon juice
2 teaspoons basil leaves (or to taste)
¼ teaspoon ground red pepper
1 tablespoon olive oil

Preparation

- Steam collards with lemon juice, basil leaves, and red pepper 20 minutes or until tender.

Topping

Ingredients

½ cup mixed salted nuts
1 Fuji apple
4 ounces Swiss cheese
2 tablespoons apricot preserves

Preparation

- Using a food processor, shred the nuts, apple, and cheese coarsely.
- Add the apricot preserves and toss the mixture together.

Nutrition Facts	
Steamed Collards with Fruit, Nut, And Cheese Topping per serving makes 6 servings	
Amount per serving	
Calories	226
Calories from fat	118
	% Daily Value *
Total Fat 13.1g	20%
Saturated Fat 4.7g	23%
Cholesterol 17 mg	6%
Sodium 156 mg	6%
Total Carbohydrate 17.9g	6%
Dietary Fiber 4g	16%
Protein 9.2g	
Percent values are based on a 2,000-calorie per day diet. Your daily values may differ.	
Additional Information 52.1% of calories from Fat 31.6% from Carbohydrates 16.3% from Protein	

Serving Suggestions

- Serve the greens hot with the cool topping added to the individual plates.
- Try sprinkling Tiger Sauce® over the top.

Equipment/Utensils

Steamer • food processor

"When you come to the end of your rope, tie a knot and hang on."
        Franklin D. Roosevelt

Fall Flavor Collards With Cranberries

Whether for Thanksgiving, Christmas, or any night during Kwanzaa, this easy collard dish reflects the tastes of the season and would be a welcome vegetable next to any roast turkey or meat. The green collards studded with red cranberries make a lovely presentation, and the sweet-sour combination from the sugar and vinegar makes this an unbeatable side dish.

Source: Cut `n Clean Greens® (http://www.cutncleangreens.com)

Ingredients

3 tablespoons olive oil
1 (8-ounce) red onion, chopped
2-3 cloves garlic, chopped
3 tablespoons balsamic vinegar
2 tablespoons brown sugar
⅓ cup dried, sweetened cranberries (such as Craisins)
1 (2-pound) bag Cut `n Clean Greens® Collard Greens
Salt and pepper
⅓ cup chopped toasted pecans

Preparation

Heat oil in a 12- to 14-inch sauté pan with a lid. When hot, add onion and sauté for about 8 minutes, adding garlic during the last minute, stirring frequently. Add vinegar, brown sugar, and most of the cranberries (reserve about 1-2 tablespoons for later).

Rinse greens and drain in a colander, then transfer greens to pan. Cook and stir (tongs work well) until wilted enough to cover with a lid. Cook, covered, stirring and turning occasionally, for 15 minutes, until greens are tender. Add another tablespoon or two of water if pan is drying up. Taste and season with a bit of salt and pepper. Stir in remaining cranberries (for a bright look). Sprinkle with pecans and serve.

Serves 6-8.

Dorothy Reinhold

Reprinted with permission from Cut `n Clean Greens®
(http://www.cutncleangreens.com)

Holiday Sweet and Sour Collards

These collards are pretty enough to serve with Thanksgiving turkey or Christmas ham. The sweet and sour taste is exceptional.

Ingredients

3 tablespoons olive oil
12 ounces (1⅓ cups) frozen diced onions
2 tablespoons minced garlic
1 pound (5 cups) frozen chopped collards
3 tablespoons balsamic vinegar
¼ cup lemon juice
⅛ teaspoon baking soda
1 teaspoon salt substitute
Dash freshly ground black pepper
Dash ground red pepper
1 seedless orange
2 teaspoons orange zest
1 can (16 ounces) whole berry cranberry sauce
2 tablespoons brown sugar
2 tablespoons dried, sweetened cranberries
Orange slices for garnish

Preparation

- Sauté the onions, garlic, and collards for 5 minutes.
- Add the vinegar, lemon juice, baking soda, salt substitute, black pepper, and red pepper. Cover and continue to simmer the collards until they are tender. Add a tiny bit of water if you must, but you will not want this dish to be juicy.
- Peel the orange and prepare 2 teaspoons of zest from the peel. Be sure that the orange has no seeds. Divide the orange into segments and grind it into juice and pulp in the blender.
- Add the cranberry sauce, orange zest, orange, and brown sugar. Simmer 5 minutes.
- Place the collards in a serving bowl. Sprinkle them with the dried cranberries, garnish with orange slices, and serve.

Equipment/Utensils

Dutch oven or sauté pan with lid • Blender • Zester

Orange Garnishes

Cut the oranges in smiles, i.e., cut them in wedges against the grain of the sections.

For God so loved the world that He gave His only begotten Son, that whosoever believeth in Him should not perish, but have everlasting life. For God sent not His Son into the world to condemn the world; but that the world through Him might be saved. John 3:16-17 KJV

♥*Heart Health Cuisine*

Mexican Collards

Entertain your mouth while you reduce your waist with this extremely healthful vegetable mixture with its bold taste. Add the hot seasoning slowly unless you are accustomed to heat.

Ingredients

16 ounces frozen chopped collards

1 package (10 ounces, 1½ cups) frozen chopped onions

⅛ teaspoon baking soda

¼ cup olive oil

2 cups chicken broth, homemade

2 tablespoons Splenda®

½ teaspoon salt substitute

Freshly ground black pepper to taste

2 tablespoons lemon juice

1 tablespoon cumin

1 tablespoon chili powder

1 can Ro*Tel® tomatoes and chilies

2 cups Mexican mixed vegetables (Jalisco style potatoes, carrots, red peppers, and green peas) or other frozen mixed vegetables

Nutrition Facts	
Mexican Collards per serving makes 10 servings	
Amount per serving	
Calories	97
Calories from fat	53
	% Daily Value *
Total Fat 5.8g	9%
Saturated Fat 0.7g	3%
Cholesterol 0 mg	0%
Sodium 190 mg	8%
Total Carbohydrate 8.8g	3%
Dietary Fiber 2.8g	11%
Protein 2.1g	
Percent values are based on a 2,000-calorie per day diet. Your daily values may differ.	
Additional Information 54.9% of calories from Fat 36.4% from Carbohydrates 8.7% from Protein	

Preparation

- Sauté the collards and onions with the baking soda and olive oil in a Dutch oven.

- Add all the other ingredients except the mixed vegetables. Cover and simmer.

- When the liquid is reduced and the collards are tender, add the mixed vegetables, return to a boil, and stop cooking. (Do not overcook the mixed vegetables. You want the peas to pop when you bite them.)

Equipment/Utensils

Dutch oven

Serving Suggestion

This satisfying high-fiber dish is ideal for weight loss. If you want to add some foods to it in order to make it more scrumptious, try serving it over rice or with some tasty sausage.

Caramelized Cauliflower and Collards

The mix of rosemary, honey, ginger, bacon, lime juice, cauliflower, and collards with caramelization—what a combination! This dish has a sophisticated range of tastes. Serve it to guests when you want them to delight in a meal.

Ingredients

2 teaspoons minced rosemary
3 tablespoons honey
2 teaspoons minced fresh ginger
½ pound sliced bacon, cut into small pieces.
1 small cauliflower broken and cut into florets
1 cup onion, finely chopped
1 tablespoon minced garlic
1 pound finely chopped frozen collards
3 tablespoons lime juice
Pinch of baking soda
Salt or salt substitute
Freshly ground black pepper to taste
1 cup chicken stock

Preparation

- In a small pan simmer the rosemary, honey, and ginger 4 minutes.
- Cook the bacon in a Dutch oven or deep pot with lid until the fat is rendered. And the bacon is crisp.
- Remove the bacon and place it on a paper towel.
- Add the cauliflower and cook it until it is browned.
- Dip it out of the pot.
- Cook the collards, garlic, and onion with the lime juice, baking soda, and other seasonings until the collards are tender.
- Toss the cauliflower with the greens, add the chicken stock, and cook until half the liquid is absorbed.
- Place the vegetables in a serving bowl. Top with the bacon and pour the honey sauce over the top. (If the honey has become hardened, heat it gently until it softens.) Serve warm.

Equipment/Utensils

Small saucepan • Dutch oven

Squash, Collards, and Creamed Potato Casserole

Ingredients

Non-stick cooking spray
¼ cup canola oil
1 cup chopped yellow onions
1 tablespoon minced garlic
1½ cups frozen chopped collards
5 cups sliced fresh yellow squash (or combination of yellow and zucchini squash)
1 tablespoon Perfect Collard Seasoning Blend™
¼ cup red wine vinegar
2 tablespoons Splenda®
2½ cup water
6 cups cubed Yukon gold potatoes or red-skinned Irish potatoes
1 stick (¼ pound) unsalted butter
Salt substitute or salt to taste
Generous amount of freshly ground black pepper
1 package dry nonfat milk (enough to make 1 quart)

Preparation

- Wash the potatoes and squash thoroughly. Don't bother to peel the potatoes, but do remove the eyes and any scarred places.
- In a large pan, sauté the onions, garlic, and collards in the canola oil until the onions are translucent.
- Add the squash, collard seasoning, vinegar, Splenda®, and 1 cup water. Continue to cook over low heat until the liquid is absorbed.
- In a deep pot, bring 1½ cups water to boil. Add the potatoes and cook until they are fork tender. Stir the butter, salt, and pepper into the potatoes. Sprinkle the dry milk into the potatoes while you whip them with an electric hand mixer.
- Stir the squash mixture into the potatoes, pour the mix into a 3-quart casserole, and heat in the oven at 350° until the casserole is brown and bubbly.

Equipment/Utensils

Large heavy cooking pan • Deep pot • 3-quart casserole

Cauliflower, Collards, and Creamed Potato Casserole

Prepare the above recipe with 32 ounces cauliflower instead of 5 cups squash. Do not add water when cooking the cauliflower.

Collards and Eggs Au Gratin

Golden Cheddar Sauce

Ingredients

¼ cup unsalted butter
¼ cup all purpose flour
1 teaspoon salt substitute
3 cups fat free Half & Half®
4 teaspoons Worcestershire sauce
4 teaspoons Tiger Sauce®
4 ounces grated sharp cheddar cheese

Preparation

- Melt the butter over warm heat.
- Stir the flour and salt into the butter. Do not brown.
- Melt the butter, stir in the flour, and add the milk and sauces. Stir until the mix is smooth as you heat it slowly. Add the cheese; continue to stir until the cheese melts.

Collards and Eggs

Ingredients

4 large eggs
2 tablespoons olive oil
5 cups (1 pound) frozen chopped collards
1 cup diced onions
2 tablespoons chopped garlic
¼ cup lemon juice
⅛ teaspoon baking soda
Salt substitute to taste
Ground red pepper to taste
Freshly ground black pepper to taste
¼ cup seasoned breadcrumbs
1 tablespoon unsalted butter

Preparation

- Preheat the oven to 350°.
- Boil the eggs. (Place them in cold water, cover the pot, and bring them to a boil. Turn the heat off. Let them sit in the warm water 15 minutes. Peel them in cool water.) Quarter them lengthwise. Set aside.
- Cook the collards. Sauté them with the onions and garlic in the olive oil 5 minutes. Add the juice, soda, salt substitute, and peppers. Set aside.
- Melt the butter and stir it into the breadcrumbs.
- Place the collards in the casserole dish. Arrange the egg quarters carefully over the top. Pour the sauce over the eggs and collards. Top them with the breadcrumbs.
- Bake 15 minutes or until the sauce thickens and bubbles.

Continued on next page

Equipment/Utensils
2 saucepans • Collard cooking pan • Small microwave dish • 2 quart casserole

Lapsang Collards

To enjoy the explosion of flavor created by the following recipe for collards with an exotic taste, you will need to use fresh collards, onions, and cilantro.

Ingredients
2 tablespoons olive oil
3 tightly packed cups fresh collards, finely chopped and stems removed
½ cup fresh green onions (tops included), finely chopped
4 stems (4" each) fresh cilantro (leaves included), finely chopped
1 teaspoon Lapsang Souchong tea leaves
1 teaspoon cumin
⅓ cup Port wine
½ cup water
Salt or salt substitute to taste

Preparation
- Pour the olive oil into the skillet; add the collards, onions, cilantro, tea leaves, and cumin. Stir-fry the mix 3 minutes over high heat.
- Add the wine while you continue to stir until the wine is evaporated. Add the water, lower the heat, and cook covered 10 minutes or until the water has evaporated.
- Check occasionally to make sure the mixture is not becoming too dry.

Equipment/Utensils
Heavy skillet with tightly fitting lid

Cooking Tips
- Basil, oregano, rosemary, and thyme make a delightful seasoning combination for vegetables, including collards.
- Tiny thin slices of lemon peel make a pretty garnish..
- Use a resealable plastic bag to marinate, crush crackers, or crush potato chips.
- Add melted butter to a resealable bag of crackers or breadcrumbs when you are topping a casserole.
- Crushed potato chips make a great casserole topping.
- Try adding chopped pecans or walnuts or slivered almonds to a casserole topping.
- Pine nuts taste delicious in many dishes.
- To roast garlic, slice it really thin and place it between two sheets of parchment paper in the oven on a cooking sheet. Toast the garlic slices on low heat until they are crisp and golden.
- Salad spinners are great for removing all the water from salad greens.
- Place a tight lid on a bowl and shake liquids to save time mixing.

Corn and Collard Timbale

Ingredients

Butter flavored non-stick cooking spray
2 cups chopped fresh tender collards
½ cup chopped onion
¼ teaspoon ground red pepper
⅛ teaspoon baking soda
3 tablespoons lime juice
⅓ cup breadcrumbs
⅓ roasted, salted sunflower seeds
2 ounces chunked Colby/Jack cheese
2 large eggs
¼ cup Fat Free Half & Half®
1 tablespoon Splenda®
2 teaspoons minced garlic
½ teaspoon salt substitute
1 cup frozen whole grain corn

Nutrition Facts	
Corn Collard Timbale per serving Makes 4 servings	
Amount per serving	
Calories	270
Calories from fat	128
	% Daily Value *
Total Fat 14.3g	22%
Saturated Fat 4.5g	22%
Cholesterol 118 mg	39%
Sodium 325 mg	14%
Total Carbohydrate 23.5g	8%
Dietary Fiber 3.5g	14%
Protein 11.9g	
Percent values are based on a 2,000-calorie per day diet. Your daily values may differ.	
Additional Information 47.5% of calories from Fat 34.9% from Carbohydrates 17.7% from Protein	

Preparation

- Preheat the oven to 325°.
- Spray 4 custard cups or 4-ounce ramekins and line the bottoms with waxed paper.
- Spray a skillet and sauté the collards and onion until the onions are translucent.
- Add the red pepper, baking soda, and lime juice. Turn off the heat.
- In the blender grind the breadcrumbs and sunflower seeds.
- Add all the remaining ingredients except the vegetables. Continue to blend until the mixture is uniform.
- Add the collards, onions, and corn. Blend until they are chopped.
- Pour the mixture into the custard cups or ramekins.
- Bake in a water bath by placing the cups inside a large roasting pan and adding hot water half way up the outside of the cups.
- Cook until a knife inserted in the middle comes out clean, about 40 minutes.
- Allow the cups to cool 10 minutes.
- Run a knife around the edges and invert onto the serving plates.

Equipment/Utensils

4 custard cups or 4-ounce ramekins • Skillet •Blender • Large cooking pan

Serving Suggestion

Top with Sauce Mornay with Colby/Jack. Over the sauce, drizzle a small amount of Tiger Sauce®.

Sauce Mornay with Colby/Jack

Ingredients

1 cup Fat Free Half & Half®
1 small onion
¼ teaspoon nutmeg
1 teaspoon crushed bay leaves
6 cloves
2 tablespoons all purpose flour
2 tablespoons unsalted butter
½ teaspoon salt substitute
½ cup (2 ounces) grated Colby/Jack
    Cheese
1 cup (2%) milk

Nutrition Facts	
Sauce Mornay, per serving Makes 4 servings	
Amount per serving	
Calories	185
Calories from fat	104
% Daily Value *	
Total Fat 11.5g	18%
Saturated Fat 7.2g	36%
Cholesterol 33 mg	11%
Sodium 177 mg	7%
Total Carbohydrate 12.3g	4%
Dietary Fiber 0.1g	0%
Protein 7.9g	
Percent values are based on a 2,000-calorie per day diet. Your daily values may differ.	
Additional Information 56.3% of calories from Fat 26.6% from Carbohydrates 17.1% from Protein	

Preparation

- Pour the cream into a small saucepan.
- Cut the onion in half and place it in the pan with the cream.
- Enclose the bay leaves and 6 cloves inside a tea strainer ball.
- Simmer the cream at low heat 10 minutes.
- Remove and discard the onion, bay leaves, and cloves.
- Meanwhile in a medium saucepan, melt the butter and stir in the flour and salt. (Do not allow the butter to brown.)
- Add the cream and stir until the mixture is smooth.
- Add as much of the milk as need to make the sauce the consistency that you would like.
- Turn off the heat and stir the cheese into the sauce.

Equipment/Utensils

Small saucepan • Medium saucepan

Definition

Timbale—a creamy mixture baked in a mold.

Thank the Lord for the blessing of your wonderful food.

Collard Timbale

Ingredients

Butter flavored non-stick cooking spray
2 tablespoons olive oil
5 cups (1 pound) frozen chopped collards
2 tablespoons minced garlic
½ cup finely chopped onion
½ cup small sliced mushrooms
⅛ teaspoon baking soda
3 tablespoons lemon juice
1 tablespoon butter
2 teaspoons Perfect Collard Seasoning Blend™
4 large eggs

Preparation

- Sauté the collards, garlic, onion, and mushrooms in the olive oil 5 minutes. Add ½ cup water, baking soda, lemon juice, butter, and Seasoning Blend. Simmer until the liquid is reduced. Allow the mixture to cool.
- Preheat the oven to 325°.
- Spray 5 custard cups or 4-ounce ramekins.
- Beat the eggs until they are foamy. Stir the collard mixture into the eggs.
- Pour the mixture into the custard cups or ramekins.
- Bake in a water bath by placing the cups inside a large roasting pan and adding hot water half way up the outside of the cups.
- Cook until a knife inserted in the middle comes out clean, about 40 minutes.
- Allow the cups to cool 10 minutes.
- Run a knife around the edges and invert onto the serving plates.
- Serve with Cheddar Cheese Sauce (next page).

Equipment/Utensils

5 custard cups or 4-ounce ramekins • Skillet •Small bowl • Whisk • Large cooking pan

Cheddar Cheese Sauce

Ingredients

3 tablespoons unsalted butter
3 tablespoons self-rising flour
¼ teaspoon black pepper
½ -¼ teaspoon red pepper
1½ cups evaporated milk
½ cup water
3 ounces grated sharp cheddar cheese

Preparation

- Melt the butter over low heat in a small saucepan. Do not allow the butter to brown.
- Remove the butter from the heat. Add the flour and peppers. Stir until the ingredients are thoroughly blended.
- Return the saucepan to low heat. Add the milk and water. Cook and stir until the sauce is smooth. Remove the sauce from the heat and stir until the cheese is smooth.

Equipment/Utensils

Small saucepan • Whisk

Studying Dorothy Reinhold's recipes on the Cut `n Clean Greens® website, I noted that she has used many of the same ingredients to cook collards that Paul and I through experimentation have learned to include. For example, balsamic vinegar, brown sugar, pepper, and lemon juice are useful to enhance the taste and texture of collards.

When I told her that we need to add all those things to our collards, she said, "Absolutely right! They need to be shown who is boss!"

Main Event Collards
Stars of the Show

Continued on next page

♥Heart Health Cuisine

Collard Green Roll-Ups

Sauté (spray of oil) until tender:

- 6 ½ ounces of peppers (red, green, yellow)
- 10 ounces of onion (1 large)
- 2 ¼ ounces of celery (½ stalks)
- 4 to 10 cloves of garlic

Stir in:

- 10 ounces of finely chopped mushrooms (Mixture of Shitake and Portobello)
- ½ cup of red wine
- 1 tablespoon of soy sauce
- 2 tablespoon of fresh lemon juice
- ½ teaspoon each of parsley, thyme, dill, marjoram (or any dried herb mixture you like)
- Pinch of pepper (red)
- 1 cup of brown rice (cooked)

Remove from heat.

Nutrition Facts	
Collard Green Roll-Ups per serving Makes 5 servings	
Amount per serving	
Calories	170
Calories from fat	9
	% Daily Value *
Total Fat 1.1g	2%
Saturated Fat 0.1g	1%
Cholesterol 0 mg	0%
Sodium 714 mg	30%
Total Carbohydrate 34.1g	11%
Dietary Fiber 6.1g	24%
Protein 6.1g	

Percent values are based on a 2,000-calorie per day diet. Your daily values may differ.

Additional Information
5.3% of calories from Fat
80.3% from Carbohydrates
14.4% from Protein

Collard Green Preparation:
Remove the thickest part of the stem from 10 large washed collard green leaves. Place the leaves into a pot of boiling water and blanch for 3-4 minutes. Remove, dry and flatten leaves on to paper towel (keep them separate).
Pre Heat Oven: 350°.

Pan preparation: Make a bed of ½ inch sliced onions in a shallow oven ready pan with cover (or use aluminum foil).

Roll-Up preparation:
Place ½ cup of mushroom mixture on upper portion of each collard green leaf. Fold and roll up. Place each roll-up (seam side down) on the bed of slice onions.

16 ounces of Tomato Sauce:
Pour 16 ounces of tomato sauce (your favorite) over roll-ups, cover pan (aluminum foil or top) and place pan in the preheated oven. Bake for 30/35 minutes. Enjoy the Collard Greens Roll-Ups with a side of salad, pasta or by themselves!

Yvette Freeman

Yvette Freeman

With Yvette Freeman's permission, we are sharing her story and collards recipe.

In 2002, Yvette Freeman achieved one of her greatest accomplishments—she lost half her size by dropping 120 pounds. When she reported to work on the NBC series *ER* (where she had played Nurse Haleh Adams for the last 12 years) no one recognized her, and that was fine. Losing weight meant she had won over diabetes and heart disease. In 2003, Yvette Freeman was named National Advocacy Ambassador for the Diabetes Association—a duty she takes very seriously.

In addition to speaking engagements about health concerns due to diabetes, heart disease and obesity, Yvette Freeman continues to perform her award-winning role of Dinah Washington, in *Dinah Was* and acting on *ER*. In 2004, Yvette recreated the role in *Dinah Was* for the Long Beach International Theater and for L.A. Theatre Works (in 2002) as part of *The Play's The Thing* (available on CD). The play, *Dinah Was*, is based on the life of legendary jazz singer Dinah Washington and won Yvette an Obie at the Gramercy Theatre, off-Broadway. The same play in 1996 in Los Angeles garnered her "Best Actress in a Musical" from the NAACP, Ovation Awards, and LA Weekly.

Born in Wilmington, Delaware, Yvette, who is one of seven children, developed her love of performing from her father, jazz pianist Charles Freeman. After she graduated from the University of Delaware with a major in Art and Theater, Yvette's life became the theater. Her first major performance was in the Broadway musical sensation *Ain't Misbehavin'*, which utilized her tremendous singing voice and led to roles on stage, television and feature films.

On television, Freeman has been a guest-star in numerous series including *Nip/Tuck, Presidio Med, The Tick, That's Life, Boston Public, Judging Amy, NYPD Blue, The John Larroquette Show, Living Single, Sisters,* and many more. Her feature film credits include roles in *Switch, Dead Again, Children of the Corn III,* and *Angus Bethune*. She was also seen in the HBO movie *Norma and Marilyn.*

In 1999, Yvette Freeman added director to her credits when she completed the American Film Institute's program Director's Workshop for Women. Her first film was *The Blessing Way*. She has gone on to write, direct and produce several short films including *Remember,* a film about Alzheimer's, which won several awards including Best Short Story for the Moondance 2004 Film Festival.

Yvette and her husband, jazz pianist Lanny Hartley, live in the Los Angeles area with their two cats, Barkley and Sam.

Catfish Wrapped In Collard Greens

Excerpted from Fish: Grilled & Smoked by John Manikowski. ©2004.
Used with permission from Storey Publishing, LLC.

The leaves of fresh collards measure approximately nine inches across, perfect for wrapping fish. By placing the greens into boiling water for about a minute and a half, then plunging them into cold water, you will retain their bright green color. Use a perforated pizza pan or grill wok.

8 blanched collard leaves
1 tomato, diced
1 cup seeded and sliced kalamata olives
6 scallions, finely chopped
4-6 garlic cloves, minced
1 tablespoon olive oil
Salt and freshly ground black pepper
4 catfish fillets, 8 ounces each
Lemon wedges for garnish
Cooked brown rice

Advance Preparation
Blanch collard leaves.

1. Preheat a grill.
2. Lay four of the collard leaves on a work surface. Sprinkle half the tomato, olives, scallions, garlic, and oil and salt and pepper to taste on each leaf.
3. Place one fillet on top of each leaf; sprinkle the remaining ingredients (including more salt and pepper, if desired) over all.
4. Top each assemblage with the remaining four greens and secure tightly with toothpicks.
5. Place in an oiled perforated pizza pan, set the pan on the grill, and lower the lid. Grill for 6 to 7 minutes. Gently turn over with a spatula and grill for 4 to 5 minutes longer, until slightly browned.
6. Place one pocket on each of four plates. Remove the toothpicks before garnishing with the lemon wedges.

Serve with brown rice.

John Manikowski

Nutrition Facts	
Catfish Per serving, rice not included Makes 4 servings,	
Amount per serving	
Calories	374
Calories from fat	117
	% Daily Value *
Total Fat 13g	20%
Saturated Fat 2.8g	14%
Cholesterol 184 mg	61%
Sodium 449 mg	19%
Total Carbohydrate 9.5g	3%
Dietary Fiber 4.4g	18%
Protein 54.8g	

Percent values are based on a 2,000-calorie per day diet. Your daily values may differ.

Additional Information
31.3% of calories from Fat
10.2% from Carbohydrates
58.6% from Protein

John Manikowski

John Manikowski is not only a chef but also an avid outdoorsman and seafood aficionado. He has filled <u>Fish Grilled & Smoked : 150 Recipes for Cooking Rich, Flavorful Fish on the Backyard Grill, Streamside, or in a Home Smoker</u> with innovative suggestions about cooking fish. He wraps small-mouthed bass in corn husks and catfish in collards.

Chef John Manikowski is truly a man for all seasons—and some might even say an overachiever. Well, that may be an exaggeration, but it's true that as a chef, hunter, artist, and writer, he excels in every aspect.

As an artist, he earned a Master's Degree from Rhode Island School of Design before teaching art for over ten years, including a year at Harvard University. The National Endowment for the Arts also awarded him a grant as Massachusetts' artist-in-residence.

For more than a dozen years, he was co-chef and co-owner of two restaurants: Charleston in Hudson, New York, (still in operation) and Konkapot in Mill River, Massachusetts.

"Both restaurants had their own gardens," he says, "and we specialized in game from early on. I recall having trouble just finding pheasant or moullard duck breasts to buy. Now game is readily available through mail order or by the vast amount of small, specialized farming ranging from pheasant, ducks (for meat as well as foie gras), on up to venison, elk, and buffalo."

His love for hunting and fishing, developed since childhood, led him to the art of cooking wild game. Showing his respect, he writes of the pheasant as "nature's feathered jewel" and his paintings and drawings show the same esteem for these wild creatures that his recipes do.

The combination of ingredients, right down to the selection of the wine, emphasizes an attention to detail in all the flavors. It is no wonder that this same man was honored for a seemingly unglamorous pork sandwich—whatever he did to it earned him the Grand National Award from the Pork Producers Council of America, and a tidy sum of cash which, we are told, went right back into the kitchen.

Recipe reprinted from <u>Fish Grilled & Smoked</u> by John Manikowski with permission from Storey Publishing, LLC, 210 MASS Mo CA Way, North Adams, MA 01247.

Those who eat well eat collards.

Pork Tenderloin

The tenderloin can be seared baked or grilled.

Trimmed pork tenderloin has only 33 calories per ounce including 9 calories of fat.

Roast
1 (10- to 12-ounce) pork tenderloin

Marinade
3 cups teriyaki sauce
½ cup olive oil
¼ cup honey
Chopped garlic
Chopped ginger (Fresh ginger is essential!)
Cilantro

Preparation
- Mix marinade ingredients together in a large bowl.
- Place the trimmed pork tenderloin in marinade and marinate overnight.
- Grill, bake or sear the tenderloin.
  - o If baking, the tenderloin should be baked at 350°F for 15 to 20 minutes.
  - o If grilling in a charcoal grill, cook the tenderloin for 12 minutes.
  - o If searing in a skillet, cook for about 6 minutes on each side.

Jim Rooker, John Martin Terranova

Jim Rooker, John Martin Terranova

Armand's, a deliciously decorated restaurant in deep French country, is housed within Chris's Flowers & Gifts located at 313 Main Street, Gramercy, Louisiana. Behind the main dining room sits a New Orleans style courtyard, where on special occasions there is enjoyable live music—not too loud.

When I asked Jim to give me his favorite recipe, he gave me two that he received from John Martin Terranova, deceased, the former executive chef of the Castle, an exquisite restaurant located in the old stables of historic Dunleith Plantation, Natchez, Mississippi.

Grilled Pork Tenderloin and Stir-Fried Collards are featured with Creamed Sweet Potatoes on the Castle's dinner menu. Jim shared his treasured recipes with me, and I'm giving them to you.

Stir-Fried Greens

The collards go with the pork loin. If you think you don't like collards, you haven't tasted these collards!

Ingredients

2 bunches greens, collards if possible
¼ pound bacon, diced
1 red onion, sliced thin
Rice wine vinegar
Salt and pepper

Preparation

- Remove stems, then cut greens into thin strips.
- Wash thoroughly.
- Render bacon until crisp, add onion and cook onion until onion is done.
- Add greens and toss in pan.
- Add salt and pepper to taste, then add vinegar and toss in pan.
- Remove from heat and keep warm.
- Serve with Sweet and Sour Sauce (recipe below).

Sweet and Sour Sauce

Words are inadequate to tell you how good this sauce is. There is extra sauce, which can be used on everything from carrots to Brussels sprouts. These recipes are for restaurant amounts and are quoted exactly as the chefs wrote them.

Ingredients

6 cups sugar
4 cups red wine vinegar
3 cups teriyaki sauce
Chopped garlic
Chopped ginger
Chopped cilantro
3 cups ketchup
Cornstarch

Preparation

- Mix sugar, vinegar, teriyaki, garlic, and ginger in a pot and bring to a boil.
- Add cilantro and ketchup and return to a boil.
- Thicken with a little cornstarch mixed with water. Serve warm.

Equipment/Utensils

Skillet (big) • Cooking pot • Large saucepan

Jim Rooker, John Martin Terranova

Chicken and Collard Casserole

Here's another tasty casserole!

Ingredients

Non-stick cooking spray
2 tablespoons olive oil
5 cups (1 pound) frozen chopped collards
12 ounces frozen seasoning blend
⅛ teaspoon baking soda
1 tablespoon sugar
⅓ cup vinegar
Salt substitute to taste
¼ teaspoon red pepper
¼ teaspoon freshly ground black pepper
8 ounces cream cheese, softened
2 cups cooked chicken, diced (Dark meat is juicier than white meat.)
1 can cream of mushroom soup
1 tablespoon dry basil
1 cup Ritz® cracker crumbs
½ stick (4 tablespoons) butter

Preparation

- Spray the baking dish or casserole.
- Sauté the collards and seasoning blend with the olive oil 5 minutes. Add the baking soda, sugar, vinegar, salt substitute, red pepper, and black pepper. Continue to cook until the collards are tender.
- Preheat oven to 375°.
- Mix the collards, creamed cheese, soup, and basil thoroughly. Transfer the mixture to the casserole.
- Crumble the crackers and sprinkle them over the top.
- Cut the butter into tiny slices and dot it over the crackers.
- Bake until the casserole bubbles, about 20 minutes.

Equipment/Utensils

9 X 13" baking pan or casserole dish • Deep saucepan, preferably with transparent lid • Mixing bowl

Alternate Method

- A quick and easy way to crumble the crackers is to place them in a resealable plastic bag.
- You can also pour the butter in there and squish it around until everything is mixed.

Ramen Noodle Casserole

Collards add variety of color, texture, and taste to this delicious and easy dish.

Ingredients

Non-stick cooking spray
1 pound bulk sausage
1 package (3 ounces) ramen beef noodles
2 cups frozen chopped collards
1 package frozen seasoning blend
1 tablespoon olive oil
4 teaspoons Splenda®
1 teaspoon lemon juice
⅛ teaspoon baking soda
1½ cups water
½ cup uncooked rice
8 ounces Velveeta® cheese spread cubed
Paprika mixed with a smidgeon of red pepper

Preparation

- Preheat the oven. (If you are cooking something else, this dish can tolerate a range of temperatures.)
- Spray the skillet if necessary and the casserole.
- Brown the sausage and remove it from the skillet. Blot the grease from the meat.
- Break the noodles into small chunks and cook them until golden brown in the oil in the same skillet and place them with the sausage.
- Sauté the collards and seasoning blend in the same unwashed skillet. Add the Splenda®, lemon juice, and baking soda. Cook the vegetables until the greens are tender.
- Cook the rice in boiling water in another pan with the lid in place. After about 5 minutes add the sausage and noodles to the rice. Include the little pack of seasoning that came with the ramen noodles. Cook until the water is absorbed.
- Combine all the ingredients (except the paprika and red pepper) and transfer them to a sprayed casserole dish. Sprinkle with paprika or parsley.
- Bake until the dish is heated throughout.

Equipment/Utensils

Large skillet • 2-quart casserole • Mixing bowl • Cooking pot with lid

Creamy Crawfish and Collards

Louisiana myth circulating on the Internet: *Collards and crawfish do not taste good when they are cooked in the same pot.*
Truth evidenced in spicemouths'™ kitchens: *Collards and crawfish taste wonderful cooked in the same pot. This recipe is proof.*
Getting started: *The crawfish tails in this recipe are unseasoned. If you plan to use some leftovers, you will need to adjust the seasonings. (Louisiana eaters never seem to have leftover crawfish.) Plan to cook a fresh pot of collards.*

Ingredients

2 pounds (a pot full) fresh collards,
    chopped and washed
4 tablespoons olive oil
2 tablespoons minced garlic
1 cup chopped onion
3 cups water
2 tablespoons red vinegar
2 tablespoons Splenda®
3 tablespoons flour
2 cups Fat Free Half & Half®
12 ounces frozen crawfish tails
2 teaspoons Madras curry powder
½ teaspoon ground red pepper
Salt substitute to taste

Nutrition Facts	
Creamy Crawfish and Collards per serving makes 8 servings	
Amount per serving	
Calories	180
Calories from fat	68
% Daily Value *	
Total Fat 7.6g	12%
Saturated Fat 1g	5%
Cholesterol 45mg	15%
Sodium 170mg	7%
Total Carbohydrate 17.1g	6%
Dietary Fiber 4.6g	18%
Protein 11g	
Percent values are based on a 2,000-calorie per day diet. Your daily values may differ.	
Additional Information 37.7% of calories from Fat 37.9% from Carbohydrates 24.4% from Protein	

Preparation

- In the soup pot, sauté the collards, onions, and garlic with 2 tablespoons olive oil.
- Add the water, add vinegar and Splenda®, and let it simmer until the water evaporates.
- In the skillet, mix the olive oil and flour. Heat, but do not brown the mix (white roux). Stir in the cream. Heat and stir until the sauce is smooth. Add the crawfish and warm gently.
- When the collards are tender and cooked down, add the crawfish mix and seasonings. Simmer approximately 5 minutes.

Equipment/Utensils

6-quart soup pot • large skillet

Suggestion: A smidgeon of liquid smoke intensifies the flavor of this dish.

Crawfish, Grits, and Collards

This recipe will require time to prepare it, but it is worth the effort.

Collards

1. Sauté 5 minutes in a stockpot:
   - 2 tablespoons olive oil
   - 5 cups (1 pound) frozen chopped collards
   - 2 tablespoons minced garlic
   - 1 cup chopped red onion
2. Add to the pot and stir:
   - 1 cup tasso or ham
   - 2 tablespoons homemade hot pepper sauce
   - 2 tablespoons lemon juice
   - 1 tablespoon lime juice
   - ¼ cup apricot preserves
   - ⅛ teaspoon baking soda
   - 1 can cream of mushroom soup
   - 2 cups water
3. Make a pass by the spice rack. Add these spices to the collards until they taste delicious to you. Start with the smallest amount listed. Once it is in the pot, you cannot remove it very easily. Taste and add:
   - 1-2 teaspoons salt substitute
   - 1-2 teaspoons basil leaves
   - ⅛-1 teaspoon ground red pepper
   - ⅛-1 teaspoon freshly ground black pepper
   - 1-2 dashes rosemary
   - 1-2 dashes nutmeg
   - 1-2 dashes cinnamon
   - 1-2 dashes thyme
   - 2-3 teaspoons Madras curry powder
   - 2-4 teaspoons chili powder
   - ½-1 teaspoon cumin
   - ½-1 teaspoon oregano
4. Simmer the collards 20 minutes or until they are tender.

Equipment/Utensils

Big heavy pot

(Continued on next page)

Grits

1. Spray a 9 x 13 x 2" glass pan:
   - Non-stick cooking spray
2. Sauté 3-4 minutes in a saucepan:
   - 1 package (1 pound) Birds Eye® Pepper Stir Fry
   - 1 tablespoon olive oil
3. Add and heat to boiling:
   - 3 cups water
   - ½-1 teaspoon salt substitute
4. Add and stir:
   - 1 cup grits
5. Cook the grits until they are very thick. Stir continuously to prevent lumps.
6. Spoon the grits and pepper into the glass pan. Spread the mixture smoothly in the pan.
7. Refrigerate the grits until they are firm.
8. Shortly before mealtime, mix:
   - 1 cup all purpose flour
   - 1 teaspoon salt substitute
   - ½ teaspoon ground red pepper
   - ½ teaspoon ground black pepper
9. Cut the grits into squares.
10. Dredge them in the flour mix and fry them in preheated oil until they are golden brown:
    - Canola oil 2 inches deep in cooking pan
11. Drain the fried grits cakes on paper towels.

Equipment/Utensils
9 x 13 x 2" glass pan • Heavy saucepan • Mixing bowl • Deep-fat fryer or cooking pot • Lid for safety • Paper towels

Crawfish

1. Sauté in a skillet with sides:
   - 1 pound crawfish tails
   - 2 tablespoons butter
   - 1 cup diced green onions
   - 1 tablespoon minced garlic
2. Melt in small saucepan:
   - 2 tablespoons butter
3. Add, stir, and cook until the sauce thickens:
   - 2 tablespoons all purpose flour
   - 2 cups Fat Free Half & Half®
4. Add the sauce to the crawfish and stir.

(Continued on next page)

5. Make another pass by the spice rack. Select seasonings from the following list to flavor the crawfish:
   - Salt
   - Ground red pepper
   - Freshly ground black pepper
   - Parsley
   - Rosemary
   - All purpose seasoning
   - Thyme
   - Madras curry powder

Equipment/Utensils
Heavy skillet • Small saucepan

Assembling the Dish
1. Layer individual plates or a large platter with the collards topped by the grit cakes and then the crawfish.
2. Garnish with the following if you wish:
   - Sliced tomatoes
   - Grated cheddar
   - Crushed red pepper
   - Paprika
   - Refrigerated dill pickle sticks

Note: In Louisiana we believe that our crawfish acquire their unique delicious taste from the mud they eat.

Shrinking Soup Cans
Throughout the cookbook we have worked hard to be consistent. There is one problem, however, that we have failed to solve. When we buy canned products and use them, we tell you how many ounces are in the products. The size of a can of cream of mushroom soup continues to change. When we started collecting these recipes, there were 11 ounces in a can; then there were 10 1/2 . The last time we checked there were 10 1/4. You'll have to excuse the soup companies.

Stuffed Onions

Ingredients

Non-stick butter spray
2 tablespoons olive oil
8 yellow onions
1 cup tender fresh collards, finely
    chopped
⅛ teaspoon baking soda
¼ to ⅓ cup red wine vinegar
Juice of 1 lime
12 ounces frozen crawfish tails
1 can (4 ounces) mushrooms, drained
1 can (4 ounces) diced green chilies
1 cup water
2 cups Fat Free Half & Half®
1 package (6 ounces) cornbread
    stuffing mix with vegetable
    seasoning pack
1 cup finely ground prepared
    breadcrumbs
2 tablespoons Madras curry powder
Dash red pepper
8 ounces grated Dutch Garden®
    smoked Gouda cheese
Paprika

Nutrition Facts	
Stuffed Onions, Per serving Makes 8 servings	
Amount per serving	
Calories	298
Calories from fat	114
	% Daily Value *
Total Fat 12.7g	20%
Saturated Fat 5.7g	28%
Cholesterol 70 mg	23%
Sodium 829 mg	35%
Total Carbohydrate 28.9g	10%
Dietary Fiber 2.7g	11%
Protein 17.2g	
Percent values are based on a 2,000-calorie per day diet. Your daily values may differ.	
Additional Information 38.2% of calories from Fat 38.7% from Carbohydrates 23.1% from Protein	

Preparation

- Spray the cooking pan.
- To prepare each onion, cut a thin slice off the bottom so the onion will sit well and not roll over. Slice off the top third of the onion and remove the skin, along with the tough outer layer. With the sharp point of the knife, cut a small hole into the top of the onion. Continue to dig with the scoop until the center of the onion is removed. Leave the 3 outer layers intact. When you remove the onion center, part of the bottom may pop out. Don't panic. Simply cover the hole from the inside with 2 pieces of onion. Prepare each onion in this manner.
- Chop and store the remaining onion pieces to use in future recipes. You will need 1 cup for this recipe.
- Cook the onions in the microwave until they are limber—approximately 3-6 minutes. The time required will depend on the number of onions you are preparing.
- Sauté 1 cup chopped onion in the olive oil. Add the collards, and baking soda. Sauté until tender.
- Add the remaining ingredients, except for the paprika, while you continue to stir. Simmer at low heat until the mixture is firm.

- Pile the dressing high into the onions. Sprinkle the tops with paprika. (If you are a spicemouth™, you may want to sprinkle some more red pepper on top.)
- Bake at 350° until the stuffing is warmed throughout. The baking time and the number of servings will depend on the size of the onions.

Equipment/Utensils

Sharp knife with a point • Cutting board • Grater • Large skillet with high sides • Small scoop, such as a metal tablespoon-size measuring spoon, melon ball scoop, or small ice cream scoop • Microwave-safe baking pan

Notes

- We selected Great Value® Stuffing Mix because of its low sodium.
- Crawfish (Cajun crustaceans) are known as crayfish in some places.

Collard Squash Dressing

This dish is made mostly from leftovers, but good enough to serve as a side at Thanksgiving! We eat it as a main course on other days. Use those frozen packages of collards and cornbread leftover from some of the recipes you have tried recently

Ingredients

Non-stick cooking spray
1½ cups sliced green onions with tops
4 cups sliced yellow squash
2 tablespoons canola oil
2 cups cooked collards (well seasoned with meat in them)
1 can cream of mushroom soup
½ cup water
½ cup fat free Half & Half®
To taste:
    Salt or salt substitute, black pepper, red pepper, parsley, sage, rosemary, thyme
4 cups crumbled cornbread (preferably one with added ingredients)
4 eggs, beaten

Preparation

- Spray a large glass casserole.
- Sauté the onions. Add the squash and continue to cook.
- Add everything else but the eggs. Simmer on low heat and stir occasionally until the mix has a thick soupy consistency. Adjust the seasonings.
- Stir in the cornbread while you continue to cook on very low heat. Beat the eggs into the dressing.
- Pour it into the casserole and bake it uncovered until it reaches the desired consistency—slightly moist. (Southern dressing should not be dry.)

Equipment/Utensils

Sharp knife • Cutting board • Dutch oven or big pot • Whisk • 3-quart casserole

Stacked Steak and Collards

Here's a way to cook a pile of good old-fashioned Southern comfort food. When you watch your family eat this dish, you won't be sorry you cooked it.

Collards

1. First you will need some cooked collard greens on hand. If you have been trying the recipes in this book, you will know by now which type you prefer. I suggest the bacon-seasoned collards.
2. Warm the collards in the microwave or in a saucepan. Set them aside.

Rice

1. Cook some rice according to the package directions. The most delicious and best smelling rice is basmati or Texas basmati. Allow approximately ¼ cup uncooked rice per person.
2. Set the rice aside.

Steak

1. Select some tenderized gravy steak or minute steak. Don't marinate it because it will be falling apart from the mauling the butcher gave it. Salt and pepper it.
2. Smear mayonnaise over each piece.
3. In the blender grind ⅔ cup honey roasted sunflower seeds with 1 cup all purpose flour and a shake of salt (or salt substitute).
4. Place the flour in a shallow dish, and coat the steak in the flour mixture.
5. (Since you will be frying a small amount of meat, use a heavy saucepan to fry it. Keep the lid handy for safety.) Pour vegetable oil to a height of 2½ to 3" in the pan. (I like to use canola oil, and sometimes I use some olive oil mixed with the canola oil.)
6. Heat the oil until it is crackling hot. Drop some of the meat into the oil. Don't overcrowd it. You want to have one layer with space for the oil to bubble up around the meat. Turn the meat once.
7. Drain the meat on paper towels. (Some of my friends insist that the best way to drain all the grease is to place the meat on newspaper, because it is more absorbent than paper towels. Don't you think that sounds nasty?)
8. Continue to cook it until all the meat has been fried.

Gravy

1. Heat a kettle of water.
2. Estimate the amount of flour that is remaining. Dip about that same amount of flour into a skillet. Don't measure it! If you mess up, you can always make adjustments. Add the remaining flour with the seeds in it. Cook the flour and oil until it is dark brown—a roux. You can cook the roux while the meat cooks.
3. Add enough water to make gravy of desired consistency. Let it boil. Taste it and toss in some red pepper and black pepper. Add salt if you need it.

Continued on next page

Finishing

1. On each plate, place a flattened heap of rice. Top the rice with about ½ cup collard greens. Layer meat over the greens, and pour gravy over all of it.
2. Slice some tomatoes thinly to make the food look pretty and have contrast.
3. Call your folks to the table. I hope you made some cornbread.

Equipment/Utensils

Whatever pot you need to cook the collards • Big pot with a lid to cook the rice (A see-through pot lid can help you keep up with it.) • Blender • 2 or 3 dishes for preparing the meat • Pan lined with paper towels • Heavy saucepan (not too deep) with lid • Kettle • Skillet

Growing Your Own Vegetables

If you grow some of your own vegetables, you will have the joy of knowing that they have not been dusted, sprayed or otherwise assaulted.

Furthermore, you will have the pleasure of harvesting them in the morning after they have spent the night under the stars. Talk about natural delight!

Sausage Collard Bake

This is a very tasty casserole, suitable for brunch as well as lunch.

Ingredients

Non-stick cooking spray
1 pound bulk pork sausage
1 cup Vidalia onion chopped
½ cup green bell pepper, chopped
16 ounces (5 cups) frozen chopped collards
1 tablespoon olive oil
2 tablespoons lemon juice
1 tablespoon orange marmalade
½ teaspoon ground red pepper (more or less)
½ teaspoon ground black pepper
½ cup milk
3 eggs
1 cup toasted breadcrumbs
1 cup low fat sour cream
⅓ cup Favorite Dipping Sauce or Thousand Island dressing
1 tablespoon brown mustard
1 tablespoon brown sugar
¼ cup pine nuts
1 cup (4 ounces) shredded or grated cheddar cheese
Some more ground red pepper
Paprika

Preparation

- Spray the baking pan and heat the oven to 350°.
- Brown the sausage with the onion, and bell pepper. Drain and rinse the sausage mixture in a colander or blot the grease with a paper towel. Set aside.
- Sauté the collards in the oil about 4 minutes. Add the lemon juice, marmalade, black pepper, and red pepper. Allow the collards to cool.
- Stir in the milk, eggs, sour cream dipping sauce, mustard, and brown sugar into the mixture.
- Combine the sausage mixture and the collard mixture.
- Stir the breadcrumbs and pine nuts into the mix.
- Spoon the mixture into the baking pan, sprinkle the pine nuts over the mixture, and bake uncovered 10 minutes.
- Spread the cheese over the casserole and top it with sprinkles of red pepper and paprika.
- Bake 5 minutes.

Equipment/Utensils

9 x 13 x 2" baking pan • 2 large pans or skillets • colander

Vienna Sausage Casserole

Making a casserole from Vienna sausages is the kind of thing that my mother and her sisters used to do. Vienna Sausage Casserole is another old-fashioned recipe with Mississippi hill country taste. On a cold night it is, as the folks used to say, hard to beat.

Ingredients

Non-stick cooking spray
4 cups fresh finely chopped collards
2 white potatoes (approximately 1 cup), thinly sliced
2 tablespoons Tone's® spicy spaghetti seasoning
2 cans (5 ounces each) Vienna sausages, drained and halved horizontally
1 can cream of mushroom soup
1 cup fat free Half & Half®
1 cup grated mozzarella cheese
1 cup grated Colby cheese
¼ pound salt free, low fat saltine crackers
Non-fat butter flavored spray
Sprinkles of crushed red pepper, paprika, and garlic powder

Nutrition Facts	
Vienna Sausage Casserole per serving makes 6 servings	
Amount per serving	
Calories	422
Calories from fat	214
	% Daily Value *
Total Fat 23.7g	36%
Saturated Fat 10.8g	54%
Cholesterol 52 mg	17%
Sodium 1337 mg	56%
Total Carbohydrate 33.1g	11%
Dietary Fiber 2g	8%
Protein 18.9g	

Percent values are based on a 2,000-calorie per day diet. Your daily values may differ.

Additional Information
50.7% of calories from Fat
31.4% from Carbohydrates
17.9% from Protein

Preparation

- Spray pan with cooking spray.
- Steam the collards and sliced potatoes 5 minutes.
- Mix the Italian seasoning, sweetener, and vinegar into the collards.
- Layer the collards, the potatoes, and the Vienna sausages inside the sprayed baking dish.
- Mix ½ cup of the cream with the soup and spread the mixture over the layers.
- Crush the crackers. An easy method is to roll them with a rolling pin while they are still in the package.
- Stir the cheeses and crackers together and layer the mixture over the other layers.
- Pour the remaining cream over the casserole.
- Spray the top with the butter-flavored spray and sprinkle the seasonings as desired.
- Bake at 400°F until the mix is bubbly and the crackers are golden brown.

Equipment/Utensils

Steamer • 9 x 9 x 2" • Bowl • Baking dish • Rolling pin

Collard Rolls And Spare Ribs

This recipe is slightly long, but the results are worth the effort. The instructions are as explicit as we could make them. If you follow the steps, the preparation is really uncomplicated.

The yield is 6 collard rolls and 6 spare ribs.

Ingredients

Non-stick cooking spray
6 collard leaves (equivalent of a cabbage)
½ cup barley, cooked (If you plan to make the soup listed below, cook enough barley for it now. That will be 2 more cups, cooked measurement.)
6 spare ribs (approximately pound)
½ pound ground lean beef
½ pound ring sausage (in casing)
1 teaspoon pumpkin pie spice
1 teaspoon garlic powder
1 tablespoon curry powder
Ground red pepper, black pepper, and salt substitute to taste
2 eggs
1 large onion, thinly sliced
1 can (14 ounces) sauerkraut
1 cup (8 ounces) beer
1 can (1 pound.) tomatoes
¼ cup packed brown sugar
⅓ cup balsamic vinegar
2 tablespoons orange marmalade
1 pint sour cream

Preparation

- Select 6 big beautiful collard leaves without holes or brown spots. Wash the leaves thoroughly.
- Cook the barley according to the package instructions. Drain any liquid.
- Crumble the beef and chop the sausage. Mix and brown them. Rinse and drain them in a colander to remove excessive grease.
- Combine the beef, sausage, barley, garlic powder, pumpkin pie spice, red pepper, curry powder, salt, and pepper. Taste the mixture and adjust it to your personal taste. Stir in two beaten eggs.
- Cut 6 spare ribs into individual pieces and brown them.
- Separate the onions into rings and place them in the bottom of a large Crock-Pot®. which has been sprayed with non-stick cooking spray.
- Rinse the sauerkraut and drain it in a colander. Layer ½ the sauerkraut over the onions.
- Layer the ribs over the sauerkraut.
- Begin cooking the ribs with the Crock-Pot® set on high.
- Trim the stems from the bottom of the collard leaves.

- Blanch the collards in boiling water 1 minute, and gently transfer them with tongs to a colander. (The leaves should be tender but firm and intact.)
- Place the base of a leaf facing you on a cutting board.
- Dollop 1/6 of the mixture in a row across the base of the leaf and begin rolling away from you.
- After a single roll, fold the sides of the leaves around ends of the mixture extending the folds to the far end of the leaf on each side.
- Continue wrapping to the end of the leaf.
- Place the rolls in a layer above the sauerkraut with end flap down.
- Add the remaining sauerkraut.
- Combine the tomatoes, brown sugar, and balsamic vinegar. Add a shake of crushed red pepper, according to your taste.
- Pour the tomato mixture over the ribs. Continue to cook on high for 3½ hours, or until the ribs are tender.
- Serve with sour cream.

Equipment/Utensils

Cutting board • Sharp knives • Large Crock-Pot® • Colander

Don't discard the leftover liquid or wash the Crock-Pot®! Instead make the easy soup shown below.

Collard and Barley Soup

- Dip the collard rolls, ribs, onions, and sauerkraut from the mixture in the Crock-Pot®.
- Add the following ingredients:
  2 cups frozen, chopped collards
  1 sliced onion, sautéed
  ½ pound ring sausage, sliced and sautéed
  2 cups cooked barley
  1 can (28 ounces) crushed tomatoes
  1 can (28 ounces) water
  1 tablespoon balsamic vinegar
  1 tablespoon basil leaves
  2 tablespoons orange marmalade
- Cook 4 hours in Crock-Pot® on high setting.

Stuffed Collard Rolls

Ingredients

Non-stick cooking spray
2 bunches fresh uncooked collard leaves
1 pound lean ground beef
1 cup finely chopped onion
1 cup finely chopped bell pepper
1 tablespoon chopped garlic
1 teaspoon Worcestershire sauce
⅛ teaspoon dry mustard
1 teaspoon prepared horseradish
Ground red pepper as desired
Salt substitute as desired
2 tablespoons Tone's® spaghetti seasoning
2 cups tomato juice

Preparation

- Spray the baking dish. Preheat oven to 350° F.
- Remove the lower part of the stems from the collard leaves.
- Wilt the collard leaves in the microwave or in a skillet of hot water. Cut the stems out of the leaves.
- Brown ground beef, onion, bell pepper, and garlic. Drain well.
- Add Worcestershire sauce, and other seasonings except spaghetti seasoning. Stir to blend well.
- Line the baking dish with a single layer of collards. Allow the top of each leaf to hang over the edge of the dish about 3".
- Place a rounded tablespoon of filling on 8 of the leaves and roll from the top of the leaf toward the stem area.
- Place the rolls, seam side down, in the baking dish.
- Blend the tomato juice and Italian seasoning.
- Pour the juice over the collard rolls. Fold the tops of the leaves that are lining the pan over the rolls. If necessary place a piece of a leaf in the middle so the rolls are completely covered.
- Spray the top of the covering leaves to keep the collards from burning.
- Bake until the temperature of an inside roll reaches 170°F, approximately 45 minutes.

Equipment/Utensils

Skillet • 13 X 9 X 2" Pyrex® baking dish • Aluminum foil

Pork-Teriyaki Stuffed Collard Leaves

Ingredients

1 (1½ pounds) pork loin roast
½ cup teriyaki sauce
½ cup uncooked rice
⅓ cup orange marmalade
1 tablespoon red wine vinegar
2 small bunches young collards
Non-stick cooking spray

Preparation

- Place the roast in a small Crock-Pot®. Cover it with the teriyaki sauce. Cook on high until it is tender—about 3½ hours.
- Remove the roast from the Crock-Pot® and chop it into small pieces.
- Preheat the oven to 325°. Spray a baking dish.
- Cook the rice according to the package instructions, but do not add salt.
- Add the pork, ⅓ cup of the teriyaki sauce and drippings, the garlic, orange marmalade, and vinegar. Stir thoroughly. (Discard the remaining sauce and drippings.)
- Wash and blanch the collard leaves. Choose longest ones. If the collards have long stems, use the stems for handles and hold them about 2 minutes in a skillet of boiling water.
- Take the leaves to a cutting board. Cut the stems off. On the larger leaves, cut approximately 2" of the stemmy spines out of the leaves.
- Dollop a blob of the mixture onto each leaf, tuck in the edges, and roll the leaves around the mixture from the tip to the spine end. Place the seams on the bottom. Spray lightly with cooking spray.
- Bake 40 minutes.

Equipment/Utensils

Small Crock-Pot® • Pot for cooking rice • 11½ X 8 X 2" Pyrex® baking dish • Skillet • Cutting board • Sharp knife

Crawfish Étouffée Collard Rolls

Rice

Ingredient

½ cup uncooked rice (Basmati is excellent.)

Preparation

- Cook the rice according to package instructions, but do not add salt. You should have about 1½ cups of cooked rice.

Sauce for Filling and Top of Rolls

Ingredients

1 can (15 ounces) tomato sauce

1 can 14½ ounces) diced tomatoes with basil, garlic, and oregano

1 tablespoon sugar

½ teaspoon rosemary

1½ teaspoons ground red pepper

1½ teaspoons black pepper

2 teaspoons Tony Chachere's® (sodium free)

3 tablespoons minced garlic

¼ cup red wine vinegar

Preparation

- Mix all the above ingredients in a blender until the tomatoes are liquefied.
- Pour the sauce into a saucepan and simmer it uncovered while you prepare the other ingredients.

Crawfish Filling

Ingredients

1 stick (¼ pound) unsalted butter

1 tablespoon olive oil

½ cup self-rising flour

1½ cups warm water

12 ounces peeled crawfish tails

1 package (12 ounces) Creole seasoning blend (onions, celery, green peppers, red peppers, and parsley)

1 cup sauce for filling and top of rolls

Preparation

- Make a dark roux by browning the flour in the butter and oil.
- Add the warm water and stir until the roux is smooth.
- Add the crawfish and seasoning blend along with 1 cup of the sauce.
- Simmer until the crawfish and vegetables are tender and enough liquid is reduced to a semi-firm consistency.
- Adjust the seasoning to taste. You may want to add some more Tony Chachere's®.
- Add the rice with minimal stirring.

Collard Leaves

Ingredients
2 bunches collards with medium large leaves
Pinch of baking soda

Preparation
- Add the baking soda to a shallow pan or skillet of water. Separate the collard leaves from the bunches; wash them.
- To tenderize the collard leaves place them into a pot of boiling water and blanch them for 1-2 minutes.
- Cut off the stemmy spines for a couple of inches into the leaves. They should be tender but firm and intact.

The Rolls
- Preheat the oven to 350°.
- Spray a 13 X 9 X 2" cooking pan with non-stick cooking spay. Line the pan with a single layer of leaves that hang over about 3". If necessary, place some leaves in the bottom of the pan.
- Place the top of a leaf facing you on a cutting board.
- Dollop some mixture in a row across the top of the leaf and begin rolling away from you.
- After a single roll, fold the sides of the leaves around ends of the mixture extending the folds to the far end of the leaf on each side.
- Continue wrapping to the end of the leaf.
- Place the rolls, seam sides down, in the pan on top of the leaves. Pour the remaining tomato sauce over the top. Be sure to drizzle the sauce over each leaf.
- Fold the leaves over the top. If necessary, place some leaves in the center. Spray with cooking spray (or coat lightly with olive oil.)
- Bake 40 minutes.

Equipment/Utensils
Pot to cook the rice • Blender • Saucepan • 2 skillets • Cutting board • 13 X 9 X 2 " • Cooking pan

About the Preceding Recipe
When you serve the rolls, garnish them with some parsley. Serve them with some grilled French bread and some iced tea.

Crawfish Étouffée

If you wish, you may serve the crawfish filling in the above recipe as simply delicious étouffée. Do not add the extra tomato sauce intended to pour over the collard rolls. Leave the étouffée soupy with plenty of liquid—like an extremely thick soup.
Also cook enough rice to spread across each plate underneath your étouffée. Serve it over rice with garlic bread.

Quick, Easy, Tasty, Nutritious

Stir-Fried Crawfish and Vegetables

Stir-fry some vegetables and crawfish when you are in a hurry but want something tongue-tingling tasty without extra calories.

We love our food spicy. Adjust the spices and vinegar according to your personal taste. If you are using previously seasoned crawfish, you may not need to add any spices.

Ingredients

1 cup uncooked rice (basmati or other)
¼ teaspoon olive oil
12 ounces frozen crawfish tails
1 pound (5 cups) Birds Eye® Pepper Stir-Fry (sliced green, red, and yellow peppers
  and white onions)
2 cups frozen chopped collards
⅛ teaspoon baking soda
Creole seasoning as desired (salt free)
Dash garlic powder
¼ cup Tiger Sauce®
¼ cup balsamic vinegar
2 teaspoons brown sugar
2 cups sliced mushrooms

Preparation

- Cook the rice according to the package directions.
- Toss all the other ingredients into a deep skillet with a lid except the mushrooms
- Cook the vegetables and crawfish until the liquid is absorbed. If you are busy, put the lid on and let them cook until they are tender. Check and stir them often.
- When most of the liquid is absorbed, add the mushrooms and cook another minute.
- Serve over rice. Four servings

Equipment/Utensils

Pot to cook the rice • Deep skillet with lid or Dutch oven

After Katrina and Rita, Louisiana has seeded the entire nation with people with palates synchronized to the Acadian (Cajun) influence.

Italian Sausage over Cauliflower

Indulge in a huge amount of tasty food including nutritious vegetables—a main dish for less than 450 calories. Use milder sausage and less pepper if you wish. Enjoy it with Sweet Potato and Collard Biscuits.

Ingredients

1 head cauliflower
1 tablespoon olive oil
½ cup frozen chopped collards
½ cup carrots, grated
½ cup celery, sliced thinly
½ cup bell pepper, diced
2 tablespoons minced garlic
1 can (10½ ounces) cream of tomato
   soup
1 cup water
1 tablespoon crushed red pepper
1 teaspoon basil
8 ounces Velveeta® cheese product,
   cubed
2 links Johnsonville® hot Italian sausage
Salt substitute to taste

Nutrition Facts	
Italian Sausage over Cauliflower per serving makes 4 servings	
Amount per serving	
Calories	431
Calories from fat	211
% Daily Value *	
Total Fat 23.5g	36%
Saturated Fat 9.3g	47%
Cholesterol 62 mg	21%
Sodium 1739 mg	72%
Total Carbohydrate 32.4g	11%
Dietary Fiber 6.1g	24%
Protein 22.7g	
Percent values are based on a 2,000-calorie per day diet. Your daily values may differ.	
Additional Information 48.9% of calories from Fat 30% from Carbohydrates 21% from Protein	

Preparation

- Break the cauliflower into medium pieces, wash, and steam. Leave the cauliflower firm, not overly tender.
- In the large skillet sauté the collards, carrots, celery, bell pepper, and garlic in the olive oil.
- Add the tomato soup and water. Simmer about 15 minutes until the liquid is reduced to a desired sauce consistency.
- Chop the sausage into small pieces and brown it in the small skillet. Rinse excessive grease from it and drain.
- Add the basil, sausage, cheese, and salt substitute to the vegetable sauce. Heat until the cheese melts.
- Serve the sauce over the cauliflower.

Equipment/Utensils

Steamer • Grater • Knife • Cutting board • Large high-sided skillet • Small skillet

Sweet Potato and Collard Biscuits

These biscuits go well with Italian Sausage over Cauliflower. Be sure to include the collards in the biscuits for interesting color and taste. This recipe will make 24 medium biscuits or 12 huge biscuits.

Ingredients

Small amount of shortening to grease the pan
2 cups self-rising flour
1 teaspoon baking powder
¼ cup sugar
1 teaspoon ground cinnamon
⅓ cup butter flavored shortening
1 cup cooked, mashed sweet potatoes
¼ cup cooked, finely chopped collards
⅔ cup fat free Half & Half®
More self-rising flour for kneading
1 tablespoon melted butter

Nutrition Facts	
Sweet Potato and Collard Biscuits per serving makes 12 servings	
mount per serving	
Calories	254
Calories from fat	120
	% Daily Value *
Total Fat 13.4g	21%
Saturated Fat 5.5g	28%
Cholesterol 9 mg	3%
Sodium 421 mg	18%
Total Carbohydrate 30.1g	10%
Dietary Fiber 1.2g	5%
Protein 3.5g	
Percent values are based on a 2,000-calorie per day diet. Your daily values may differ.	
Additional Information 47.2% of calories from Fat 47.3% from Carbohydrates 5.5% from Protein	

Preparation

- Combine 2 cups flour, baking powder, sugar, and cinnamon. Cut in shortening with pastry blender until the mixture resembles coarse meal. Add the sweet potatoes, collards, and cream. Mix vigorously.
- Turn the dough onto a floured surface. Knead until the dough has a smooth consistency.
- Pat the dough to a thickness of ½". Cut the biscuits with the biscuit cutter.
- Place the biscuits on the cooking sheets and bake until golden brown—about 20 minutes. Brush with melted butter.

Equipment/Utensils

Cooking sheets or baking pans • Pastry blender• Cutting board or pastry board • Biscuit cutter • Butter brush

Nutrition Note

- In calculating the nutritional value of these biscuits, we have allowed 2 teaspoons shortening to grease the pan and ½ cup self-rising flour to knead the biscuits.

Skillet Supper Sandwiches

You will need to start with some good biscuits, such as Ruth's (next page. Lately I've been serving Pillsbury® Oven Baked Extra Large Easy Split™ biscuits with 280 calories per biscuit. They can be found in the frozen section of the grocery.

They taste just like Mama's, and as they bake, they become ragged looking like hers. With a gentle nudge, they will divide into 2 sections.

Ingredients

1 tablespoon olive oil
2 cups chopped tender fresh collards
2 ounces sliced tasso
1 cup sliced fresh mushrooms
1 tablespoon lemon juice
1 tablespoon lime juice
3 eggs

Preparation

- Heat the oil in the skillet.
- Add the collards, tasso, and mushrooms. Cook rapidly until all ingredients are hot. Do not overcook.
- Scoot the ingredients to one side, and scramble the eggs in the empty space.
- Just before serving, tilt the hot skillet and add the juices. As they absorb and evaporate, the dish will sizzle and steam like fajitas.

Nutrition Facts	
Filling Only, Per serving	
Makes 2 servings	
Amount per serving	
Calories	231
Calories from fat	141
% Daily Value *	
Total Fat 15.7g	24%
Saturated Fat 3.2g	16%
Cholesterol 334 mg	111%
Sodium 325 mg	14%
Total Carbohydrate 5.5g	2%
Dietary Fiber 1.7g	7%
Protein 17g	

Percent values are based on a 2,000-calorie per day diet. Your daily values may differ.

Additional Information
61% of calories from Fat
9.5% from Carbohydrates
29.4% from Protein

Equipment/Utensils

Large skillet with sides

Serving Suggestions

Serve with a variety of add-ons, such as sliced fresh tomatoes, feta cheese, spicy mustard, Wal-Mart Southwest Spicy Sweet Hot Mustard®, salt, black pepper, crushed red pepper, and Madras curry powder.

Ruth's Old-Fashioned Biscuits

My sister Ruth has been cooking great biscuits since she could remember. Since her family is dieting, she greases the cooking pan with non-stick cooking spray instead of yummy bacon drippings. Her food is always delicious.

Ingredients

2 cups self-rising flour
2 tablespoons shortening
¾ cup milk (approximately) any
    kind of milk—buttermilk is good
More self-rising flour (about ¼ cup)
Non-stick cooking spray

Preparation

- Blend the shortening into the flour until it is in pieces about the size of small peas.
- Mix the milk into the flour.
- Make the mixture as moist as possible, and still have it in good condition to handle.
- Form the dough into a ball.
- Sprinkle flour on a cutting board; lift the dough onto the board.
- Flour your hands. Knead.
  - o Ruth's method: Shape the dough into biscuits by rolling them in your hands. Place them in a greased pan.
  - o Alternate method: Sprinkle flour thinly over the top; pat dough to 1" thick. Cut it with a biscuit cutter; place the biscuits in a greased pan.

Nutrition Facts		
Ruth's Biscuits, Per serving Makes 6 servings		
Amount per serving		
Calories		216
Calories from fat		47
		% Daily Value *
Total Fat 5.4g		8%
Saturated Fat 1.6g		8%
Cholesterol 2 mg		1%
Sodium 613 mg		26%
Total Carbohydrate 36.5g		12%
Dietary Fiber 1.3g		5%
Protein 5.8g		
Percent values are based on a 2,000-calorie per day diet. Your daily values may differ.		
Additional Information 21.7% of calories from Fat 67.5% from Carbohydrates 10.7% from Protein		

- For crusty biscuits, place them an inch apart; for thick, soft biscuits, make the edges touch. Bake 18 to 20 minutes at 450°.

Equipment/Utensils

Bowl • Cutting board • Baking pan

Ruth Ishee

Collard Patch Cuisine

Our cuisine is the result of the fusion of varied cooking styles, including

- Down-home Mississippi cooking, the epitome of Southern good eating
- Hot and spicy Texas cooking, the essence of Southwestern fare
- Varied Louisiana gastronomy, the heart of Cajun and Creole food

Pork Loin Roast
With Collard Dressing

Pork Loin Roast

Ingredients

Non-stick cooking spray
1 (2-pound) boneless pork loin roast
3 tablespoons light soy sauce
1 can (12 ounces) beer
2 teaspoons Jamaican Jerk seasoning
1 cup barbecue sauce

Preparation

- Place the roast, which should be well trimmed, into the Crock-Pot®, which you have sprayed.
- Pour the remaining ingredients over the roast and cook it on a high setting until it is tender.

Note

- Jamaican Jerk is a potent seasoning mix containing onions, chili, salt, garlic, nutmeg, black pepper, allspice, paprika, and ginger. Since some of the ingredients are whole seeds, the mixture has an interesting texture. It gives a special flavor to barbecued meat and fish.
- If you are within 500 miles of Central Market in Dallas, don't hesitate to drive there to buy some.

Collard Dressing

Ingredients

Non-stick cooking spray
1 box (8½ ounces) Jiffy® corn muffin mix
1 egg
⅓ cup Fat Free Half & Half®
1 tablespoon olive oil
5 cups (16 ounces) frozen chopped collards
2 cups chopped onion
½ cup chopped bell pepper
⅛ teaspoon baking soda
¼ to ½ cup lemon juice
⅛ to ¼ cup balsamic vinegar
½ cup water
1 package (20 ounces) frozen creamed corn

Continued on next page

1 can (10 ¾ ounces) mushroom soup
1 small jar (4 ounces) chopped pimiento
1 teaspoon hot sauce
1 tablespoon Madras curry powder
6 ounces grated Dutch Garden American® cheese
2 eggs, beaten

Preparation

- Preheat the oven to 400º.
- Spray the small cooking pan.
- Mix the corn muffin mix, 1 egg, and the Fat Free Half & Half®.
- Bake the cornbread while you prepare the other ingredients.
- Sauté the collards, onion, and bell pepper in the olive oil. Add the baking soda, lemon juice, vinegar, and water. Simmer until the water is absorbed.
- Add the corn, soup, and pimiento. Continue to simmer.
- Crumble the cornbread into the mixture. Add the hot sauce and curry.
- Allow the mixture to cool. Then add the cheese and the 2 beaten eggs.
- Spoon the dressing into the casserole dish.
- Bake until the center of the dressing is set, 30 to 40 minutes.

Notes

- Collards are tasty when they are tart. If you prefer less tartness, adjust the vinegar and lemon juice according to your taste.
- Dutch Garden American® cheese has an excellent taste with a hint of cheddar-like sharpness but a smoothness like cheese spread. It is easy to grate.
- Do not add sweetener to the collards. The corn and corn muffin mix are sweet enough.
- Contact the authors for nutritional information.
- There are times when you may not want your mascara to stream down your cheeks or when you are too busy to chop onions. Seasoning blend—a tasty mixture of chopped seasoning vegetables such as onions, celery, green peppers, red peppers, and parsley—can be substituted for chopped onions in most recipes.
- Also there are frozen chopped onions.

Equipment/Utensils

Crock-Pot® • Small baking pan • Mixing bowl • Dutch oven • Cutting board •
• Knife • Grater • 2-quart casserole dish

Serving Suggestion

1. Serve the roast and dressing with sweet orange marmalade.
2. The collard dressing with pimiento in it is colorful enough to grace a Christmas buffet.

Louisiana Redneck Beans

Here is the ultimate comfort food for a redneck woman. It's tastes so good you will not want to share it. Cook yourself a batch—it's easy to prepare.

Ingredients

Non-stick cooking spray
1 onion (about 1 cup) coarsely chopped
1 can (15 ounces) Ranch Style® beans
½ of a 12-ounce can Treet® (Virginia Baked Ham Taste), cubed
1 tablespoon honey
Leftover collards (cooked by a basic recipe)
2 ounces processed cheese food, cubed
Tiger Sauce®

Preparation

- Spray a medium-sized skillet with the cooking spray and sauté the onion. Add the beans. Cook them gently until most of the liquid is absorbed. Add the Treet® and honey. Warm the mixture thoroughly.
- Spread a layer of collards on your plate. Microwave it until the plate is hot on the bottom. Layer cheese cubes over the collards
- Spoon half the bean mix on top.
- Add some Tiger Sauce®.

This recipe yields 2 servings.

Equipment/Utensils

Skillet • Knife • Cutting board

Late Night Wrapped Snack

If you are eating alone, hide the leftover beans in the back of the refrigerator. Some late night when you want to serve a special snack, whisk 4 eggs. Scramble them with the leftovers and the other half of the can of Treet®, diced. Serve the mix with large warm tortillas as wraps. Lay a big wilted collard leaf over each tortilla before rolling the ingredients.

Curried Lamb Roast

Lamb, customary meat of the Middle East, has a matchless taste, but many people in the United States miss this culinary delight. The seasonings included remove the gamy taste that some people dislike about lamb.

Ingredients

1 boneless leg of lamb roast (approximately 5 pounds)
1 tablespoon minced garlic
1 teaspoon rosemary
6 sprigs (4" each) mint, chopped
1 tablespoon Madras curry blend
⅓ cup balsamic vinegar
3 tablespoons Tiger Sauce®
¼ cup water
1 cup Port wine
3 large carrots
3 medium white potatoes
12 fresh collard leaves
Additional vinegar
Additional Tiger Sauce®

Preparation

- Thaw the roast.
- Preheat the roaster to 400°F.
- Place garlic, rosemary, mint, curry, vinegar, Tiger Sauce®, and water in blender. Blend until the mixture is smooth without large particles. Pour the mixture into a small bowl and add the wine.
- Using the syringe, inject the roast with as much liquid as possible.
- Cut the carrots into sticks and the potatoes into cubes. Place a layer of the carrots and potatoes on the bottom of the pan.
- Wash the collards and trim the stems. Roll the collards, and secure them with toothpicks. Place a layer of collard rolls over the carrots and potatoes.
- Place a rack inside the roaster, place the pan containing the vegetables on top of the rack, place the other rack on top of the pan, and put the roast on top of the rack. Cook until the roast reaches an internal temperature of 180°F.
- Remove the vegetables from the gravy and sprinkle vinegar over them before serving.
- Allow the roast to cool and slice it. Serve with Tiger Sauce®.

Equipment/Utensils

Roaster oven • Large glass cooking pan • Racks • Meat injecting syringe • Blender • Toothpicks • Meat thermometer

Curried Shrimp and Chicken With Collards and Rice

An Asian flavored casserole

Ingredients

1 cup uncooked basmati rice
2 tablespoons olive oil
5 cups (16 ounces) frozen chopped collards
2 tablespoons minced garlic
1 package (about 10 ounces) frozen seasoning blend
¼ cup lemon juice
1 tablespoon crushed basil leaves
2 tablespoons Splenda®
⅛ teaspoon baking soda
Salt substitute to taste
Ground red pepper to taste
Freshly ground black pepper to taste
3 tablespoons Madras curry
1½ cups low sodium chicken stock or broth
1 pound large cooked and peeled shrimp.
1 cup Kraft® Creamy Poppy seed Dressing
1 cup sliced mushrooms
1½ cups cooked and deboned chicken

Preparation

- Cook the rice and set it aside.
- In a large heavy pan or Dutch oven sauté the greens, garlic, and seasoning blend until the onions are translucent.
- Add the lemon juice, basil, Splenda®, baking soda, salt substitute, red pepper, black pepper, curry, and broth or stock. Cover and cook until the liquid is absorbed.
- Add the remaining ingredients and rice. Heat thoroughly.

Equipment/Utensils

Pan for cooking pasta • Heavy pan or Dutch oven • 3-quart casserole

Suggestions

This recipe makes a large amount. Place it in a 3-quart casserole and store it until you are ready to heat it. Then warm it in the oven.

Use some of this dish as stuffing for baked squash.

Asparagus-Collard Green Linguine

One of the most delicious lunch entrées you can imagine is Asparagus-Collard Green Linguine. Careful shopping is essential. Select really tasty ham with a sweet, smoky taste and linguine of excellent quality. Use frozen, not canned, asparagus.

Ingredients

2 packages (9 ounces each) Green
    Giant® frozen asparagus without sauce
1 teaspoon salt substitute
2 tablespoons olive oil (divided)
1 pound linguine
2 cups frozen chopped collards
2 cups chopped Vidalia onions
1 tablespoon balsamic vinegar
⅛ teaspoon baking soda
8 ounces thinly sliced and chopped cured
    Virginia ham
Dash black pepper
Dash crushed red pepper
1 can cream of mushroom soup
8 ounces grated mozzarella cheese
½ cup light sour cream
½ cup ricotta cheese

Nutrition Facts
Asparagus-Collard Green Linguine
Per serving
Makes 11 servings, 1 cup each

Amount per serving	
Calories	333
Calories from fat	103
	% Daily Value *
Total Fat 11.4g	18%
Saturated Fat 4.7g	23%
Cholesterol 28 mg	9%
Sodium 672 mg	28%
Total Carbohydrate 38.8g	13%
Dietary Fiber 3.8g	15%
Protein 18.6g	

Percent values are based on a
2,000-calorie per day diet.
Your daily values may differ.

Additional Information
31% of calories from Fat
46.7% from Carbohydrates
22.4% from Protein

Preparation

*   Cook the asparagus according to package instructions. (Place unopened pouches in vigorously boiling water in a large uncovered saucepan. Boil 18 minutes. Turn the pouches over halfway through heating time.).
*   Remove the pouches.
*   Cook the linguini by boiling 6 quarts of water with 1 teaspoon salt substitute and 1 tablespoon olive oil. Add the linguini to vigorously boiling water. Cook 11 minutes. Stir lightly to separate occasionally. Drain in a colander and return to the pot to keep it warm.
*   Sauté the collards and onions in olive oil until they are tender. Add the vinegar and baking soda.
*   Toss all the ingredients together.
Serve immediately.

Equipment/Utensils

Large saucepan for cooking asparagus • Large pot for cooking spaghetti • Colander •
Large skillet

Collard-Crawfish Alfredo

If you don't tell the people the truth about Collard-Crawfish Alfredo, they may think they are eating spinach; but collards taste better than spinach.

If you don't tell them, they will think you stood over the hot stove all afternoon; but this dish is quick and easy. It is so special and pretty that people will think you are celebrating a special occasion, but don't tell them it is economical.

Who says collards and crawfish are incompatible? What's wrong with mixing Italian sauce with chilies? What happens if you combine all of the above? The answer is a flavor explosion no one will forget!

Ingredients

1 jar (16 ounces) Classico® Alfredo
    sauce
12 ounces frozen crawfish tails
2 teaspoons olive oil
2 cups frozen chopped collards
1 can (4 ounces) diced green chilies with
    juice
⅛ teaspoon baking soda
2 teaspoons balsamic vinegar
Salt substitute to taste
Shake of black pepper
12 ounces seashell macaroni
Parmesan cheese
Crushed red pepper

Nutrition Facts	
Collard-Crawfish Alfredo per serving makes 8 servings	
Amount per serving, Parmesan not included	
Calories	322
Calories from fat	119
	% Daily Value *
Total Fat 13.3g	20%
Saturated Fat 5.3g	27%
Cholesterol 95 mg	32%
Sodium 510 mg	21%
Total Carbohydrate 37g	12%
Dietary Fiber 2g	8%
Protein 13.7g	
Percent values are based on a 2,000-calorie per day diet. Your daily values may differ.	
Additional Information 37% of calories from Fat 46% from Carbohydrates 17% from Protein	

Preparation

- Empty the sauce into the saucepan. Rinse the jar with a tablespoon of water. This classic sauce with its cracked pepper and aged Parmesan cheese taste is too good to waste!
- Drop the crawfish into the sauce and simmer the mixture on the back burner.
- Heat the oil in the skillet. Add the collards, chilies with juice, baking soda, and vinegar. Sauté while stirring frequently until the collards are tender.
- Cook the seashell macaroni according to the package directions and drain.
- Add the collards and then the macaroni to the crawfish and sauce. Salt to taste.
- Serve with Parmesan cheese and crushed red pepper.

Equipment/Utensils

Deep saucepan • Skillet • Deep pot to cook past • Colander

Chorizo-Collards Lasagna

Tim Ellis told us he worked on this recipe for more than a year to perfect it. Actually it's a Mexican flavored lasagna. We wrote what he told us.

Ingredients

16 ounces lasagna pieces (18 pieces)
24 ounces beef chorizo
1 quart fresh collards, finely chopped
1 cup chopped red onion
1 can (10 ounces) Ro*Tel® original diced tomatoes and green chilies
1 can (14½ ounces) diced tomatoes
1 can (4 ounces) chopped green chilies
1 can (15 ounces) tomato sauce
2 teaspoons cumin
¼ teaspoon cinnamon
3 tablespoons peach preserves
1 teaspoon Mexican oregano
2 pounds grated Colby/Monterey Jack cheese
30 ounces part-skim ricotta cheese
4 eggs
4 ounces Parmesan cheese
Paprika
Parsley
Crushed red pepper

Preparation

- Cook the lasagna according to directions on package. Do not overcook. Drain well. Place the noodles in single layers to cool.
- Place the chorizo in the Dutch oven. Add 1 cup water and cook. Dip the oil off the sausage. Add the collards and onions to the chorizo and continue to cook.
- Add the canned ingredients, cumin, cinnamon, preserves, and oregano. Continue to cook; stir occasionally. Cook uncovered 30 minutes.
- Combine half the grated cheese with the ricotta cheese and eggs. Mix thoroughly.
- Assemble the lasagna. Begin with 1 cup sauce in each pan. Place 3 pieces of lasagna over the sauce. Continue with layers of the cheese/egg mix, lasagna pieces, more sauce, ½ the remaining cheese, another layer of lasagna, then a small amount of the sauce, and the remaining cheese.
- Top with the Parmesan. Sprinkle with paprika, parsley, and crushed red pepper.
- Bake until the mixture bubbles, about 30 minutes.

Equipment/Utensils

• Dutch oven • Pot to cook lasagna • Colander • Two 13 X 9 X 2" cooking pans

Tim Ellis

Tim Ellis

The old Ellis boy, who lives in east Texas, is known for his vociferous opinions. Having lived all his life in the Big Piney close to Canton—he ranges in the Big Piney, you know, all the way down to Toledo Bend—he looks about a hundred years old. He is crusty like a swamp alligator. He is probably no more than thirty-six, but you can never tell about alligator hide.

He just comes out of the woods at certain seasons of the year. He goes online at the public library in Canton when he comes into town. He has to get his liver cleaned in February—that's the occasion for one of his trips to town. He goes to the Trade Days mostly to sell alligator meat. He sells pickled alligator meat and alligator hides. When he leaves the Big Piney to come to town, he hitchhikes through Tyler on Texas 64.

Nobody ever has ever seen him any farther southeast than Brachfield on FM 840E, but mostly he can be seen hitchhiking between Henderson and Canton on Highway 64. Sometimes he'll stop off in Tyler, but they ask too many questions in Tyler, and Tim don't like no nosy people. In Canton they don't have a tendency to ask too many questions. You can stay longer in the Canton area without people getting too curious.

♥*Heart Health Cuisine*

Vegetable Garden Spaghetti Sauce

Ingredients

2 tablespoons olive oil
1 cup frozen chopped collards
1 cup fresh zucchini, sliced
1 cup fresh yellow squash, sliced
1 cup chopped onions
1 can (28 ounces) crushed tomatoes
1 can (8 ounces) tomato sauce
½ cup fresh sliced mushrooms
⅛ teaspoon baking soda
3 tablespoons lemon juice
2 tablespoons sugar or Splenda®
2 tablespoons minced garlic
¼ cup Tone's® spicy spaghetti seasoning
1 teaspoon cinnamon
Salt substitute to taste
Black pepper and red pepper to taste

Nutrition Facts	
Vegetable Garden Spaghetti Sauce per serving makes 6 servings	
Amount per serving	
Calories	125
Calories from fat	44
	% Daily Value *
Total Fat 5g	8%
Saturated Fat 0.7g	3%
Cholesterol 0 mg	0%
Sodium 214 mg	9%
Total Carbohydrate 16.4g	5%
Dietary Fiber 4.5g	18%
Protein 3.8g	
Percent values are based on a 2,000-calorie per day diet. Your daily values may differ.	
Additional Information 35.3% of calories from Fat 52.6% from Carbohydrates 12.2% from Protein	

Preparation

- Sauté the collards, zucchini, yellow squash, and onions in the olive oil. Stir in the baking soda as the vegetables cook.

- Add the remaining ingredients and simmer until the vegetables are tender but firm. Limit stirring.

Knife •Cutting board • Dutch oven

Serving Suggestions

- Serve over spaghetti or other pasta.
- Top with meatballs or skillet-browned Italian sausage links if desired.
- Serve with grated mozzarella cheese.
- Sprinkle Parmesan over the top.
- Serve the sauce over spaghetti squash or cauliflower for a delicious, low-calorie alternative to pasta.

About Salt

Unless you are required medically to restrict your potassium intake, use salt substitute to lower the sodium content. (Most processed foods have excessive amounts of sodium built in that cannot be eliminated.)

Spaghetti

For pasta, follow the package directions.

We are including the nutrition facts related to spaghetti noodles for your reference. The nutritional information is for ¾ cup cooked, enriched, without added salt.

The basic method for cooking spaghetti is to boil it in a big deep pot with plenty of water, a small amount of olive oil, and salt to taste. Place the noodles in vigorously boiling water, and cook about 4 minutes. Be careful to place them in small increments. Adding too many at once or adding them to under heated water can cause them to stick together.

If you like your spaghetti al dente, you can always test it by throwing a piece at the wall. If it sticks, it is al dente. Soon the wall will become sticky if you cook spaghetti often.

Pour the spaghetti into a colander and rinse it with hot water. Then you can return it to the pan, which has been removed from heat.

Nutrition Facts	
per serving of spaghetti noodle 1 serving	
Amount per serving	
Calories	145
Calories from fat	6
	% Daily Value *
Total Fat 0.7g	1%
Saturated Fat 0.1g	1%
Cholesterol 0 mg	0%
Sodium 1 mg	0%
Total Carbohydrate 29.8g	10%
Dietary Fiber 1.8g	7%
Protein 5g	

Percent values are based on a 2,000-calorie per day diet. Your daily values may differ.

Additional Information
4.1% of calories from Fat
82.1% from Carbohydrates
13.8% from Protein

The above instructions are the American way of cooking spaghetti. Some Italians have a different method. Here it is:

When the spaghetti reaches the al dente stage, drain some of the liquid—about a cup of it—and pour it into the spaghetti sauce. Dip the spaghetti pasta from the liquid where you cooked it and add the noodles to the sauce.

About Parmesan

Parmesan when young, soft and slightly crumbly is eaten on bread. But when well aged, let us say up to a century, it becomes Rock of Gibraltar of cheeses and really suited for grating.

It is easy to believe that the so-called "Spanish cheese" used as a barricade by Americans in Nicaragua almost a century ago was none other than the almost indestructible Grana, as Parmesan is called in Italy.

Quoted from *The Complete Book of Cheese,* 1955, by Bob Brown

About Cheddar

The first American cheddar was made soon after 1620 around Plymouth by Pilgrim fathers who brought along not only cheese from the homeland but a live cow to continue the supply. Proof of our ability to manufacture cheddar of our own lies in the fact that by 1790 we were exporting it back to England.

It was called cheddar after the English original named for the village of Cheddar near Bristol. More than a century ago it made a new name for itself, Herkimer County cheese, from the section of New York State where it was first made best. Herkimer still equals its several distinguished competitors, Coon, Colorado Blackie, California Jack, Pineapple, Sage, Vermont Colby and Wisconsin Longhorn.

The English called our imitation Yankee, or American, cheddar, while here at home it was popularly known as yellow or store cheese from its prominent position in every country store; also apple-pie cheese because of its affinity for the all-American dessert.

The first cheddar factory was founded by Jesse Williams in Rome, New York, just over a century ago and, with Herkimer County cheddar already widely known, this established "New York" as the preferred "store-boughten" cheese.

An account of New York's cheese business in the pioneer Wooden Nutmeg Era is found in Ernest Elmo Calkins' interesting book, *They Broke the Prairies*. A Yankee named Silvanus Ferris, "the most successful dairyman of Herkimer County," in the first decades of the 1800's teamed up with Robert Nesbit, "the old Quaker Cheese Buyer."

They bought from farmers in the region and sold in New York City. And "according to the business ethics of the times," Nesbit went ahead to cheapen the cheese offered by deprecating its quality, hinting at a bad market and departing without buying. Later when Ferris arrived in a more optimistic mood, offering a slightly better price, the seller, unaware they were partners, and ignorant of the market price, snapped up the offer.

Similar sharp-trade tactics put too much green cheese on the market; so those honestly aged from a minimum of eight months up to two years fetched higher prices. They were called "old," such as Old Herkimer, Old Wisconsin Longhorn, and Old California Jack.

Although the established cheddar ages are three, fresh, medium-cured, and cured or aged, commercially they are divided into two and described as mild and sharp.

The most popular are named for their states: Colorado, Illinois, Kentucky, New York, Ohio, Vermont and Wisconsin. Two New York Staters are called and named separately, Coon and Herkimer County. Tillamook goes by its own name with no mention of Oregon. Pineapple, Monterey Jack and Sage are seldom listed as cheddars at all, although they are basically that.

Quoted from *The Complete Book of Cheese*, 1955, by Bob Brown

Collard Pizza

Fresh homemade pizza—yum! This recipe makes 8 servings.

Ingredients

1 teaspoon olive oil
1 cup chopped onions
1 tablespoon minced garlic
1 cup frozen finely chopped collards
½ teaspoon salt substitute
1 teaspoon basil
1 teaspoon thyme
1 teaspoon oregano
½ teaspoon crushed red pepper
½ teaspoon black pepper
1 tablespoon lemon juice
1 cup part-skim ricotta cheese
Pizza crust dough (13½ ounces) from the dairy case
3 ounces shredded part-skim mozzarella cheese
1 cup thinly sliced tomatoes
1 cup sliced mushrooms
1 ounce chopped ham

Preparation

- Sauté the onions, garlic, and collards, in the saucepan 2 minutes over high heat.
- Add the salt substitute, spices, pepper, and lemon juice.
- Add ½ cup water and cook until the collards are dry. Then allow the collards to cool.
- Preheat the oven to 450°F.
- Prepare the pizza dough according to instructions; partially bake it.
- When the collards have cooled, stir the ricotta cheese into the collard mixture.
- Spread the cheese-collard mixture over the partially cooked dough crust.
- Top the pizza with the remaining ingredients.
- Bake until the crust browns and the cheese melts. Cut into 8 slices.

Equipment/Utensils

Pizza pan • Medium saucepan • Pizza cutter or kitchen scissors

Quick and Tasty Pizza

Ingredients

1 can (8 rolls) reduced fat crescent rolls
2-3 teaspoons canola oil
1 cup thick spaghetti sauce
1 cup frozen chopped collards
1 teaspoon Perfect Collard Seasoning Blend™
1 cup (or more) sharp cheddar cheese
½-1 cup mixed cheeses

Preparation

- Remove the rolls. Keep them in 1 piece. Place the piece of dough on an oiled baking sheet. Pinch the dough together to mend any holes. Press the dough as flat as possible.
- Bake the dough at 450° 3 minutes.
- Remove the dough from the oven. Roll it flat and fold the edges.
- Sauté the collards in a tiny bit of oil. Add the seasoning blend and stir.
- Spread the spaghetti sauce over the partially cooked dough.
- Layer the collards over the sauce and spread the cheese over the collards.
- Bake at 475° until the cheese melts and the edges of the crust are lightly browned.
Serve hot.

Equipment/Utensils

Pizza pan • Medium saucepan • Pizza cutter or kitchen scissors

Vegetable Bacon Pizza

Ingredients

1 tablespoon olive oil
1 cup frozen chopped collards
1 cup fresh spinach, torn into small pieces
½ cup chopped onions
1 tablespoon minced garlic
½ cup grated zucchini
⅛ teaspoon baking soda
1 tablespoon Tone's® Spicy Spaghetti Seasoning
1½ cups (6 ounces) grated mozzarella cheese
2 ounces Hormel® Real Bacon Pieces
1½ cups Ragu® Chunky Pasta Sauce
Non-stick cooking spray
Pizza crust dough (13½ ounces) from the dairy case

Continued

Preparation

- Prepare the crust according to package instructions. Pre-bake on a sprayed cooking pan as directed in a very hot oven.
- In a skillet sauté the vegetables. Add the baking soda and spaghetti seasoning.
- Begin building the pizza by lightly covering the crust with sauce.
- Spread the vegetables over the sauce and add another layer of sauce.
- Next, distribute the cheese over the top and sprinkle the bacon on top.
- Return the pizza to the oven and cook until it bubbles, the cheese is melted, and the crust is golden brown.

Equipment/Utensils

Pizza pan • Medium skillet • Grater • Pizza cutter or kitchen scissors

Collard Tahini Pasta

Ingredients

12 ounces vegetable macaroni
3 slices bacon, diced into small pieces
1 cup chopped red onions
1 cup chopped frozen collards
1 jar (4 ounces) sliced pimiento
2 tablespoons minced garlic
½ cup chopped or sliced black olives
2 tablespoons honey
½ cup cooked turkey sausage or cooked lamb
1 tablespoon basil
1 teaspoon whole oregano
1 teaspoon rosemary leaves
1 teaspoon ground sage
1 teaspoon tarragon leaves
1 teaspoon crushed red pepper
1 teaspoon salt or salt substitute
15 ounces part-skim ricotta
1½ cups tahini
½ cup balsamic vinegar
1 cup milk

Preparation

- While the other ingredients are cooking, prepare the macaroni according to the package directions. Drain.
- In a large high-sided skillet, cook the bacon.
- Add the onions and collards. Cook until the onions are tender.
- Add the remaining ingredients and continue to cook over low heat until the ingredients are blended.
- Add the mix to the cooked macaroni and sprinkle Parmesan cheese on top.

Continued

Serving Suggestion

Collard Tahini Pasta is delicious with the following:

- Spread a layer of minced garlic—the kind that is canned in a jar—onto a baking sheet. Bake at 275° until the garlic is brown and crisp.
- Spread the garlic onto small serving plates, one for each person. Sprinkle some herbal seasonings over the garlic. Cover the garlic and seasonings with extra virgin olive oil.

Serve with sliced and heated crusty rolls to dip into the olive oil.

Collard Tahini Pasta Casserole I

Whisk some eggs and milk. Stir it into the leftover Collard Tahini Pasta. (The leftover pasta will need some moisture.) Spoon the mixture into a casserole dish that has been coated with cooking spray. Top the casserole with chopped onions, grated cheese, and croutons.

Bake at 350° until the mixture bubbles.

Collard Tahini Pasta Casserole II

Stir cream of mushroom soup into the leftover Collard Tahini Pasta. (The leftover pasta will need some moisture.) Spoon the mixture into a casserole dish that has been coated with cooking spray. Top the casserole with chopped onions, grated cheese, and croutons.

Bake at 350°.

Collard Stuffed Manicotti

Ingredients

2 cups frozen chopped collards
1 tablespoon balsamic vinegar
1 teaspoon sweetener
½ teaspoon salt substitute
⅛ teaspoon baking soda
¼ teaspoon ground red pepper
1 package (8 ounces) manicotti
Non-stick cooking spray
2 jars (28 ounces each) marinara sauce
2 eggs
1 container (15 ounces) part-skim ricotta cheese
4 cups (16 ounces) shredded mozzarella cheese
1 cup (4 ounces) grated Parmesan cheese
1 tablespoon dried parsley

Nutrition Facts	
Collard Stuffed Manicotti per serving makes 12 servings	
Amount per serving	
Calories	350
Calories from fat	141
	% Daily Value *
Total Fat 15.5g	24%
Saturated Fat 8g	40%
Cholesterol 74mg	25%
Sodium 972mg	40%
Total Carbohydrate 29.4g	10%
Dietary Fiber 3.1g	12%
Protein 22.8g	
Percent values are based on a 2,000-calorie per day diet. Your daily values may differ.	
Additional Information 40.3% of calories from Fat 33.6% from Carbohydrates 26.1% from Protein	

Preparation

- Steam the collards with the vinegar, sweetener, salt, soda, and red pepper 30 minutes.
- Cook the manicotti according to package directions. Rinse and drain.
- Spray a 9 X 13 X 2" glass pan.
- Pour 1 jar of marinara sauce into the pan.
- In large bowl, mix the eggs, ricotta cheese, 3 cups mozzarella cheese, ½ cup Parmesan cheese, and parsley. Stir in the collards. Add salt if desired.
- Fill the cooked manicotti with the cheese mixture and arranged the filled manicotti in the baking dish.
- Top with the remaining sauce and cheese.
- Bake covered at 350°F 45 minutes

Equipment/Utensils

Steamer • Large pot • 9 X 13 X 2" • glass pan • Large mixing bowl

Note

- The nutritional value included with this recipe is based on the use of commercially prepared marinara sauce.
- Check out Mike's Marinara Sauce in *Flavored with Love*. It's excellent.

Red Peppers Stuffed With Crabmeat and Steamed Collards

Ingredients

1 small bunch fresh tender collards
8 baby carrots
Lemon juice
Pinch baking soda
Cayenne pepper
1 teaspoon Splenda®
Salt substitute
2 teaspoons extra virgin olive oil
1 large tender red bell pepper
1 can (6 ounces) crabmeat
2 teaspoons balsamic vinaigrette
Seasoned salt
1 small red onion
Madras curry

Preparation

First, you will need to steam some collards and carrots. Select some tender fresh collards. Wash the leaves, remove the stems, and roll the leaves like cigars. Cut then in tiny ribbons. I prefer to use kitchen scissors; however, I have observed cooks who used a cutting board and knife.

Place the collards and about 8 baby carrots in a steamer. Put enough water to allow the vegetables to steam until they are tender. My steamer needs about 15 minutes of cooking time to accomplish the task. Sprinkle a generous amount of lemon juice and a tiny pinch of baking soda over the collards. If the manufacturer's instructions allow you, place some seasonings directly over the collards. I like a shake of cayenne pepper, some black pepper, a teaspoon of Splenda®, and some salt substitute. Or you may want to sprinkle some collard seasoning mix.

If you are not allowed to add stuff like that while the collards are steaming, toss them in after the collards cook. You will be amazed at the tenderness of steamed collards. After you remove them from the steamer, toss 2 teaspoons of extra virgin olive oil into the mix.

Next, cut a large tender red bell pepper lengthwise. Remove the seed and ribs. Microwave the pepper until it is al dente.

Meanwhile, rinse a 6-ounce can of crabmeat in the colander to remove excess salt. Add 2 teaspoons of balsamic vinaigrette, a shake of seasoned salt, a shake of basil, and any other seasoning you may want. I needed more cayenne! Mix the spices with the crabmeat, and lightly toss the collards into the mix. Set the carrots aside. Gently spoon the mixture into the pepper halves.

Microwave the stuffed pepper halves until they are warm throughout. While they are cooking, slice a red onion.

Make it look pretty. Place the pepper halves on small individual plates. Garnish them by placing carrots around them and raw onion rings on top. Sprinkle a shake of Madras curry over the top.

Stir-Fry with Pasta

Let each person design his own meal. Have a skillet ready for each person. Each skillet needs to be about the size of a plate.

- Have on hand:
    Precooked tri-colored noodles
    Marinara sauce
    Alfredo sauce
    Pesto
    Crushed red pepper
    Oregano
    Grated Parmesan or Roman cheese
    Canola or olive oil
    White wine
- Have containers of the following:
    Fresh chopped collards (tender ones)
    Finely chopped red onions
    Sliced mushrooms
    Fresh chopped mixed vegetables (yellow squash, zucchini, broccoli florets, cauliflower florets—whatever you have available)
    Sliced black olives
    Sliced bell peppers (green, red, yellow, or orange)
    Sliced jalapenos
    Peeled shrimp
    Crumbled cooked bacon
    Cooked meatballs
    Diced ham
- Pour a tablespoon of oil in each skillet and let each person select his own combination.
    (If the collards are not tender, begin with them. Add some lemon juice and baking soda to the collards as they cook.)
- Cook the vegetables first for a short time—no more than a couple of minutes.
- Add the other ingredients as you choose, and place them on each plate. Finish with the cheese.

Jerk Pork and Collards With Cornbread on Top

An easy one-pot meal—try it! Aaron, who lives next door, likes it.

Paul buys Jamaican jerk seasoning in bulk at Central Market in Dallas. It does not seem to be quite as hot as some others we have tasted. You may want to half the amount in this recipe until you are sure about the heat.

Jamaicans flavor their food with hot and spicy jerk seasoning, which goes well with pork, the perfect food to eat with collards.

Crock-Pot® Jerk Pork Chops
1. For each pound pork chops add the following to your Crock-Pot® or slow cooker:
   - 2 tablespoon jerk seasoning
   - 1 tablespoon lime juice
   - ¼ cup brown sugar
   - 1 teaspoon mustard
2. Cook slowly until the chops are tender. (Cook at least 3 pounds and save the leftovers for sandwiches.)
3. Remove the fat and bones; chop the meat. Save the sauce and plan to use some of it for flavoring.

The Meal
Ingredients
Non-stick cooking spray
2½ cups (8 ounces) frozen chopped collards
1 cup chopped onions
2 cups chicken broth (homemade low sodium)
⅛ teaspoon baking soda
1 can (14.5 ounces) diced tomatoes
1 cup chopped jerk pork
Some sauce from the bottom of the Crock-Pot®
1 small box cornmeal mix
1 egg
1 tablespoon cooking oil
½ cup milk

Preparation
- Heat the oven to 375 °.
- Spray the skillet.
- Sauté the onions and collards in the skillet.
- Add the broth and the tomatoes. Cover the skillet and allow the mixture to simmer a few minutes to tenderize the greens and reduce the liquid.
- Add some of the sauce to flavor the mixture, as you desire. Lower the heat.

Continued

- Stir the cornmeal mix, egg, oil, and milk together.
- Spoon the cornmeal batter over the collard mixture.
- Bake approximately 30 minutes or until the bread is firm and starting to brown. Do not overcook. Test it to make sure there is still some moisture in the bottom of the skillet. Add more liquid if needed.

Serve it hot.

Equipment/Utensils

Crock-Pot® • 10¼ cast iron skillet with lid • Bowl

Chicken-Vegetable-Biscuit Pie

Ingredients

2 tablespoons canola oil
1 large onion (about 1 cup), chopped
1 tablespoon minced garlic
1 cup cooked collards, drained
2 cups raw spinach leaves, torn
1 cup frozen mixed vegetables (Jalisco style potatoes, carrots, red peppers, and green peas)
1 can (13 ounces) chicken breast in water
1 can (12 ounces) fat-free evaporated milk (divided)
2 cans (10.5 ounces) cream of mushroom soup
As desired: rosemary, Creole seasoning, salt, black pepper, red pepper
2 cups Bisquick® biscuit mix
1 egg, beaten
Non-stick cooking spray

Preparation

- Heat the oven to 375°.
- Sauté the onion and garlic in the oil until the onions are translucent.
- Add the other vegetables and chicken. Lower the heat but continue to cook.
- Set aside ½ cup milk.
- Add the remaining milk, the soup, and enough water to cover everything. Stir.
- Add seasonings as desired. (Since the collards are precooked, it is unfeasible to give exact amounts of seasonings to use.)
- Stir the egg, ½ cup milk, and biscuit mix together.
- Drop the biscuit dough by spoonfuls over the vegetables.
- Bake about 30 minutes or until the top is brown.

Equipment/Utensils

10¼" cast iron skillet • Bowl

Collard Salads
Unsurpassed Greens

Netherland Salad

Vincent Fields, who is married to my niece Judi, gave me this recipe, an heirloom from his mother, who was the chef for the governor of Kentucky. It appears exactly the way she wrote it except for the addition of the item enclosed in brackets.

Netherland Salad has a beautiful presentation, exquisite enough to serve to ladies at a luncheon; yet it is hearty enough to satisfy a man-sized appetite.

Mrs. Fields has allowed the cook some liberty by not including the amount of eggs, asparagus, or olives to be used. I boiled 3 eggs and used 1 for the salad dressing. For 2 servings, I used an entire can (15 ounces) of extra long asparagus spears and ½ small can (4.25 ounces) of sliced olives. If I were serving this salad to a group of ladies, I would probably drizzle a small amount of dressing on top and provide more dressing for the ladies to add as needed.

From the Executive Mansion

Netherland Salad

This recipe is designed to make 2 servings.
¾ head lettuce, Julienne
½ cup baked ham, Julienne
1 tablespoon chopped dill pickle
½ cup tomatoes, Julienne
Sliced eggs
Sliced black olives
Asparagus spears
[2 fresh collard leaves]

Dressing
1 teaspoon chopped chives
1 finely chopped hard-boiled egg
3 tablespoons mayonnaise
2 tablespoons vinegar
3 tablespoons olive oil
1 teaspoon Worcestershire

Mix well. Pour on salad.

Notes
- To prepare each collard leaf:
  - Select broad, tender, crisp collards.
  - Pinch off the stems.
  - Wash each leaf and pat it dry.
  - Place the leaf on a paper towel.
  - Microwave 20-25 seconds.

- A collard leaf (which is delightfully edible) underneath a salad creates a palate where you can construct the pretty salad with a contrast of color and texture. The edges of the leaf provide an intriguing dark blue green border on the plate.

Equipment/Utensils
Knife • Cutting board • Whisk • Small bowl

Vincent Fields
(We added the collard leaves.)

Delicious and Tender Baby Collard Leaves

For all you collard greens lovers out there who grow your own collards, here is a tip.

Collard farmers cut off the whole plant when they harvest the crop. Not so when you grow your own.

Y'all know, when you grow your own collards, you pick your collard leaves starting at the bottom and cut the leaves as they mature. This extends the growing season.

However, at some point the plants will start to "bolt," that is to make a flowering head. When that happens, break off the tops with the budding flowers. (You can use these in a tasty salad.) The smaller leaves will grow larger but only about half the size of a mature leaf or less. Harvest them for very tender and deliciously tasty greens to add to salads.

I call them "baby collards."

You can also use them for sandwiches in place of lettuce. Their slightly peppery taste adds a spicy sensation that other mixes of lettuce or sprouts get only with something like radish leaves or sprouts. Baby collard leaves are better because they have a slightly bitter addition, and they are more nutritious.

Baby collard greens are delightfully tender and are not at all "stemmy." They don't need any work other than rinsing before you add them to your sandwiches or salads. Don't pass up the opportunity to enjoy this delicious and healthy addition to your meals.

Paul

Collard Curls

Note from Lynn Salter: Here is a great way to include raw greens into your diet. Raw, uncooked foods are considered LIVE with the enzymes and nutrients intact, where as when we cook our food we kill the enzymes and therefore considered DEAD food. Our bodies do not benefit from the nutrients that were in the food. We still enjoy the taste, but the enzymes fuel our bodies and help us maintain optimum health.

Ingredients

1 bunch collard greens
1 bunch red or green chard
Dressing:
¼ cup sweet onion, diced
2 garlic cloves, diced
2 tablespoons unpasteurized apple cider vinegar
3 tablespoons cold pressed extra virgin olive oil
1 tablespoon raw, unfiltered honey
1 tablespoon flaxseed, freshly ground (I use a coffee mill for this purpose only!)
½ teaspoon dry mustard
⅛ teaspoon stevia (see note below)
½ teaspoon Celtic sea salt

Preparation

- Wash the greens, dry and cut out the rib going almost all the way down the middle of each leaf.
- Lay the greens on top of each other and then fold in half. Roll the entire bunch into a tight roll. (Depending on the number of leaves you'll most likely need to do this several times to use all the greens.) Starting at one end of the roll, cut into very thin slices. Put the slices into a large bowl and set aside.
- In a small bowl, mix the dressing ingredients and blend well.
- Pour the dressing over the greens and toss until they are well coated. Cover and let sit overnight in the refrigerator for maximum flavor.

Serving suggestion: Add sliced almonds and red bell pepper, sliced thin. Toss. Serves 3-4. Keeps for 2-3 days in the refrigerator.

For more information on how to add whole foods into your diet and improve your health visit my website, http://www.Whole-Food-and-Healing.com, or contact me at info@whole-food-and-healing.com and request my newsletter.

To your health, Lynn Salter

Stevia

Stevia, native to Paraguay, is pronounced "steh-via." It is an herb and has been used as a sweetener and flavor enhancer for centuries. It is extremely sweet, in fact up to 300 times sweeter than sugar, with its own unique flavor. The great thing about Stevia is it contains no calories, no carbohydrates, and no artificial chemicals. It comes in single serving packets and concentrated powder form, which I used in this recipe.

Crawfish Tortellini Salad

Ingredients

½ cup thinly sliced green onions with tops
1 small jar artichoke hearts, drained
1 cup small fresh mushrooms
1 cup large pitted ripe olives
1 cup fresh red bell pepper, sliced
1 cup thinly sliced carrots
12 ounces frozen crawfish tails
1 cup olive oil
1 teaspoon salt-free Creole seasoning
½ cup red wine vinegar
¼ cup lemon juice
1 tablespoon spicy mustard
1 teaspoon Splenda®
¼ teaspoon crushed red pepper
½ teaspoon freshly ground black pepper
Salt substitute to taste
1 tablespoon minced garlic
1 teaspoon cumin
1 tablespoon fresh parsley, chopped
1 tablespoon fresh basil, chopped
1 cup seedless golden raisins
1 package (14 ounces) cheese tortellini
4 ounces (¼ cup) feta cheese
4 cups tender baby collard leaves, chopped
4 cups Romaine lettuce, torn into small pieces

Preparation

- Place the first 6 ingredients in a big bowl.
- Place ¾ cup olive oil in the blender. Add the vinegar, lemon juice, mustard and all the remaining powdered seasonings. Blend until it is well mixed. Stir in the parsley and basil.
- Pour the blended dressing over the ingredients in the bowl and marinate them covered at least 2 hours in the refrigerator.
- Sauté the crawfish in ¼ cup olive oil and Cajun seasoning about 5-7 minutes. Even though there will be other seasoning mixed with the tortellini, each individual crawfish needs its own spiciness. You don't want those crawfish to get lonesome. After you sauté them long enough to catch the seasoning, set them aside to cool.
- Cook the tortellini according to the package directions. Cook it al dente. Drain it in the colander and allow it to cool.
- Toss the crawfish, tortellini, and raisins with the vegetable mixture.
- When you serve the salad, place it over the greens. Garnish it with feta cheese.

Cooking Tips

Instead of crawfish, substitute 1 of the following:

> 3 cups white chicken meat, cooked and chopped
> 1 pound jumbo shrimp, peeled and deveined

If the feta cheese is a block, cube it.

Quick, Easy, and Tasty Pasta Salad

Sauté a small sliced onion, some garlic, and a cup of collards in virgin olive oil until they are tender. You may need to sprinkle some baking soda on the collards and stir that in. Add about two teaspoons of something sweet.

Look around in the cabinet for some pasta, and cook it according to the package directions. Don't overcook it; leave it al dente. Rinse it and return it to the pan.

Meanwhile, wash and cut some romaine and tear some other lettuce to go with it. Set that aside.

To the collards, add any of these you like: sliced baby carrots, sliced olives, artichoke hearts with the liquid included, toasted nuts or seeds, pimientos, thinly sliced celery, peppers of choice, grated cheese of choice, sliced smoked turkey or chicken, pepperoni, diced ham, drained English peas, canned and drained garbanzo beans.

Stir in some dry Italian seasonings. Add some Italian salad dressing or light mayonnaise. Maybe you would prefer to add some more olive oil and vinegar or lemon juice. Add salt or salt substitute, black pepper, and red pepper.

Toss all that together and let it chill. Serve it over the lettuce. Top it with bacon bits or croutons. You may want to add some nuts or seeds on top.

Cutting Collards

When you need really fine collards, use kitchen scissors or a sharp knife with a cutting board to remove the stems. Roll 3-4 leaves into a cigar shape. Cut horizontally down the middle. Then snip or slice as finely as possible into shrivels.

About Flowerbeds

Collards are pretty in flowerbeds. In the fall we tuck collard plants between chrysanthemums to add greenery. When cold weather comes and the mums die down, we trim them back to make more room for the collards.

Curried Chicken and Collard Salad

Ingredients

2 pounds boneless, skinless chicken breasts
Salt substitute to taste
Black pepper to taste
Red pepper to taste
Dash rosemary
4 tablespoons olive oil
½ cup water
3 tablespoons lemon juice
½ cup sliced green onions (including tops)
½ cup finely chopped baby collards or very tender collards
1 cup finely sliced celery
½ cup seedless white grapes, halved
2 cups low-fat mayonnaise
½ cup Riesling wine
½ cup Major Grey's chutney
¼ cup Madras curry powder
Romaine lettuce
1 cup roasted salted cashews

Preparation

- Sprinkle salt substitute, black pepper, red pepper, and rosemary over the chicken breasts.
- Sauté the chicken breasts in 3 tablespoons olive oil about 3 minutes per side.
- Add the water and lemon juice. Lower the heat, cover the pot, and simmer until the chicken is done—about 30 minutes.
- When the chicken cools, chop it into large cubes.
- Sauté the green onions and collards about 30 seconds, just long enough to warm them.
- Blend the mayonnaise, wine, chutney, and curry powder until smooth to make the salad dressing.
- Combine the chicken, onions, collards, celery, and grapes.
- Add enough salad dressing to moisten the salad.
- Refrigerate the salad 4 hours.

Serving the Salad

- Spread the cashews over the servings.
- Serve the salad over romaine leaves
- Provide the extra salad dressing to be added as needed.
- Include some tasty crackers, cornbread muffins, or interesting rolls.

North Louisiana Bean Salad

Bean salad is music to the mouth. This salad is one to prepare ahead of time and store in the refrigerator. Serve it in a bowl by itself or on lettuce leaves.

It complements something special, such as salmon roll and crackers or ham sandwiches, to make a stay-at-home supper a special occasion to share with the ones you love or to enjoy during an enthralling movie.

Ingredients

1 can (14½ ounces) cut green beans
1 can (15½ ounces) garbanzos (chick peas)
1 can (15¼ ounces) black beans
1 can (15½ ounces) light red kidney beans
1 jar (7 ounces) diced pimientos
½ cup finely chopped fresh collards
1 medium (about 1 cup) thinly sliced onion
1 cup olive oil
½ cup balsamic vinegar
3 tablespoons Splenda®
1 tablespoon garlic powder
1 teaspoon salt substitute
Dash ground red pepper
Freshly ground black pepper to taste

Preparation

- Drain the beans and pimientos (the first five ingredients) in a colander.
- Steam the collards until they are tender.
- Lay the onion slices on top of the collards and steam 30 seconds.
- Remove the collards and onion slices from the steamer. Rechop the collards with scissors. Toss the ingredients lightly and transfer them to a storage container.
- Mix the remaining ingredients in a blender to make a delectable and pour them over the salad.
- Chill in the refrigerator 1 hour.

Equipment/Utensils

Colander • Saucepan with lid and steamer rack • Knife • Scissors • Sealed 2-quart container • Blender

Coleslaw

The shreds of collards add beautiful dark green color to give the slaw a rich appearance. The poppy seeds add interesting texture.

Ingredients

16 ounces shredded green cabbage and carrots

16 ounces (1 pint) Kraft® Creamy Poppyseed Dressing

½ cup finely shredded tender fresh collards

Preparation

- Mix the ingredients and chill.

Nutrition Facts	
Coleslaw, per serving makes 8 servings	
Amount per serving	
Calories	92
Calories from fat	18
% Daily Value *	
Total Fat 2g	3%
Saturated Fat 3.5g	18%
Cholesterol 0 mg	0%
Sodium 460 mg	19%
Total Carbohydrate 17.6g	6%
Dietary Fiber 1.4g	6%
Protein 0.8g	

Percent values are based on a 2,000-calorie per day diet. Your daily values may differ.

Additional Information
19.7% of calories from Fat
76.9% from Carbohydrates
3.5% from Protein

Wilted Collard Salad

Here's another delightful salad. This recipe makes 2 servings.

Ingredients

4 slices bacon
2 cups fresh tender collards, sliced in 2″ strips
½ teaspoon baking soda (for washing collards)
2 tablespoons sliced black olives
10 grape tomatoes
4 teaspoons Parmesan cheese
2 shakes red wine vinegar

Preparation

- Fry the bacon until it is crisp. Drain and crumble it.
- Wash the collards in plenty of water and the baking soda. Rinse and pat dry.
- Wilt the collards in the bacon drippings. Pat the grease from the collards.
- Place the collards in two salad bowls. Douse them with vinegar and arrange the remaining ingredients on the salad.
- Serve immediately.

Nutrition Facts	
Wilted Collard Salad, per serving Makes 2 servings	
Amount per serving	
Calories	374
Calories from fat	316
	% Daily Value *
Total Fat 35.2g	54%
Saturated Fat 13g	65%
Cholesterol 40 mg	13%
Sodium 579 mg	24%
Total Carbohydrate 6.3g	2%
Dietary Fiber 2.4g	10%
Protein 8.2g	
Percent values are based on a 2,000-calorie per day diet. Your daily values may differ.	
Additional Information 84.5% of calories from Fat 6.7% from Carbohydrates 8.8% from Protein	

Equipment/Utensils

Skillet

Bacon Drippings

Paraphrased from an anonymous forward circulating on the Internet:

If you are moving from the North to the South, start saving all your bacon grease. We will tell you what to do with it.

Making salad is one thing to do with it. Not too many years ago, folks in the rural South defined salad as wilted greens—any kind of greens. They grew tender unheaded lettuce in the garden, tender young collards, turnip greens, mustard greens, and immature cabbage. All these greens they called salad greens.

They tossed the greens in hot bacon drippings and served them with cornbread. Usually they included fresh green onions in the meal.

Falling from the Sky Salad

Paul designed the tasty salad depicted in the following recipe. He said the idea came to him out of the blue. Ideas came to him like falling rain. "I added ham," he stated, "because a pig ran between my legs. I never could catch a pig in a corner because I was bowlegged from riding Smoky all those years bareback. Too many free associations! I'm going to start charging for some of them."

Salad, Ingredients

2 fresh collard leaves
3 cups chopped lettuce
1 cup finely chopped collards (frozen), sautéed with a bit of olive oil, a pinch (⅛ teaspoon) of baking soda, and 1 teaspoon sweetener
1 cup Cajunized* ham (ham with Cajun seasoning added)
2 tablespoons sweet pickle relish
2 tablespoons chopped green onions, including tops
½ cup chopped tomatoes
½ cup grated carrots
½ cup grated sharp cheddar cheese

Salad, Preparation
Layer the salads on plates in the order listed. 2 servings

Dressing, Ingredients
1 finely chopped hard-boiled egg
4 tablespoons light mayonnaise
3 tablespoons vinegar
3 tablespoons olive oil
2 tablespoons lemon juice
1 teaspoon Pickapeppa® sauce
1 teaspoon sweetener

Dressing, Preparation

Mix well. Serve the dressing on the side.

Equipment/Utensils
Knife • Cutting board • Whisk • Small bowl

Paul

Eat salad slowly. Savor the flavors. Savor life.

Asian Cabbage, Collard, And Fruit Salad

Ingredients

2 cups chopped green onions (including tops)
2 cups finely chopped tender baby collards
1 cup thinly sliced celery
16 ounces shredded green cabbage and carrots (packaged slaw mix)
1 cup slivered almonds
1 cup unsalted sunflower seeds
2 packages (3 ounces each) chicken flavored ramen noodles
1 cup golden raisins
1 cup Mandarin oranges, drained
½ cup Splenda®
½ cup rice vinegar
¾ cup sesame oil
¼ cup pineapple juice
2 tablespoons lemon juice
1 teaspoon ground ginger
½ teaspoon ground white pepper
½ cup chow mien noodles

Preparation

- Be sure to chop the green onions, collards, and celery very finely.
- In a large bowl combine the onions, collards, celery, slaw mix, almonds, and seed.
- Crumble the ramen noodles and stir them into the mix. Add the fruit.
- Place the seasoning packets from the noodles in the blender with the remaining ingredients except the chow mien noodles. Blend until combined.
- Stir the dressing into the salad mix.
- Transfer the salad into the salad bowl.
- Cover and refrigerate at least 2 hours before serving.

Equipment/Utensils

Cutting board • Scissors • Knife • Large missing bowl • Blender • Tall, clear 3-quart salad bowl • Plastic wrap

About Red, Black and White, Pepper

White pepper is black pepper with the outer black skins removed. It is used in light-colored food with delicate tastes.

- Red is immediate.
- Black is delayed.
- White is persistent.

Layered Texianne Salad I

8 to 10 servings

Dressing

Ingredients

⅓ cup chopped fresh cilantro
½ cup lime juice
½ cup. olive oil
½ cup. sour cream
1 tablespoon honey.
½ teaspoon salt substitute
½ teaspoon freshly ground black pepper
¼ teaspoon crushed red pepper
1 teaspoon cumin

Preparation

- Blend the ingredients until they are smooth.
- Scrape the sides of the blender with a rubber spatula.

Salad

Ingredients

8 ounces romaine lettuce, shredded
1 quart tender fresh collard leaves, wilted and shredded
1 cup fresh tomatoes, chopped
1 (15-ounce) can black beans, rinsed and drained
1 small red onion, chopped
1 cup light sour cream
8-ounces grated Colby and Monterey Jack-cheese blend
2 cups frozen whole kernel corn
1 (6-ounce) can sliced ripe olives, drained
2 cups crushed tortilla chips

Preparation

- Combine the greens.
- Layer the ingredients a 3-quart tall glass bowl.
- Pour the salad dressing over the salad immediately before serving.

Equipment/Utensils

Blender • Rubber spatula • 3-quart tall glass bowl

Layered Texianne Salad II

Ingredients

8 slices bacon, pan fried, drained, and crumbled
2 cups finely chopped fresh tender collards
½ cup chopped bell pepper
½ cup grated carrots
½ cup grated onions
¼ cup sweet pickle relish
1 cup frozen whole kernel corn,
½ teaspoon seasoned salt
2 cups shredded Romaine
2 cups frozen English peas
2 cups light mayonnaise
1 cup light brown sugar
1 can (4 ounces) diced green chilies
½ teaspoon cumin
½ cup sliced ripe olives
1 cup (4 ounces) grated Colby/Jack cheese blend
¼ cup salsa

Preparation

- Fry the bacon, drain it, and pat the excessive grease with paper towels. Crumble it.
- Drop the cup of chopped collards into a small amount of the hot bacon drippings and remove them immediately.
- Layer all the ingredients in the salad bowl in the order listed except the bacon.
- Cover the salad with clear plastic wrap and chill the salad 4 hours
- Add the bacon just before serving.

Equipment/Utensils

Skillet • Cutting board • Scissors • Knife • Tall, clear 3-quart salad bowl • Plastic wrap

Serving Suggestion

Serve with tortilla chips.

Mixed Greens Caesar Salad

Dressing

Ingredients

2 soft boiled eggs (gently boiled 2 minutes and transferred immediately from heat to cold water),
½ cup fresh lemon juice
½ cup canola or extra virgin olive oil
1 bulb garlic, sliced (less if you wish)
Salt or salt substitute
Freshly ground black pepper
Dash Worcestershire sauce

Preparation

- Blend the ingredients just enough to mix the eggs and chop the garlic.
- Refrigerate 1 hour or longer.

Salad

Ingredients

Approximately 1½ cups each raw:
    Tender finely chopped collards
    Baby spinach leaves
    Romaine lettuce, torn into bite-sized pieces
    Sliced mushrooms
One of the following (individual serving sizes):
    Grilled chicken breast
    Anchovy filets
    Grilled salmon
    Grilled shrimp
    Sautéed crawfish tails
As much as you like:
    Sliced avocados
    Tomato wedges
    Hormel® bacon bits or fried bacon, drained and crumbled
    Parmesan cheese
    Seasoned croutons

Preparation

- Toss the vegetables.
- Stack an ingredient from the second group on top of the greens.
- Garnish with the ingredients in the third group.
- Before serving add the salad dressing or serve it in small separate bowls beside the salad.

The Story of Caesar Salad

Caesar Caradini was an Italian restaurateur and chef who lived in San Diego. His restaurant was located in Tijuana, Mexico, so that he could sell alcohol during the Prohibition era.

In 1924 Caesar or one of his associates created Caesar salad. There are many stories about the salad. Julia Child ate it when she was young and later contacted Caesar's daughter, who told her what it contained. One story is that he created it for Julia.

Another story is that it was created for a group of Hollywood stars partying at Tijuana. Even though this story is plausible, it is probably not accurate.

The most common story is that he ran out of supplies one Fourth of July and invented something with the food he had on hand. This story is considered to be the correct one. The legend is that he made a dramatic show of tossing the salad beside the table.

Hotel César is located in downtown Tijuana, where it is still possible to eat a Caesar salad made by the original recipe.

Try not to gossip.

Fresh Salad

Select some tender collard greens and baby spinach greens. Add some red onion ring slices or maybe some sliced mushrooms.

Serve it with Favorite Dipping Sauce.

Favorite Dipping Sauce

Use our Favorite Dipping Sauce with salad, meat or seafood. Use it for dipping chips or raw vegetables.

Ingredients

1 cup light mayonnaise
½ cup ketchup
¼ cup canola oil
1 tablespoon minced garlic
½ cup chopped onion
1 hardboiled egg, chopped
¼ cup lemon juice
¼ cup water
2 tablespoons brown mustard
2 tablespoons brown sugar
2 teaspoons Worcestershire sauce
¼ teaspoon ground red pepper
¼ teaspoon black pepper
Dash of salt substitute
1-2 teaspoons horseradish (optional)

Preparation
Blend the ingredients until the sauce is smooth. Store it in the refrigerator overnight.

Equipment/Utensils
Sharp knife • Cutting board • Blender

Avoid pride.

Soups and Gumbos
Partly Creole and Other Lip-Smacking Sources

Hoppin' John Collard Soup

Hoppin' John is a traditional New Year's Day dish of black-eyed peas and rice, reputed to bring good luck and fortune. The rice is said to bring fertility into the home and in the field. Black-eyed peas represent coins. When eaten alongside cooked collards, which represent folding money, you are on the right track to paving the way for a good year!

This recipe combines all of the important New Year's Day elements into a flavorful and easy soup. For variety, you may substitute Cut `n Clean Greens® Kale or Cut `n Clean Greens® Mustard for the collards if you like, or use a bag of Cut `n Clean Greens® Country Mix blend, which combines collards, mustard and turnip greens in one bag.

Source: Cut `n Clean Greens® (http://www.cutncleangreens.com)

Ingredients

4 tablespoons olive or canola oil
2 onions, chopped
2 carrots, cut into thin coins
2 ribs celery, chopped
8 ounces cooked ham, cut into ¼-inch dice
¼ teaspoon red pepper flakes
¼ teaspoon dried thyme leaves
2 bay leaves
2 garlic cloves, minced
1 (1-pound) bag Cut `n Clean Greens® Collard Greens
2 (15- or 16-ounce) cans low-salt, fat-free chicken broth (about 4 cups broth)
4½ cups water
½ teaspoon sugar
2 (15- or 16-ounce) cans black-eyed peas
2 teaspoons apple cider vinegar (or use hot pepper vinegar)
2-3 cups cooked rice (optional)

Preparation

Heat oil in a stockpot and over medium heat sauté onion, carrots, celery, ham, pepper flakes, thyme leaves and bay leaves for about 7-8 minutes, stirring occasionally. Add garlic and sauté for another minute.

While onion mixture is cooking, chop collard greens so they are a bit finer. To do this, grab a small handful and place on a cutting board. Using a chef's knife, chop them by first making vertical cuts through the pile, and then horizontal cuts through the pile. Continue chopping handfuls of collards in this manner until they are all chopped smaller. (This step may be omitted, but it yields a more refined looking soup.)

Add collards, chicken broth, water and sugar to the pot and return to a boil. Stir collards down into the boiling liquid, cover, reduce heat to low and boil gently for 30 minutes.

Drain peas and place one can of peas in a wide, flat bowl or on a large plate. Mash with a fork, or with a potato masher. Add both mashed and whole peas to the pot, and boil gently, covered, for another 20 minutes.

Stir in vinegar and season with freshly ground pepper if needed. (Be careful of adding additional salt because the ham, broth and peas will have been seasoned with salt already.)

To serve, put a small scoop of cooked rice in the bottom of each soup bowl, and ladle soup over it.

Pass additional hot pepper vinegar or hot pepper sauce at the table, for those who like additional zing.

Serves 4-6.

Dorothy Reinhold

Reprinted with permission from Cut `n Clean Greens® (http://www.cutncleangreens.com)

Terry's Collard Soup

Terry is recognized as an outstanding cook in north Louisiana.

Ingredients

2 cups cooked kidney or red beans
1 pound beef shank or beef tips
8 ounces Italian sausage
⅔ cup split peas
2½ teaspoons salt
6 cups or 2 bunches of fresh collards (washed, rinsed, and chopped fine)
2 cups peeled and chopped red-skinned, white potatoes (2 potatoes)
2 cups coarsely chopped cabbage

Preparation

- Brown beef and sausage in a skillet.
- Stir the meat into the drained beans. Add peas and salt.
- Cover the mix with water.
- Reduce to simmer.
- Cook the mixture 2 hours.
- Discard bones if any.
- Add collards, potatoes, and cabbage.
- Cook 30 minutes.

Continued

Equipment/Utensils

Skillet • Cutting board • Scissors • Knife

Terry Chrisman

Notes

- The beef tips are easier because you don't have to remove the bones.
- The split peas are optional. The soup is just as good without them. Terry's friend uses sauerkraut instead of cabbage and omits the salt.

Serving Suggestions

- You can serve the soup over rice, if you wish, or eat it from a bowl without the rice.
- Cornbread is essential.

Terry said:

My husband is making me a Cajun cook shack out of 160-year-old barn wood. He's building it out of my grandfather's old barn tin and wood. A cook shack has two sides closed and two sides open. It is like a lean-to, and it will house our crawfish boiler pot, a barbecue pit, and a fish fryer.

I'm planning to fix a bottle tree in my yard.

The Ordeal of Getting Paul to Share His Chili Recipe

Paul is the one who cooks chili. Since I needed a chili for several purposes, I needed him to give me his to share with you. I spent an inordinate amount of time and energy acquiring this recipe. I don't know why he was retaining it for himself.

Obtaining a *Complete* Chili Recipe

(If you would like nutritional information about the chili, please write us.)

Paul had been telling me for months about his remarkable chili. (With the first cold snap, I require chili. I can cook chili, but don't tell anybody.) He makes it Texas style, which for him—among other things—is conceptually without beans.

In Mississippi we don't miss an opportunity to eat beans. I told him that if he made it as spicy as I predicted he would—he has one of the spiciest mouths I've ever known, while I'm only a moderate spicemouth™—I would need to cook beans.

"BEANS?" he shouted incredulously. "You won't need beans, I promise."

At midnight at an undisclosed place where he could enjoy private alchemy, he combined the ingredients for his lip-smacking, palate-prickling, water-guzzling, gullet-frying, rib-wrenching, tummy-twisting, inimitable Texas chili. The following day, I found the chili. It was tasty, but I cooked beans.

Before making the chili, he told me that in the past he usually had added carrots, sometimes had added okra, and would consider adding collards. He had also been

Continued

sticking his nose inside the Jamaican Jerk bag when he was contemplating the chili. (I thought he would never stop sneezing!) Maybe during the wee hours of the morning, he decided to omit some ingredients; or maybe he had been putting me on.

Since I needed a chili recipe for chili dip, I had insisted he write down his recipe. For that reason, I was aware of some of the omitted ingredients. When he reappeared, he said, "I deliberately left the okra out because I want the flavors to meld. I didn't want it to be too spicy.

Although I was not aware of the spicy quality of okra, I did not question that remark.

He continued, "I usually add barbecue sauce, but I just haven't added it yet."

"Is this your usual recipe?" I asked.

"Yes."

By then I was soaking red beans. "The only beans I have in the house are red ones," I explained. "Usually I use pintos."

Paul said, "Maybe you should cook some rice."

"No, I don't think I'll need it." You see, I was not going to give him a chance to cool his mouth with rice after he had disparaged my beans.

Trying to appease me, he offered, "You can stir the beans into the chili if you want to."

"No!" I insisted. "Then it wouldn't be Texas chili."

Paul, being concerned about what people would think of his recipe, said, "We don't have to tell people we added the beans."

Finally, Paul listed all the ingredients, but he failed to see the purpose of writing the directions. I was begging Paul to tell me exactly how he makes chili.

"Everybody knows how to make chili," he said.

"No, they don't. You have to tell us what to do."

He said, "Throw everything in there, double some of them up, and call it chili."

I hope you enjoy Paul's magnificent chili, which he prepares beginning at midnight. The ingredients are hitherto undescribed and cannot be equivolated.

Months passed. In a nonchalant manner, I again demanded the instructions for his mysterious method of cooking chili. Again he equivocated by saying. "Use the dump technique. Put it on the fire. Dump it all in."

Making Use of All That Chili

- When you cook a big pot of chili, it may not be possible to use it all in sauce for the Vegetable Monkey Bread recipe following the chili. Therefore you may need to eat some of it plain.
- Or you could stir into beans or make chili bread. (See the cornbread section.)
- I like it on hotdogs. In order to get plenty of the chili, I make my hotdog open-faced and eat it with a fork.
- Use some to make Cousin Mary's **Cream Taco au Paul**.
  - ○ Brown and drain 1 pound lean ground beef.
  - ○ Heat 2 cups Paul's chili in a saucepan with the meat.
  - ○ Add
    2 cans original Ranch Style® beans
    1 can Ro*Tel® tomatoes
    1 can diced tomatoes
    1 cup cream,
    1 pound Velveeta®
  - ○ Heat all that together until it cooks down and thickens.
  - ○ Serve it in soup bowls that are lined with Fritos®. On top place some grated cheddar or Colby, sour cream, guacamole, and a few jalapeños.

  Talking about good! This is comfort food ideal for a cold, rainy day. There are no collards in it, but we feel obligated to help you with your leftovers.
- Layer some rice in plates, followed by a layer of cooked collards. Top it off with chili and a small amount of cheese.

About Vegetable Monkey Bread

- On the page after the chili recipe you will finally find the reason for including this chili recipe, in addition to the impressive quality of the dish: Serve it with Vegetable Monkey Bread.
- Try serving the bread with a chili-cheese dip. Heat equal parts of volume of chili and Velveeta® together.
- Vegetable Monkey Bread is good with **Chili Con Queso** made by sautéing an onion, heating 2 cups of cubed Velveeta® with a can of Ro*Tel® tomatoes and green chilies. Put some cumin and a shake of cayenne in that.
- Or you may want to serve the Monkey Bread with Cheez Whiz®. Simply remove the lid and warm the sauce in the microwave.

Paul's Midnight Chili

Ingredients

2 pounds ground turkey, or other warm-blooded beast of choice, though rattlesnake
   does very well, too
1 can (29 ounces) tomato puree
1 can (29 ounces) Ro*Tel® tomatoes and green chilies—mild
1 cup fresh collards, chopped
2 medium onions, chopped
¾ cup chili powder
½ cup balsamic vinegar
½ cup lemon juice
½ cup minced garlic
½ cup Splenda®
¼ cup olive oil
¼ cup dark brown sugar
¼ cup curry powder
¼ cup oregano
⅓ cup mustard, prepared
⅛ cup basil
⅛ cup ground cinnamon

Preparation

Phew! Here are the secret directions for cooking the chili:

- Far up Crock-Pot®.
- Dump in all ingredients except Ro*Tel® tomatoes and green chilies—mild.
- Cook it till it looks like chili.
- Dump in Ro*Tel® tomatoes and green chilies—mild, juice and all.
- Cook it 30 more minutes.
- Serve it straight.
- For the non-spicemouths™ and people from "New York City" in your group, you
  can add it to beans or rice.
- Stop any flowing blood and apply Band-Aids® as needed.

Equipment/Utensils

Skillet • Crock-Pot® • Sharp knife • Cutting board • Measuring utensils • Band-Aids®

                                                                            Paul

A Word about Chili

I have known some women who could make good chili, but making great chili is a
man's thing. (Girls, it's smart to play along with this idea, which Paul calls *le setup.)*

                                                                        Mary Lou

Vegetable Monkey Bread

Ingredients

1 stick (¼ pound) unsalted butter
6 ounces lean bacon, cooked and crumbled
1 cup frozen finely chopped collards
Non-stick cooking spray
12 ounces frozen seasoning blend
⅛ teaspoon baking soda
1 teaspoon lemon juice
1 tablespoon apricot preserves
1 jar (4 ounces) chopped pimentos, drained
1 cup (4 ounces) grated Colby cheese
4 cans biscuits (8 per can) cut in halves

Nutrition Facts	
Vegetable Monkey Bread, per serving Makes 32 servings	
Amount per serving	
Calories	154
Calories from fat	78
	% Daily Value *
Total Fat 8.6g	13%
Saturated Fat 3.4g	17%
Cholesterol 16 mg	5%
Sodium 306 mg	13%
Total Carbohydrate 14.3g	5%
Dietary Fiber 2.6g	10%
Protein 4.6g	
Percent values are based on a 2,000-calorie per day diet. Your daily values may differ.	
Additional Information 50.8% of calories from Fat 37.2% from Carbohydrates 12% from Protein	

Preparation

- Preheat oven to 350º.
- Melt the butter. Pour enough butter into the bundt pan to grease it thoroughly.
- Fry the bacon until it is very crisp. Crumble enough lean bacon to fill a ½ cup-measuring cup.
- Sauté the collards and seasoning blend in a non-stick cooking spray. Add the baking soda, juice, preserves, and pimentos.
- Cook until the liquid is absorbed. Set aside to cool.
- While the mixture cools, place a layer of biscuits in the pan.
- Now that the mixture is cool, stir the bacon and cheese into it.
- Layer ⅓ of the vegetable-bacon-cheese mixture onto the biscuits. Drizzle the butter over the layers.
- Continue to repeat the layer and finish with a layer of biscuits on top.
- Bake 30 to 40 minutes. The biscuits should be golden brown, and a knife inserted should be slightly moist when removed.
- After the bread cools slightly, loosen it around the edges and invert it onto a plate.

Equipment/Utensils

Bundt pan • Skillet • Sauce pan • Knife • Cutting board • Grater

Chicken Vegetable Stock

A useful staple . . .

Ingredients

Some chicken, such as 2 boneless
  chicken breasts
An assortment of vegetables, perhaps:

- Carrots
- Collard stems
- Green bell peppers
- Celery tops
- Garlic
- Cabbage

Some herbs and seasonings:

- Lemon juice
- Thyme
- Rosemary
- Parsley
- Poultry seasoning

(Avoid salt and pepper because you will
add those when you use the stock in a
dish.)

Nutrition Facts	
Chicken Vegetable Stock, per serving Makes about 30 servings	
Amount per serving	
Calories	**13**
Calories from fat	9
	% Daily Value *
Total Fat 1g	**2%**
Saturated Fat 0g	0%
Cholesterol 0 mg	0%
Sodium 40 mg	**2%**
Total Carbohydrate 0g	0%
Dietary Fiber 0g	0%
Protein 1g	
Percent values are based on a 2,000-calorie per day diet. Your daily values may differ.	
Additional Information 69.2% of calories from Fat 0% from Carbohydrates 30.8% from Protein	

Preparation

- Place the ingredients into a soup pot.
- Fill the pot to within 2" of the top.
- Bring to boil and then lower heat.
  Simmer 1½ hours; then cool.
- Strain the mix through a colander. Save the meat to be used in other dishes.

Equipment/Utensils

Knife • Cutting Board • 2 big cooking pots • Colander

About Stock

Many recipes, especially soup, require broth or stock. Although most of the available
canned or packaged broths, as well as bouillon mixes, add sensational flavor to food, they
contain too much sodium to use in substantial amounts on a regular basis. The solution is
to make broth and keep a supply on hand.

Making stock is uncomplicated. Most recipes recommend specific amounts of items.
Popular stocks are made with chicken, which blends well with a variety of foods. The
secret is not to use much of any one ingredient, because you don't want one ingredient to
dominate the taste.

If you have included meat with noticeable fat content instead of chicken breasts, chill the stock and remove the congealed fat. Because of the vagueness of the amounts in the recipe, the nutritional information is an estimate based on reviews of typical broth and stock recipes.

Chicken Stock

When you smoke a whole chicken on the grill, you may have some leftover skin and bones that you are too busy to pick. Don't allow great food to head for the trash. Here's a suggestion to save that investment in flavor and nutrition.

- Place the skin and bones of smoked chicken in the Crock-Pot®. Add a few shakes of seasonings, such as poultry seasoning, parsley, sage, rosemary, thyme, and oregano. Cover it with water. Cook overnight on low.
- The next day, strain the liquid. Since the texture of food is often enhanced by the pieces of spice and chicken, I strain the liquid through a colander. To remove more of the little morsels, strain it through a sieve.
- Store the liquid in the refrigerator. After it cools, skim the solid fat off the top.
- Pick through the bones to find the pieces of chicken and save them for future use.

Collard and Barley Soup

The recipe for collard and barley soup is located on page 109 because its base is the liquid from the recipe on that page.

About Alligators

In Louisiana it is legal to hunt alligators. The season starts in early September and lasts until early October every year. People hunt alligators for their skins and for the edible tail meat.

(Source: http://www.zatarain.com)

Nutritional Value of Alligator Meat

Approximate values for 4 ounces of raw gator meat:

        Calories—110
        Fat—2 grams
        Carbohydrate—0 grams
        Protein—24 grams

Source: http://www.gatorama.com/recipes

French Onion Collard Soup

The collard pieces will give a sprinkling of color and a hint of added irresistible flavor.

Ingredients

French onion soup prepared from mix
1 tablespoon finely chopped frozen collards for each cup of soup
1-2 teaspoons olive oil
1-3 thin slices toasted French bread
3 tablespoons grated Gruyère cheese per serving

Preparation

- Prepare the onion soup according to directions. (Don't try to divide the package into smaller servings. It's too difficult to get a good mixture of all the flavors.)
- Preheat the oven to 450°.
- Place individual crocks on a baking sheet.
- Sauté the collards until they are heated. Pour them into the soup mixture and stir thoroughly. Save a few for a garnish.
- Assemble each serving by ladling soup into the crocks. Fill each crock about ⅔ full.
- Top each serving with French toast and then cheese. Sprinkle a few pieces of collards on each to garnish.
- Broil or bake until the cheese melts and browns slightly. Serve hot.

Equipment/Utensils

Crocks or other small ovenproof bowls • Baking sheet • Soup ladle

♥ *Heart Health Cuisine*

Mexican Collard and Black Bean Soup

Thin soup with a hearty taste…

Ingredients

Non-stick cooking spray

½ cup chopped onions

16 ounces frozen chopped collards

10 ounces cooked skinless chicken breast, diced

⅛ teaspoon baking soda

5 teaspoons salt substitute

2 tablespoons Splenda®

3 tablespoons chili powder (without sodium)

1 tablespoon cumin

1½ tablespoons oregano

2 tablespoons minced garlic

12 cups Chicken Vegetable Stock

1 can (10 ounces) Ro*Tel® diced tomatoes and green chilies

1 can (15.5 ounces) Trappey's® Seasoned Black Beans

Nutrition Facts	
Collard and Black Bean Soup, Per serving Makes 16 servings (1 cup each)	
Amount per serving	
Calories	84
Calories from fat	22
	% Daily Value *
Total Fat 2.3g	4%
Saturated Fat 0.2g	1%
Cholesterol 14 mg	5%
Sodium 187 mg	8%
Total Carbohydrate 6.6g	2%
Dietary Fiber 2.4g	10%
Protein 9g	
Percent values are based on a 2,000-calorie per day diet. Your daily values may differ.	
Additional Information 26.1% of calories from Fat 31.3% from Carbohydrates 42.7% from Protein	

Preparation

- Spray a soup pot.
- Sauté the onions.
- Add all the other ingredients except the Ro*Tel® and Trappey's®.
- Boil 15 minutes and lower the heat. Simmer 1 hour.
- Add the Ro*Tel® and Trappey's® and continue to cook 2 minutes.

Equipment/Utensils

Knife • Cutting Board • Big soup pot • Colander

Incredible Nutrition!

Mexican Collard and Black Bean Soup is a delicious delight that is a pleasure to eat without regard to the low calorie count, low amount of sodium, and high fiber. It is full of antioxidants.

Sweep the Kitchen Soup

A collard stem is a treasure you will not want to squander—a collard stem is a terrible thing to waste.

A few collard stems add color and texture to collards, but too many stems are undesirable. Raw collard stems are chewy snacks devoid of excessive calories, but too many stems become tiring. Although collard stems freeze well, they occupy valuable space in a crowded freezer. I suggest you solve the collard-stem crisis by making soup.

- Evaluate the scrumptious tidbits of vegetables, meats, and collard concoctions stored in small containers throughout the refrigerator and freezer.
- Select only the ones that are pristine. Chop them and toss them into your Crock-Pot®.
- Add some chopped collard stems, chopped onions, minced garlic, tomato paste, various spices, lemon juice, vinegar, something sweet, and something starchy. Rice, noodles, or potatoes—any or all of these will serve the purpose. Adjust the cooking time for the starchy foods.
- Cook the mix until the ingredients are al dente.
- Toss in some canned tomatoes and canned or frozen English peas and continue to cook until the latest additions have had a chance to boil.

Equipment/Utensils

Large Crock-Pot®

Serving Suggestions

- Serve with grated Parmesan or blocks of your favorite cheese added to the tops of the bowls while the soup is steamy hot.
- Slowly toast some old bread that you have sprayed with butter spray and sprinkle with garlic. Toasting it slowly makes it crunchy.
- Serve it with biscuits or cornbread. Spicemouths™ like Mexican cornbread with soup.

Selecting Collard Leaves

- The bottom leaves, known as *lugs,* are the least desirable because they are tough.
- The smallest leaves are the most tender, but they lack the popular distinct flavor collard lovers desire.
- The middle leaves are the best because they are both full-flavored and tender.

Collards are considered by some to be an aphrodisiac.

Collard Chili Soup

If you would like to cook some tasty, low-calorie dishes, try this soup for lunch. It is possible to enjoy the robust flavor without consuming bulky calories.

Ingredients

1 package (12 ounces) frozen Pictsweet® Seasoning Blend
2 cups frozen chopped collards
2 tablespoons minced garlic
1 tablespoon olive oil
12 ounces chicken broth
2 cans (total of 16 ounces) tomato sauce
1 can (28 ounces) diced tomatoes
2 cups salsa
⅛ cup chili powder or to taste)
⅛ cup oregano (or to taste)
½ cup lemon juice
1 tablespoon Splenda®
⅛ teaspoon baking soda
Salt substitute and pepper to taste

Preparation

- Sauté the seasoning blend, collards, and garlic in the olive oil.
- Add the remaining ingredients and cook on high 15 minutes.

Nutrition Facts	
Collard Chili Soup, per serving makes 8 servings	
Amount per serving	
Calories	132
Calories from fat	37
	% Daily Value *
Total Fat 4.3g	7%
Saturated Fat 0.6g	3%
Cholesterol 0 mg	0%
Sodium 975 mg	41%
Total Carbohydrate 19.6g	7%
Dietary Fiber 14.3g	57%
Protein 4.2g	
Percent values are based on a 2,000-calorie per day diet. Your daily values may differ.	
Additional Information 28% of calories from Fat 59.3% from Carbohydrates 12.7% from Protein	

Equipment/Utensils

Soup Pot

Notes

- Spicemouths™ will enjoy adding Madras curry powder at the table.
- A tiny bit of grated extra sharp cheddar in each bowl of soup is scrumptious.

The Difficulty of Preparation

Don't judge the difficulty of a recipe by the length of the ingredient list. Frequently all that is required is tossing ingredients into a pot and allowing the ingredients to simmer until they smell irresistible. Judge the work and skill required by the directions, not the number of items required.

Bonne Terre Swamp Stew

We are telling you up front to cook this recipe at your own risk. Tim Ellis gave it to us, and he declares it is the authentic method to cook it. The trouble we had was finding some alligator meat to cook. When we caught up with him, he was fresh out—he had sold all he had caught. Since Tim has been nice to us, since his food always tastes exotic, and since we could not resist the idea of combining alligator meat with fresh collards, we had no choice but to pass his recipe on to you.

Ingredients

1 quart alligator meat (See below.)
Meat tenderizer
Creole seasoning (like Tony Chachere's®)
Enough buttermilk to cover it
½ cup bacon drippings (grease)
2 big onions
2 garlic bulbs
A small mess of collards, washed and cut up in fine slivers
3 quarts homemade stock (cooked up from chicken, turkey, pork, or whatever you've got)
2-3 ribs celery (You can't cook a pot of anything in Louisiana or Texas without including onions, celery, and bell pepper.)
1 bell pepper (Choose your favorite color.)
Salt, black pepper, and cayenne pepper
¼ cup sugar
Vinegar juice (Hot pepper sauce, pickle juice, or jalapeño pepper juice will work.)
A double handful of whole baby okra

Preparation

- Alligator meat can be gamy, and it can be tough. Properly prepared, it has a delicate taste and a tender quality. When you clean it wash it plenty and strip off all the fat. Cut it in 1" strips. Beat the fool out of it with your meat mallet.
- After you dress your alligator meat, store it in washed-out milk cartons. If you wash the cartons out and get them clean and then sun them till they are dry, then you'll have some good containers. Pack it in boxes and cover it with water. Fold the top down and close it tight. Place a big rubber band around it.
- Then sprinkle meat tenderizer all over it. Leave it with the tenderizer on it about 30 minutes. Then you want to marinate it in lemon juice at least 30 more minutes.
- Sprinkle a light powdering of Creole seasoning on it and place it in the milk. Leave it there for another 30 minutes or longer. Or just leave it in the icebox overnight.
- Wash it off. The rest of this recipe is going to be easy.
- In a thick skillet start browning the flour with halve the bacon grease. Cook it on low, and stir it every once in a while.
- In your big stewing pot, put the rest of the bacon grease. Chop up the onions and slice the garlic in thin pieces. Brown them in that grease. Put the celery and bell pepper in there too. Fill the pot up with collards, and pour 2 quarts of the stock in there. When they wilt down, put some more collards till you get all of them in there.

Put the Ro*Tel® on top of the greens. Shake in some salt, black pepper, and cayenne pepper. Put the sugar and vinegar juice in there too.

- When the roux in the skillet gets as dark as you can make it without burning it, pour in the other quart of stock. Don't pour it in cold unless you want a big splattering mess. Instead have it warmed ahead of time. Stir that up until you don't have any lumps.
- Gradually spoon all the roux over into the collards after they've cooked down.
- Cook it all until it is tender. Then put the okra on top and cook it a little more. Add some more seasoning if you need it.

I suppose you could cook it with chicken. Alligator and chicken don't taste alike. If they did, why would anybody bother to eat chicken?

Tim Ellis

Equipment/Utensils

Sharp knives• Cutting boards • Heavy skillet • Soup Pot

Turkey's Boot

"It was at least 20 feet long," Turkey Thomas blurted breathlessly! "I never seen such a 'gator! And his mouf was at least a yard wide and gaped open a yard and a half! I'm tellin' you it was a prehistoric dinosaur!"

"But the world record 'gator was only 19'3"" Junior reminded his brother, Turkey.

However, that's hard to accept when you've just lost a new 6" Carolina GORILLA® Boot off your right foot in the mouth of this "monster." That 'gator just grabbed his boot and rolled. Out popped his foot! It was too easy for that 'gator! Maybe he should have bought that Great Oak 8" Logger. At least it wouldn't have come off so easy, he reasoned, agonizing more over the $59 cost than the fact he nearly lost his foot.

It simply couldn't have been the 6' animal he dragged dead limp out of the gravel pit yesterday afternoon after the hailstorm. And it was a good 'un, too. Golf ball and baseball sized hail stones fell all through those parts pretty well messing up the crops, roofs, pickups, and the few cars in the area.

Turkey had gone out to check the place left to the family when his father died. In the back of the property at the gravel pit he noticed a sizeable log at the shoreline. He figured he needed to check that out since there were no trees around that gravel pit. On closer inspection, he saw that "log" was an alligator!

Alligator? Here in south Arkansas? Naw, 'gators *never* get this far up! But that sure was what it was! He found a long stick and went to check it out. He poked gently at first then more vigorously with no response. That 'gator was dead!

Turkey sure didn't want to be that 'gator's next meal. But he'd heard how mounted 'gator heads were selling for $99 in New Orleans. He didn't mind taking some of those south Louisiana folks' money. After carefully deciding that the 'gator was dead, he loaded it in his pickup and took it back up to the house and laid it out on the back porch.

Continued on p. 173

Collard and Cauliflower Soup

Ingredients

3 tablespoons olive oil
2 tablespoon all purpose flour
1 cup tender fresh collards, chopped
1 bunch green onions with tops, finely chopped
16 ounces frozen cauliflower, finely chopped
1 quart Fat Free Half & Half®
1 pint chicken broth without added salt
Dash of salt substitute
Red pepper as desired
Black pepper as desired
½ teaspoon nutmeg
½ teaspoon cinnamon

Preparation

- Sauté the collards, green onions, and cauliflower in 1 tablespoon olive oil until the vegetables are tender.
- Blend them with the Half & Half®.
- Add the seasonings.
- In the cooking pot stir 2 tablespoons olive oil with the flour. (Do not brown the flour.) Add the chicken broth and cook while stirring until the mixture is smooth.
- Return the vegetables to the pot and heat the soup until it bubbles.
- Serve it hot with more spices sprinkled on top.

Serving Suggestions

Top the soup with croutons, french fried onions, grated cheese, or thin cucumber and tomato slices.

Turkey's Boot *(continued)*

Poppin' a beer top, he slid down in the easy chair to admire his new 6" Carolina GORILLA® Boots. Still exuding the smell of new shoe leather, they worked really well in the soggy soil of south Arkansas. He was as proud of his tough new shoes as he had been of his turkey call last year. Does life get any better?

Next morning Turkey sharpened his huntin' knife to skin that 'gator and head to New Orleans. Out the back door he went to an *empty* porch! That 'gator was missin'!

Now, 6' 'gators don't just disappear without a trace. There has to be a reason—maybe two reasons. Ol' Bugler, Turkey's award winnin' 'coon dog was number one. But it was unlikely Bugler could've got off with that 'gator by hisself. The number two suspect was Ol' Blue Eyes, Turkey's seventy-pound Catahoula Cur. Now, Blue Eyes could've got off with that 'gator 'specially with Bugler's help. But where on earth were those two? Bugler and Blue Eyes must've drug that 'gator off in the woods fer some good eatin'.

Continued on p. 175

Recipe for Collard Newbies

Collard Stew

Here is a stew full of healthy vegetables. If you have never eaten collards, this recipe would be a great starting point. The flavors blend together nicely; no single flavor dominates.

This tasty stew is easy to prepare. While you are cooking breakfast, you can toss the ingredients into your slow cooker and let it cook until evening.

Ingredients

1½ pounds lean stew beef
4 large carrots, peeled and cut in large
    pieces or 2 cups peeled fresh baby
    carrots
1 package (12 ounces) seasoning blend
1 can (10 ounces) Ro*Tel® diced
    tomatoes and green chilies
1 pound frozen chopped collard greens
¼ cup hot pepper sauce
½ cup sweet pickle juice
¼ cup orange marmalade
6 small potatoes, cut in large chunks
Dash of black pepper
Salt substitute to taste
Sprinkle of crushed red pepper
¼ cup cornstarch
2 cups water
2 cups fresh mushrooms, sliced
1 can (28 ounces) diced tomatoes

Nutrition Facts	
Collard Stew, per serving	
Makes 24 servings	
Amount per serving	
Calories	128
Calories from fat	11
	% Daily Value *
Total Fat 1.2g	2%
Saturated Fat 0.4g	2%
Cholesterol 17 mg	6%
Sodium 88 mg	4%
Total Carbohydrate 21.5g	7%
Dietary Fiber 5.1g	20%
Protein 7.7g	

Percent values are based on a 2,000-calorie per day diet. Your daily values may differ.

Additional Information
8.6% of calories from Fat
67.3% from Carbohydrates
24.1% from Protein

Preparation

- Place the beef, carrots, seasoning blend, Ro*Tel®, collards, pepper sauce, pickle juice, marmalade, potatoes, black pepper, salt, and red pepper into the Crock-Pot® in the order listed.
- Dissolve the cornstarch into the water and stir the mixture until it is smooth.
- Pour it into the Crock-Pot® and set the switch on high.
- After the ingredients cook down, push the potatoes into the collards.
- After 2-3 hours add the mushrooms. Continue to cook until the ingredients are tender—all day.
- Thirty minutes before serving, stir the ingredients and add the diced tomatoes.

See the notes on the next page.

Notes

- Seasoning blend is a frozen mixture of onions, celery, green peppers, red peppers and parsley flakes.
- The pepper sauce is the vinegar poured from a bottle of hot peppers that have been soaking therein.
- I should not admit the truth, but the truth is that sometimes I cannot keep cornstarch from lumping without the help of the blender.
- If you prefer, substitute 1 can cream mushroom soup for the water and cornstarch.
- Peel the potatoes if you must. We like ours unpeeled.
- If the dish tastes a bit spicy while it is cooking, don't panic. The tomatoes and rice will absorb the spice.

Equipment/Utensils

Large Crock-Pot® or other slow cooker

Where Are the Beans?

When I fed some of the stew to Paul (the man who does not eat beans in his chili) to test his opinion, he said, "Where are the beans? When you add the mushrooms, you could add a small package of frozen green lima beans. I thought stew had lima beans in it."

Even though I did not serve him any lima beans in the stew, he cleaned his plate with his bread. The next time I cook Collard Stew for Paul, I'll include the beans.

Serving Suggestions

Serve the stew over rice, sprinkle grated cheddar over the top, and serve with toasted French bread or some of the various types of cornbread included in this cookbook.

Turkey's Boot (continued)

Turkey was **mad.** Those two good-fer-nuthin' flea bags had got off with his $99 'gator head! All they did was eat, sleep, and hunt. The only time they was any good was huntin'.

'Bout that time, Turkey heard a whimper. Lookin' around he saw Blue Eyes limpin' up to the house. He had a flap of skin peeled off his right front leg hangin' down around his paw. Was that a 'gator bite? Turkey looked closer and carefully laid the skin back on the bare leg meat. There were two other puncture wounds close to the rip. Ol' Blue Eyes had nearly got *eaten* by that 'gator! No sooner had Turkey figured out what happened to Blue Eyes than Ol' Bugler crept quietly and warily toward the porch apparently afraid there was still "something" on it. That 'gator must've attacked those boys from the porch. They hadn't ever seen a beast that wouldn't run for a tree when they showed up!

Turkey grabbed his walkin' stick and headed to the gravel pit with revenge as much as the $99 in mind. Sure 'nough there was that "log" on the bank on the far side of the water about 200 yards away. Turkey sprinted back up to the house and returned with his 12-gauge shotgun: the one he used to "herd" fish.

Continued on p 176

Turkey's Boot *(concluded)*

He wasn't sure whether killing a 'gator with a shotgun was illegal as it was with fish, but he figured he could "herd" it onto the bank like he did the fish. He poled his flat-bottomed boat across the pond toward that "log." As he got about 20 yards away, the 'gator started to slip toward the water.

Turkey fired at the mud between the 'gator and the water. The 'gator whirled around and headed for the tall grass of the upper bank. But he still wanted the safety of the water. As Turkey put his right foot out of the boat into the mud and reached back to get his 12-gauge, that 'gator lunged hissing and grabbed his booted foot with a vise-grip that would have torn his foot clear off had it not been for the boot's protective steel toe. Instead it merely jerked his prized new 6" Carolina GORILLA® Boot plumb off his foot!

"Merely"? ***"Merely"!*** "Merely," indeed! It was ***his*** boot in that 'gator's chompin' mouth as he plunged into the deep water! Now Turkey was fightin' mad! Dogs are one thing—even the $99 head pales by comparison with losin' a 6" Carolina GORILLA® Boot!

Turkey spent the next two days stalking that 'gator with his shotgun unconcerned about the legality of his method. He ***had*** to get his boot back!

Sure 'nough one evening that 'gator was on the near bank. Turkey took aim with his deer rifle for the heart/lung area. He certainly didn't want to hit him in the stomach and risk damaging his boot, nor did he want to ruin that $99 trophy head. It was a clean shot and the 'gator lay still. Havin' been fooled more than once by this 'gator Turkey approached cautiously. Pokin' it with his walking stick he decided it was at last a ***dead*** 'gator.

He indeed did get the 'gator's head, but more importantly, he found his prized right boot in the beast's stomach. Its plastic parts had survived the 'gator's digestive system rather well to Turkey's great relief.

Turkey's friend, Boudreaux, from Breaux Bridge, Louisiana, urged him to salvage at least the 'gator's tail meat for frying or gumbo. Turkey loved that 'gator gumbo! But was that a hint of chicken flavor or boot leather?

Paul Elliott

South-by-Southwest Green Stew

La Texianne Cuisine™….   The okra provides a taste of Louisiana, while the jalapeños and chili-spiced flavors say Texas.

This satisfying and nutritious vegetarian stew requires little effort to cook. The recipe makes a huge amount, which can be enjoyed for days with variations. Contact the authors for nutritional information.

- Place these ingredients in the soup pot:
  2 tablespoon olive oil
  5 cups chopped fresh cabbage
  5 cups chopped collards (frozen or tender fresh)
  5 cups seasoning blend (frozen chopped onions,
  5 cups water
  1 cup liquid from jalapeños
  ⅛ teaspoon baking soda
  2 teaspoons salt (or to taste)
  ½ cup Splenda®
- Simmer 30 minutes. Add the following:
  2 cups whole tiny potatoes (unpeeled)
  2 cups frozen whole okra
- Simmer 30 minutes or until the potatoes are tender. Add:
  1 can Ro*Tel® diced tomatoes with green chilies
  12 ounces Mild Mexican Velveeta®, cubed
- Cook on very low heat until the cheese melts. Do not overly stir. (The okra and potatoes are delicate.) If you want to rev up the flavor, add small amounts of these:
  Curry powder
  Lemon juice

Place a layer of rice topped by a layer of spicy chips on each plate. Ladle the stew on top.

Comment
We dig around and find those tasty little potatoes first.

Paul insists that women gossip but men discuss the news.

Jamaican Collard Stew

Sweet and sour and slightly spicy—Jamaican Collard Stew will make you want to jump up and dance.

Collards are similar to calalloo, which is a green leafy vegetable popular in the Caribbean Islands.

Ingredients

1 tablespoon canola oil
1 pound frozen collards, finely chopped
1 cup finely chopped onion
½ cup green onions with tops, sliced
2 tablespoons minced garlic
1 tablespoon chopped fresh parsley
2 quarts chicken stock
½ cup vinegar
½ teaspoon thyme
¼ cup Pickapeppa®
2 ounces tasso, chopped
2 ounces lean salt pork, rinsed to remove superfluous salt
1 can (15 ounces) Coco Lopez® cream of coconut
2 cups sliced okra
1 can crabmeat
4 ounces chicken, chopped and cooked
Salt substitute
Freshly ground black pepper to taste
Ground red pepper to taste

Preparation

- Place all the ingredients in the stockpot except the coconut cream, okra, crabmeat, chicken, salt substitute, and peppers.
- Simmer the stew until all the different foods included are tender (an hour or 2).
- Add the remaining ingredients and simmer 10 minutes. Adjust the spices.

Equipment/Utensils

Stockpot• Knife • Cutting board

North Louisiana Collard Gumbo

This quick and easy version of a Louisiana staple is a blending of Southern flavors. (I started to call it a marriage: but since it has a hint of New Orleans, a strong component of African tradition, a kick of Tex-Mex, the tenderness of Georgia, and the practicality of north Louisiana, I realized it would be polygamy.)

Ingredients

½ cup finely chopped bacon (preferably ends and pieces—select lean pieces)
⅓ cup minced garlic
1 package (12 ounces) frozen seasoning blend (onions, celery, green and red peppers, parsley flakes)
1 pound finely chopped fresh collards (tender Georgia collards if you can find them or baby collards)
1 can (4 ounces) chopped green chilies
1 can (10 ounces) diced tomatoes and green chilies
1 package (4.5 ounces) Zatarain's New Orleans Style® Gumbo Base
8 cups water
¼ cup lemon juice
1 tablespoon Splenda®
1 tablespoon liquid from pickled jalapeños
Shake of crushed red pepper (According to your taste—you can always add more, but you can't take it out.)
Salt (to taste)
Black pepper (to taste)
6 ounces sliced tasso
1 package (14 ounces) cocktail smokies (sliced)
1 cup sliced okra

Preparation

- Brown the chopped bacon.
- Add the garlic, seasoning blend, and collards. Stir and sauté about 5 minutes.
- Add everything else except the smokies (which toughen when overcooked) and the okra (which gets mushy when overcooked).
- Simmer until it smells good, the collards are tender, and you've had time to cook some rice and set the table.
- When you put the rice on to cook, add the smokies and okra.
- Serve with gumbo filé and rice.

Variations and Other Comments

- Our friend Terry omitted the smokies and added a huge undisclosed amount of tasso.
- Because of variable factors, nutritional analysis is not included; it is, however, available.
- Paul, the Spicemouth™ and official taster, likes curry in his gumbo. When I cook for him, we compromise. I place a box of Madras curry powder by his plate. Also he

likes huge amounts of crushed red pepper. He keeps his "crushed red" handy. "Once it's in my bowl," he insists, "It's my business."

- For more well-researched and tried gumbo recipes prepared by my friends and family, visit http://www.fwlcookbook.com/. Click on GUMBO.

About Gumbo

Gumbo, as defined in Merriam-Webster dictionaries, is a soup thickened with okra pods or filé and containing meat or seafood and usually vegetables. According to *The Joy of Cooking,* the word "gumbo" is derived from *quingombo,* an African Congo word for okra. Louisiana gumbo is a soup thickened either with okra or filé, which is a powder made from ground sassafras root.

When you make gumbo, you are allowed to substitute ingredients liberally. Gumbo is something delicious that Louisiana people cook with whatever meats they have available. The best gumbo has more than one type of meat.

People in the Mississippi and Louisiana hill country often add vegetables that the south Louisianans with French heritage find shocking. It's all good!

About Roux

Roux, the basis of gumbo, is made by browning flour and butter oil until it is very dark for Cajun gumbo or light brown for Creole gumbo. Always cook the flour long enough to remove the raw taste and to initiate the swelling of the starch granules.

When you prepare roux, use the heaviest pot you have. The heavier the pot is, the prettier the roux will be.

Cajun cooks will tell you to begin heating water in your kettle before you start making the roux in order to avoid changing the temperature of the roux and making it lumpy by pouring cold water into it. I heat the water because my mama always failed to do so. She would brown flour and fat. Then she would dump in some cold liquid, usually delicious bouillon straight from the refrigerator or cool water. Although she stirred vigorously enough to prevent lumps, her concoction would emit steam to start a train…and burn her hands.

I have looked at countless recipes. Some of them call for equal amounts of flour and oil or butter. Other cooks feel that it is important to use slightly more oil than flour.

Cook the roux slowly and stir it often. If you cook it too fast, it will suddenly become uncontrollably hot and burn to a black stinky mess. For Cajun roux, you will want the mix to be as brown as you can get it without burning.

Collard Greens Gumbo

If you have really mature collards with tough stems, make Collard Greens Gumbo. The earthy vegetable taste is one of our favorites.

Ingredients

2 pounds fresh collards (big leaves and stems)
1 bunch parsley
½ cup olive oil
½ cup all purpose flour
1 quart chicken and vegetable stock
1 huge Vidalia onions (about 3 cups) onions, chopped
¼ cup red wine vinegar
¼ cup lemon juice
2 tablespoons Splenda®
1-4 tablespoon Swampy Land Seasoning or other seasoning blend (The recipe for Swampy Land Seasoning is on the next page.)
1-4 tablespoons Trappey's ® Jalapeño Sauce
¼ pound chopped tasso (or ham)
½ pound sliced andouille (or other sausage)
3 cups diced cooked chicken
3 cups diced Yukon gold potatoes or russet potatoes
1 can (8 ounces) oysters
1 can (14.5 ounces) tomatoes, diced

Preparation

- In a deep, heavy stockpot, brown the flour in the oil to make a roux. Warm the chicken broth in a saucepan to prevent a big splash and to avoid lumps. When the flour is brown, add the onions and sauté them. Pour the broth into the pot and stir to prevent lumps.
- Grind the collards and the parsley in a blender or food processor. (Add some water to the blender if you need to because you will need to fill the stock pot anyway.) Pour the ground greens into the stockpot and continue to stir.
- Add the seasonings, tasso, andouille, and potatoes, along with enough water to thin the mixture to a desired consistency, heat it until it bubbles, cover it, and cook over medium heat 30 minutes. Stir it occasionally.
- Lower the heat and continue to simmer the gumbo for approximately 30 minutes. Check it occasionally and stir it. Be sure to scrape the pan.
- Add the chicken, oysters, and tomatoes. Adjust the seasoning to your preference.

Serving Suggestions

- While the gumbo is cooking, prepare something to go with it, such as cornbread, baked sweet potatoes, basmati rice or basmati rice mixed with frozen whole kernel corn.
- Serve with gumbo filé.

Swampy Land Seasoning

This seasoning recipe is a delightful blend of some ingredients that are great on several foods, including collards. The recipe on the previous page has Swampy Land Seasoning listed as an ingredient.

Ingredients

2 tablespoons paprika
2 tablespoons salt substitute
2 tablespoons garlic powder
2 tablespoon onion powder
1 tablespoon black pepper
1 tablespoon cayenne pepper
1 tablespoon oregano
1 tablespoon thyme

Preparation

- Mix.
- Store in tightly sealed jars.

Notes

- Shake before using.
- Add to recipes in place of salt.
- Before using potassium chloride, check with your doctor. People with abnormal renal functions need to monitor potassium consumption.
- Swampy Land Seasoning lends a tasty variation to many dishes.
- This seasoning can be used at the table instead of salt.

Borrowed from *Flavored with Love.*

Collard Patch Herbal Seasoning

Here's another seasoning blend. Mix as you would for the above recipe.
This one is nice to stir into rice that you are serving with collards; or if you prefer a milder seasoning than the Swampy Land Seasoning in the collard recipes, try substituting the Herbal Seasoning.

2 tablespoons salt substitute
2 teaspoons garlic powder
1 teaspoon rosemary
1 teaspoon dried parsley
1 teaspoon thyme
1 teaspoon sage
1 teaspoon tarragon
½ teaspoon black pepper
¼ teaspoon red pepper

Red River Gumbo

Texianne ™ gumbo—what happens when a Texas cook and a Louisiana cook pour ingredients into the same pot. Red River Gumbo has received rave reviews.

Ingredients

1 cup small red beans
⅓ cup all purpose flour
⅓ cup olive oil
1 chopped onion (approximately 1 cup)
1 chopped green bell pepper (approximately 1 cup)
1 cup chopped celery
4 cups finely chopped fresh collards
6 ounces Richard's tasso, finely chopped
1 can Ro*Tel® diced tomatoes with green chilies
2 cups cooked, diced pork or other meat of choice
2 tablespoons chili powder
¼ cup lemon juice
2 tablespoons butter
1 pound crawfish tails
2 cups frozen mixture of okra, tomatoes, and onions
Salt to taste
Ground pepper to taste

Preparation

- Soak the beans overnight, empty the water cover again with fresh water, and cook until they are tender:
- Make a roux in the Dutch oven by browning the flour in the oil. Add the onion, bell pepper, celery, collards, and tasso. Stir and continued to heat. Add enough warm water to cover the mixture as it continues to cook.
- Add the Ro*Tel®, pork, chili powder, lemon juice, and red beans; keep the pot simmering. Add water as needed.
- Sauté the crawfish tails in butter until they are warmed throughout.
- After the gumbo has cooked until the vegetables are slightly tender, add the tomato-okra mixture and crawfish.
- Adjust the seasonings by adding salt and red pepper as desired. Simmer until all the ingredients are warm throughout and the flavors are starting to smell so good you have to eat it.

Equipment/Utensils

Large cooking pot • Dutch oven • Knife • Cutting board • Skillet

Notes

- Serve with gumbo filé. Texas basmati rice is tasty with Red River Gumbo.
- For nutritional information consult the authors.

Fish Couvillion

When we featured this recipe in http://collardpatch.blogspot.com, we were astonished at the huge number of people who went to the blog to obtain it.

This recipe makes a big bunch.

Eat it over rice and collards for a delicious, unforgettable treat. Paul brings up the subject of couvillion every few days. He says it would be good with alligator meat in it. Hmmm?

Ingredients

1 tablespoon cooking oil
2 bags frozen seasoning blend
1 pound catfish fillets
1 pound ocean perch fillets
1½ cups all purpose flour
½ teaspoon baking soda
2 teaspoons salt substitute
½ teaspoon black pepper
½ teaspoon ground red pepper
½ teaspoon cumin
1 teaspoon oregano
½ teaspoon rosemary
2 teaspoons garlic powder
1 teaspoon onion powder
2 teaspoons chicken bouillon powder
2 teaspoons curry powder
2 teaspoons chili powder
1 tablespoon dry parsley flakes
½ teaspoon thyme
2 teaspoons Splenda®
1 small can cream of mushroom soup
1 small can chopped tomatoes and green chilies (Ro*Tel® or other brand)
1 small can tomato sauce
Water
1 cup (uncooked measurement) Texmati® long grain American basmati brown rice prepared according to directions
1 batch Perfect Collard Greens

Preparation

- Toss the oil and seasoning blend into the pot to sauté while you prepare the fish.
- Now prepare the fish. You may need to remove the skin. To make that job easy, microwave the fish about 30 seconds and then scrape the skin away.
- Mix the flour in a bowl with a secure top. Or if you prefer, place the flour in a sealable freezer bag. Add all those dry seasonings, close the container, and shake them. Coat the fish thoroughly.

- Open the 3 canned ingredients and place them near the cooking pot. Remove about ¾ of the seasoning blend, which has cooked down by now.
- Assemble the couvillion in layers. The bottom layer will be the seasoning blend remaining in the pot. Continue with layers of fish, followed by a third of each of the canned ingredients. When you reach the top layer, which should be the onion mix, sprinkle the remaining flour mixture. Cover the top.
- Add enough water to cover the couvillion.
- Cover and simmer over very low heat until the ingredients have caressed each other, the liquid has turned light brown and thick, the fish is flaky, and the flour tastes cooked. If your pot is not thick enough, you may need to lift the ingredients off the bottom to prevent sticking. Do not stir it!
- On the plates spread a layer of collards.
- Then spread a layer of rice.
- Top it off with couvillion.

Equipment/Utensils

Bowl • Large cooking pot

Breakfast and Brunch Collards
Delicious Day Starters

Huevos Collards

Preparing Huevos Collards is easy, even though there are 3 little preparations required. The presentation and taste are extraordinary.

Collards

Ingredients

1½ cups water
2 tablespoons olive oil
1 package (16 ounces) frozen chopped collard greens
1 huge onion (or 2 large) onions—about 2 cups, chopped
¼ cup lemon juice
1 tablespoon balsamic vinegar
2 tablespoons orange marmalade
⅛ teaspoon baking soda
1 teaspoon basil leaves
½ teaspoon cumin
Salt substitute, crushed red pepper, and freshly ground black pepper to taste

Preparation

- In a large heavy pan or Dutch oven, heat ½ cup water with the oil until it is very hot.
- Add the greens and onions. Cover and cook five minutes.
- Add the remaining ingredients and cook until almost all the liquid has evaporated.

Huevos

Ingredients

Non-stick cooking spray
1 pound smoked sausage (in casing), chopped
8 eggs
1 cup (4 ounces) sharp cheddar cheese, cubed

Preparation

- In a large sprayed skillet, cook the sausage.
- Scramble the eggs with the sausage. When the eggs start to firm, add the cheese.
- Continue to cook and scramble until the eggs are set and the cheese has melted.

Tortillas

Ingredients

8 flour tortillas (burrito size)

Preparation

- Warm the tortillas for a few seconds in the microwave.

Continued

Equipment/Utensils

Dutch oven with lid • Thick skillet

Warming Tortillas

- You may warm an entire pack of tortillas in the microwave in the pack. (Remove the metal tie!)
- There are some neat warmers available, which are useful for warming smaller amounts.
- Here's an easy and quick method to warm 2-3 tortillas: place them on a microwave-safe dinner plate and invert another plate on top.

Serving the Huevos Collards

- Pile the eggs on a platter with the collards.
- Have each person spoon a row of eggs beside a row of collards onto a tortilla and wrap them.

Paul

Huevos Collards Picantes

On a morning when you want to cook something special for someone special, try this uncomplicated recipe for fancy-tasting eggs.

Ingredients

Non-stick cooking spray
½ cup finely chopped green onions, including tops
1 cup finely chopped fresh uncooked tender collards
⅛ teaspoon baking soda
2 teaspoons lime juice
4 eggs
½ teaspoon cumin
½ teaspoon crushed red pepper
2 ounces Colby Jack cheese blend

Preparation

- In a liberally sprayed skillet sauté the onions and collards at high heat 3-4 minutes until tender.
- Add the lime juice and baking soda. Stir thoroughly.
- In a small bowl whisk the eggs with the cumin and red pepper.
- Cube the cheese into chunks and add it to the eggs.
- Spray the skillet more if needed and add the eggs to the vegetables.
- Scramble the eggs until they are set and the cheese is softened. Leave visible pieces of melted cheese in the eggs.

Nutrition Facts	
Huevos Collards Picantes, per serving Makes 2 servings	
Amount per serving	
Calories	**268**
Calories from fat	171
	% Daily Value *
Total Fat 19g	29%
Saturated Fat 8.8g	44%
Cholesterol 449 mg	150%
Sodium 382 mg	16%
Total Carbohydrate 4.5g	2%
Dietary Fiber 0.9g	4%
Protein 19.8g	
Percent values are based on a 2,000-calorie per day diet. Your daily values may differ.	
Additional Information 63.8% of calories from Fat 6.7% from Carbohydrates 29.5% from Protein	

Equipment/Utensils

Cutting board • Sharp knife • Skillet • Small mixing bowl • Whisk

Serving Suggestions

- Top with hot thick and junky salsa and crisp tostados.
- Serve turkey sausage on the side.   Paul

Collard Cheese Soufflé

Ingredients

Non-stick cooking spray
4 eggs
1 cup Fat Free Half & Half®
1 cup breadcrumbs
½ cup red onion, grated
¼ cup green onions with tops, finely
    chopped
1 cup cooked collards
1 cup Swiss cheese, grated
½ to 1 teaspoon salt
1 teaspoon crushed red pepper
Paprika and/or ground red pepper for
    garnish

Preparation

- Preheat the oven to 350º.
- Spray the casserole dish.
- Beat the eggs and stir in the cream. In a separate bowl combine the breadcrumbs, onions, collards, cheese, salt, and red pepper. Pour the eggs and cream into the mixture.
- Spoon the soufflé into the casserole, sprinkle paprika and/or ground red pepper, and bake until it is firm— approximately 30 minutes.

Nutrition Facts	
Collard Cheese Soufflé, per serving Makes 8 servings	
Amount per serving	
Calories	**182**
Calories from fat	66
	% Daily Value *
Total Fat 7.2g	11%
Saturated Fat 3.5g	18%
Cholesterol 119 mg	40%
Sodium 236 mg	10%
Total Carbohydrate 17.5g	6%
Dietary Fiber 1.3g	5%
Protein 11.6g	
Percent values are based on a 2,000-calorie per day diet. Your daily values may differ.	
Additional Information 36.2% of calories from Fat 38.4% from Carbohydrates 25.4% from Protein	

Equipment/Utensils

2 mixing bowls • Grater •
2-quart casserole

Warnings

- The seasonings in the soufflé are slightly warm, adjusted to the taste of a mild spicemouth™. The amount of pepper in a dish is always a personal preference, requiring fine-tuning.
- This soufflé is so tasty that it may not be possible to stop eating it once you start, even if you have not previously been aware of the delicious flavor that collard can add.

Serving Suggestions

- Drizzle with Tiger Sauce®.
- Eat Collard Cheese Soufflé for breakfast, for lunch, or for dinner. Or warm you a square of it in the microwave when you cannot forget it is waiting for you in the refrigerator.

Collard Soufflé

Ingredients

Non-stick cooking spray
5 eggs, separated
2 cups creamed collards, cooked
Dash of salt substitute
¼ teaspoon cream of tartar

Preparation

- Spray a casserole dish.
- Preheat the oven to 350º.
- Beat the egg yolks thoroughly and stir the creamed collards (which should not be hot) into the yolks. Add a dash of salt.
- Beat the egg whites until they stand in peaks. Add the cream of tartar and continue to beat until it is blended into the eggs.
- Fold the collard-egg yolk mixture into the egg whites.
- Transfer the mixture to the pan.
- Bake until a knife inserted in the middle comes out clean.

Bacon-Collard Pie

Your guests will say, "This quiche is delicious! What's in it?"

Ingredients

Unbaked deep 9″ pie shell
9 slices bacon
2 teaspoons olive oil
1 cup finely chopped onion
1 cup chopped frozen collards
⅛ teaspoon baking soda
2 tablespoons lemon juice
2 teaspoons Splenda®
⅓ cup grated Parmesan cheese
½ cup grated Swiss cheese
4 eggs
2 cups Fat Free Half & Half®
Dash ground black pepper
Dash ground red pepper
¼ teaspoon nutmeg

Preparation

- Preheat the oven to 450°F. Prick the pie shell bottom with a fork and bake for 5 minutes. Set aside.
- Fry the bacon slowly; turn it frequently until crisp. Drain the bacon on paper towels and crumble it. Set aside

Nutrition Facts	
Bacon-Collard Pie, per serving Makes 8 servings	
Amount per serving	
Calories	**279**
Calories from fat	139
	% Daily Value *
Total Fat 15.7g	24%
Saturated Fat 8.7g	43%
Cholesterol 143 mg	48%
Sodium 831 mg	35%
Total Carbohydrate 21.5g	7%
Dietary Fiber 0.6g	2%
Protein 13.4g	

Percent values are based on a 2,000-calorie per day diet. Your daily values may differ.

Additional Information
49.9% of calories from Fat
30.9% from Carbohydrates
19.2% from Protein

Ingredients

Non-stick cooking spray
5 eggs, separated
2 cups creamed collards, cooked
Dash of salt substitute
¼ teaspoon cream of tartar

Preparation

- Spray a casserole dish.
- Preheat the oven to 350°.
- Beat the egg yolks thoroughly and stir the creamed collards (which should not be hot) into the yolks. Add a dash of salt.
- Beat the egg whites until they stand in peaks. Add the cream of tartar and continue to beat until it is blended into the eggs.
- Fold the collard-egg yolk mixture into the egg whites.

Collard Omelets

The preparation of these omelets is uncomplicated; the results are impressive.

Ingredients

2 teaspoons olive oil
½ cup frozen chopped collards
1 small stick celery, sliced thinly
½ cup chopped mushrooms
2 ounces chopped ham
2 tablespoons high quality barbecue
    sauce
2 ounces cubed Monterey jack cheese
4 large eggs
Non-stick cooking spray

Nutrition Facts	
Collards Omelets, per serving Makes 2 servings	
Amount per serving	
Calories	389
Calories from fat	259
	% Daily Value *
Total Fat 28.8g	44%
Saturated Fat 10.3g	52%
Cholesterol 466 mg	155%
Sodium 859 mg	36%
Total Carbohydrate 6.6g	2%
Dietary Fiber 1.7g	7%
Protein 25.8g	
Percent values are based on a 2,000-calorie per day diet. Your daily values may differ.	
Additional Information 66.6% of calories from Fat 6.8% from Carbohydrates 26.6% from Protein	

Preparation

- Stir-fry the collards, celery, and mushrooms in the olive oil at a high temperature in the saucepan. Stir in the ham and barbecue sauce. Cover and simmer over low heat 5 minutes. Check occasionally to make sure the mixture is not burning and stir it when you check it. Turn the heat off and layer the cheese over the mix. Do not stir. Set aside.
- Whisk the eggs. Spray the skillet generously and heat it until it is very hot. Pour half the eggs into it, lower the heat, and cook the omelet until the eggs begin to set. Place half the collards mixture on one half the top of the eggs. Flip the uncovered half onto the covered half and transfer to a warm plate.
- Prepare the second omelet with the remaining ingredients.

Equipment/Utensils

Small well-cured iron skillet (8" across the top) • Heavy-duty saucepan with tightly fitting lid • Whisk• Cutting board • Sharp knife

Notes

- Collard omelets go well with warm flour tortillas.
- Since each omelet will require only about 1½ minutes to cook, be sure to have your dining companion and all the other food you plan to serve ready when you start. If you prefer, use butter instead of cooking spray.

Bacon Collard Omelet

Cooking this omelet is really simple. I am including all the little procedures and the reasons for them.

If you don't need all these directions, skip them. On the other hand, if you have not yet cooked a perfect omelet, these directions will enable you to do so.

Bacon Collard Omelet is big enough to make 2 delicious, rich servings.

Ingredients

4 slices bacon, finely chopped (or the equivalent in lean bacon ends and pieces)
1 cup finely chopped, fresh uncooked tender collards
1 small Roma tomato
¼ cup red onion
¼ cup ricotta cheese
¼ cup Colby/Jack cheese, grated
4 large eggs
Sprinkle salt substitute
Non-stick cooking spray
Dash red pepper
Freshly ground black pepper to taste
Dash paprika
6 slices pickled jalapeños
Parsley

Nutrition Facts	
Bacon Collard Omelet, Per serving Makes 2 servings	
Amount per serving	
Calories	301
Calories from fat	230
	% Daily Value *
Total Fat 25.5g	39%
Saturated Fat 10.2g	51%
Cholesterol 38 mg	13%
Sodium 481 mg	20%
Total Carbohydrate 6.5g	2%
Dietary Fiber 1.5g	6%
Protein 11.2g	
Percent values are based on a 2,000-calorie per day diet. Your daily values may differ.	
Additional Information 76.5% of calories from Fat 8.6% from Carbohydrates 14.9% from Protein	

Preparation

- Fry the bacon in the skillet until it is crisp and the fat is rendered.
  Add the collards to the bacon and sauté them until they are tender.
- Transfer the bacon and collards to the steamer. (Using a stovetop steamer is a convenient way to remove the grease from the bacon. Place warm water in the saucepan, add the steamer rack, place the mixture inside, and cover with a lid. Heat at low temperature until you are ready for the bacon. The steamer will allow the excessive bacon drippings to drip down in the water.)
- Chop the tomato and onion. (Don't place them with the bacon—they need to be crisp.) In a small bowl, stir them with the cheeses. Save a few pieces of the tomato and a tablespoon of the grated cheese to garnish the omelet.

Continued

- In another bowl, whisk the eggs. Sprinkle some salt substitute into the eggs.
- Spray the inside of the skillet thoroughly. Be sure to include the sides.
- Heat the skillet until it is too warm to touch, but not until it smokes and burns. Add the eggs. Top them with red pepper and grind some fresh black pepper over them.
- Allow them to cook on medium heat about 2 minutes.
- Spread the tomato-cheese mixture over half the omelet; then top the mixture with the bacon and collards.
- Let the omelet cook until it is almost set. Then flip the plain side onto the covered side.
- With the spatula, make sure that the omelet is not stuck. Loosen it if necessary. Cut it in half and transfer it to the plates.
- Garnish the omelets with the tomato pieces, cheese, paprika, and parsley.
- Smile as you serve it with muffins on the plates.

Equipment/Utensils

Medium-sized (10" well-cured heavy stainless steel skillet Heavy-duty saucepan with tightly fitting lid • Steaming rack • 2 small mixing bowls • Cutting board • Sharp knife• Whisk • Stainless steel spatula

Southwestern Eggs Rolled In Crepes With Collards

What a fine way to start a day!

Ingredients

In addition to the ingredients in the crepes and scrambled eggs, you will need enough tender collard leaves to cover each crepe.

Preparation of Collard Leaves

- Select some tender baby collard leaves, wash them, and remove the stems.
- Drain them on a paper towel.

Paul

Paul's Basic Crepes

These basic crepes can be used with breakfast fillings or with dessert fillings

Ingredients

2 eggs
2 tablespoons vegetable oil
1⅓ cups (2% butterfat) milk
1 cup all purpose flour
½ teaspoon salt substitute

Preparation

- Whisk ingredients.
- Make crepes with crepe maker.

Equipment/Utensils

Mixing bowl • Crepe maker

Cooking and Storing

- Cook all the batter at once and stack them. The recipe will yield 16 (6") crepes.
- To store the leftovers, place sheets of waxed paper between the crepes and seal them in an airtight container.

Nutrition Facts	
Paul's Basic Crepes, per serving Makes 8 servings	
Amount per serving	
Calories	71
Calories from fat	49
	% Daily Value *
Total Fat 5.4g	8%
Saturated Fat 1.2g	6%
Cholesterol 56 mg	19%
Sodium 40 mg	2%
Total Carbohydrate 2.5g	1%
Dietary Fiber 0g	0%
Protein 3.1g	
Percent values are based on a 2,000-calorie per day diet. Your daily values may differ.	
Additional Information 68.6% of calories from Fat 14% from Carbohydrates 17.4% from Protein	

Paul

Paul's Southwestern Eggs

Fill collard-lined crepes with these delicious eggs.

Ingredients

6 eggs
½ cup (2 ounces) grated cheddar cheese
½ teaspoon garlic powder
2 teaspoons chili powder (without sodium)
1 teaspoon ground cumin or oregano
1 tablespoon bacon drippings

Preparation

Scramble

Equipment/Utensils

Mixing bowl • Skillet

Assembling the Crepes

- The diners can assemble the crepes at the table.
- Line each crepe with a single layer of tender collard leaves.
- Place a row of the eggs on top of the collards.
- Sour cream is an optional topping.
- Roll and eat.

Nutrition Facts	
Paul's Southwestern Eggs, per serving Makes 4 servings	
Amount per serving	
Calories	217
Calories from fat	158
% Daily Value *	
Total Fat 17.6g	27%
Saturated Fat 7.3g	37%
Cholesterol 337 mg	112%
Sodium 251 mg	10%
Total Carbohydrate 1.1g	0%
Dietary Fiber 0g	0%
Protein 13.6g	
Percent values are based on a 2,000-calorie per day diet. Your daily values may differ.	
Additional Information 72.9% of calories from Fat 2% from Carbohydrates 25.1% from Protein	

Paul

Hot Link Collard Eggs

Here's another example of the way a man can cook breakfast. Yum!

Paul uses Hot Link Collard Eggs as filler for crepes. (See the crepes recipe on p. 196.)

Ingredients

1 small yellow onion, chopped
1 cup finely chopped tender baby
    collards with stems removed
1 hot links, finely chopped
1 tablespoon olive oil
6 eggs
⅔ cup grated cheddar
1 tablespoon oregano
1 teaspoon cumin
½ teaspoon salt substitute
1 tablespoon Frank's Red Hot Sauce—
    Chile 'n Lime®

Preparation

- Sauté onions, collards, and hot links in olive oil in a heavy skillet.
- Whisk the other ingredients together—the eggs, cheese, and spices—in a mixing bowl
- Pour all the ingredients into the skillet; cook and stir, as you would scramble eggs.

Nutrition Facts	
Hot Link Collard Eggs, per serving Makes 4 servings	
Amount per serving	
Calories	290
Calories from fat	205
	% Daily Value *
Total Fat 22.8g	35%
Saturated Fat 9.1g	46%
Cholesterol 350 mg	117%
Sodium 486 mg	20%
Total Carbohydrate 3.7g	1%
Dietary Fiber 0.7g	3%
Protein 17.5g	
Percent values are based on a 2,000-calorie per day diet. Your daily values may differ.	
Additional Information 70.7% of calories from Fat 5.1% from Carbohydrates 24.2% from Protein	

Equipment/Utensils

Collard patch • Cutting board • Sharp knife • Large skillet with deep sides • Mixing bowl • Whisk

Paul

Notes

- If Frank's Red Hot Sauce—Chile 'n Lime® is unavailable, substitute 1 teaspoon Louisiana Hot Sauce® and 1 teaspoon lime juice.
- Nutritional values vary with different types of sausage links and sauces.
- Sometimes Paul, the Spicemouth™, adds chili powder.
- Finely chopped tender collard leaves can be substituted for baby collards.

Collard Crepes

These crepes have a light, spicy flavor and a pretty green color. They are paper-thin.

Ingredients

Non-stick cooking spray
1 cup finely chopped baby collards with
    stems removed
3 chopped green onions (approximately
    1 cup)
2 eggs
1½ cup milk (2% butterfat)
2 tablespoons canola oil
½ teaspoon salt substitute
¼ teaspoon dry thyme
Dash white pepper
Dash nutmeg
1 cup all-purpose flour

Nutrition Facts	
Collard Crepes, per serving (2 crepes) Makes 8 servings	
Amount per serving	
Calories	128
Calories from fat	41
	% Daily Value *
Total Fat 4.6g	7%
Saturated Fat 1.2g	6%
Cholesterol 57 mg	19%
Sodium 45 mg	2%
Total Carbohydrate 16.6g	6%
Dietary Fiber 1g	4%
Protein 5.2g	
Percent values are based on a 2,000-calorie per day diet. Your daily values may differ.	
Additional Information 32% of calories from Fat 51.8% from Carbohydrates 16.2% from Protein	

Preparation

- Sauté the collards and onions 3-4 minutes in a skillet that has been sprayed with non-stick cooking spray. (The collards will shrink to ¼ cup.) Set them aside to cool.
- Place all the ingredients except the flour in the blender and blend
until the mixture is smooth with only a few dark green flecks.
- Add the flour in increments and continue to blend until all the ingredients are thoroughly combined.
- Cook on an electric crepe maker.

Assembling the Crepes

- Place 1½ tablespoons to 2 tablespoons filling in a row near the end of each crepe.
- Roll the crepe so that the seam is on the bottom.

Topping Suggestions

- Colby and Jack cheese melted over the tops
- Sour cream
- Salsa
- Cilantro as a garnish or wrapped inside the crepes

Paul

Chili Verde Crepe Filling

Since we need to eat Chili Verde Filling often because it is irresistible, we make a huge batch and store it. You may want to half this recipe.

Mike's recipe for green chili in <u>Flavored with Love</u> was the inspiration for this crepe filling. In cold weather, he makes it and feeds it to Christie. It is one of their comfort foods.

Ingredients

Non-stick cooking spray
2½ pounds lean boneless pork back
2 tablespoons butter
½ cup green onions including tops
½ cup Vidalia onions
14 ounces diced green chilies with juice
1½ cups water
2 teaspoons salt substitute
½ teaspoon freshly ground black pepper
2 teaspoons Crystal® hot sauce
2 tablespoons lime juice
2 tablespoons Splenda®
2 tablespoons melted butter
2 tablespoons flour

Nutrition Facts	
Chili Verde Crepe Filling, per serving Makes 24 servings	
Amount per serving	
Calories	**85**
Calories from fat	35
	% Daily Value *
Total Fat 3.9g	6%
Saturated Fat 1.9g	9%
Cholesterol 35 mg	12%
Sodium 57 mg	2%
Total Carbohydrate 2.3g	1%
Dietary Fiber 0.1g	0%
Protein 10.2g	
Percent values are based on a 2,000-calorie per day diet. Your daily values may differ.	
Additional Information 41.2% of calories from Fat 10.8% from Carbohydrates 48% from Protein	

Preparation

- Cube the pork in small pieces and brown it in a sprayed skillet. The yield should be approximately 4 cups.
- Place the pork in the Crock-Pot®.
- Sauté the onions until they are shiny in two tablespoons butter.
- Add the onions to the pork.
- Add the chilies, water, salt substitute, pepper, hot sauce, and lime juice.
- Brown the flour and butter.
- Scrape the sides of the skillet and add the flour and butter.
- Stir the mix and cook in the Crock-Pot® for 3 hours.
- If you are not ready to serve the crepes, leave the filling on warm until you have the crepes ready.

Equipment/Utensils

Sharp knife • Cutting board that can be washed in hot water with soap • Large skillet • Crock-Pot®

Scrambles

You may add many different ingredients to Scrambles. This recipe is a suggestion. You will have 4 generous servings.

Ingredients

½ cup each:
  Diced potatoes
  Chopped onions
  Frozen chopped broccoli
  Frozen chopped collards
  Frozen diced bell peppers
  Frozen whole kernel corn
5 large eggs
½ cup cream cheese, cut in blocks
½ cup grated Colby/Jack cheese
2 teaspoons Madras curry powder
Shake of red pepper
Shake of salt or salt substitute
½ pound chopped Cajun sausage
1 tablespoon minced garlic
⅛ teaspoon baking soda
1 tablespoon jalapeño slices, chopped
1 small tomato, chopped
1 tablespoon lime juice

Preparation

- Chop the vegetables finer if preferred or needed.
- Whisk the eggs with the cream cheese and grated cheese. Add the curry powder, red pepper and salt to the eggs; whisk the mix some more.
- Brown the sausage, potatoes, and onions.
- Add the broccoli, collards, bell peppers, corn, garlic, and baking soda; continue to stir-fry them until the potatoes are almost tender. Do not overcook.
- Add the jalapeños, tomato, and lime juice.
- Pour the egg mixture into the skillet and scramble all the ingredients together until the eggs are set.

Variations

- Use another meat if you prefer, such as ham or salami.
- Select other vegetables, such as mushrooms or English peas, as you wish.

Serving Suggestions

- Roll into crepes or flour tortillas.
- Serve with sauce as desired, perhaps zesty steak sauce or barbecue sauce.
- Try Vidalia® Blossom Sauce.

Collard Hash Eggcups

Corned beef hash has a retro taste, which the collard cooks have updated to cause an explosion of enhanced flavor. The eggcups are neat enough to serve ladies at a brunch, but they have a hearty flavor that men will ravish. Serious epicures will enjoy eating two servings each.

Ingredients

Non-calorie canola cooking spray
2 teaspoons olive oil
1 cup finely chopped fresh baby collards
⅛ teaspoon baking soda
1 tablespoon red wine vinegar
1 tablespoon orange marmalade
1 tablespoon minced garlic
15 ounces corned beef hash
1 teaspoon Madras curry
1 teaspoon oregano
½ teaspoon sage
1 tablespoon A-1® steak sauce
4 medium eggs
Ground red pepper
Paprika

Nutrition Facts	
Collard Hash Eggcups per serving makes 4 servings	
Amount per serving	
Calories	231
Calories from fat	127
	% Daily Value *
Total Fat 14.1g	22%
Saturated Fat 5.3g	27%
Cholesterol 82mg	27%
Sodium 591mg	25%
Total Carbohydrate 14.9g	5%
Dietary Fiber 1.5g	6%
Protein 11g	

Percent values are based on a 2,000-calorie per day diet. Your daily values may differ.

Additional Information
55.1% of calories from Fat
25.8% from Carbohydrates
19.1% from Protein

Preparation

- Spray the ovenproof bowls with cooking spray.
- Wash the collard leaves, roll them, and snip them into short, thin shreds. Prepare enough to fill one well-packed measuring cup.
- Sauté the collards in the olive oil over high heat 3 minutes.
- Turn off the heat; add all the remaining ingredients except the eggs, red pepper, and paprika.
- Stir the mix thoroughly and check the seasonings.
- Divide the mixture among the 4 bowls; make an indentation in the middle of each.
- Crack each egg carefully and drop an egg into each bowl.
- Spray a small amount of cooking spray over each egg.
- Sprinkle red pepper and paprika on the tops as desired.
- Bake at 350° until the eggs are set. Personal preferences may vary.

Equipment/Utensils

4 small (7 ounce size) round stoneware ovenproof bowls • Kitchen scissors • Medium skillet

Serving Suggestions

Add one of your favorite toppings, such as Tiger Sauce®.

Note

The calorie count of different brands of corned beef hash can vary as much as 300 calories per 15 ounces. For calculation we used Hormel® because of its lower calorie and fat content.

Angels and Saints

The experiences I am sharing with you in this little story are simply the truth with no embellishments, although the supernatural quality of these events may make them seem unbelievable.

My mind has been going through these events for several months. Today, when I finally decided I would absolutely have to tell you what happened, Paul, not knowing what I was writing, turned the television on to the Discovery Channel to watch "Extreme Machines" featuring perilous bicycle feats that are scary to watch. There are stunt riders who can soar over fifteen feet above the ground and downhill mountain bikers.

Last year I was riding my bike—actually it is an adult tricycle with two wheels on the back—to take a break from writing. (A person can have too much fun writing, you know.) As I turned a corner, I noticed that my handlebars were slightly loose. I thought, "I need to hurry and finish my ride so I can go home and check on these handlebars." Can you believe what I did next? I increased my speed!

I drove up a little hill. As I started down it, I suddenly realized that I was holding handlebars not connected to my bicycle! There were no good choices of places to go. To the left was the other side of the street. If I went over there and a car approached, the driver could have failed to see me. A serious wreck could have resulted. There was little chance of continuing to go straight ahead because the tricycle was wobbling. Steering was impossible, and the brakes were inoperative. To the right I saw a deep ditch. Going clockwise I saw my neighbor's driveway. I supposed if I kept going down it I could hit her house. I remember thinking that I was glad she was not at home because she would have been upset. The left edge of the driveway, which was becoming closer to me at that time, had an edge as sharp as a knife. I had no choice and no control.

Before I could choose to jump, the tricycle threw me into the air. As I continued to hold my handlebars, I flew upward with no idea of where I would land! My life flashed before me. I've heard that expression, but suddenly it developed a new meaning for me. Then I laughed. Somehow I visualized myself and realized how funny I looked—a woman of an age I like to call *ripe*—flying through the air and holding those handlebars.

Continued on p. 206

Appetizers And Snacks

Let's Have a Party!

Collard Greens Puffs

*Everyone—including kids!—loves this versatile appetizer that looks a bit like a cookie. (Perhaps don't tell the kids they are **vegetable** cookies.) You can serve them hot from the oven or at room temperature; either way is fine. The batter must rest in the refrigerator for at least 1 hour to firm up; so start this recipe with enough time to spare. The blue cheese in the salad dressing adds a subtle hint rather than a wallop; so even if you have a blue cheese avoider in your house, you'll still be safe with these.*

Source: Cut `n Clean Greens® (http://www.cutncleangreens.com)

Ingredients
1 (1-pound) bag Cut `n Clean Greens® Collard Greens
2 eggs
2 tablespoons dried minced onion
½ cup (2 ounces) shredded sharp or extra sharp Cheddar cheese
½ cup bottled creamy blue cheese salad dressing (low-fat version works fine)
2 tablespoons butter, melted
¼ teaspoon garlic powder
1 (8.5-ounce) package corn muffin mix (such as Jiffy® brand)
⅓ cup honey mustard, purchased or homemade (optional; see following recipe)

Preparation
Bring 6 cups water and 1 teaspoon salt to a boil in a large pot. Add greens, stir to submerge, and boil for 15 minutes, stirring once or twice to ensure even cooking. Drain well in colander, pressing on greens with the back of a spoon to remove excess water. When cool enough to handle, place greens on cutting board, mass them together and chop much more finely.

While greens are cooking and cooling, mix eggs, onion, cheese, salad dressing, butter, and garlic powder in a large bowl. Stir in cooked, chopped greens and dry muffin mix. Cover and refrigerate batter for at least 1 hour, so batter will firm up and is easier to handle.

Heat oven to 350°. Mist cookie sheets with non-stick baking spray. With a spoon, drop tablespoonfuls of batter onto the prepared sheet, as you would drop cookie batter. The puffs will not spread; so you may place them as close as 1" apart.

Bake puffs for 13-15 minutes. Remove sheet from oven and, using a spatula, place puffs on a serving platter to serve immediately, or place them on a cooling rack.

They are good whether straight from the oven, re-heated and served slightly warm, or served at room temperature. Accompany with a honey mustard dip if you wish, although they are excellent plain.

Makes 36 puffs.   Dorothy Reinhold
Reprinted with permission from Cut `n Clean Greens® (http://www.cutncleangreens.com)

Homemade Honey Mustard

Place about 5 tablespoons Grey Poupon Dijon® mustard in a small bowl; stir in 2 tablespoons honey. You may increase or decrease amount of honey to suit your personal preference.

Dorothy Reinhold

Reprinted with permission from Cut 'n Clean Greens®
(http://www.cutncleangreens.com)

Angels and Saints *(continued)*

I landed in the juniper bush on the left side of the driveway. Except for receiving a few scratches and being pinned under the branches of the bush, I was fine. (Almost fine—little did I realize that I would be sore for a month and require the good doctor to give me physical therapy every day!)

The hilarity continued. I could not reach my cell phone because the limbs were poking into my back. Finally I broke the limbs and reached my phone, which was dying. It had enough charge remaining to make one brief call. "Paul, I'm all right, but I've had a little bike wreck. There's no need to come get me."

"I'll be right there," he said. When he arrived, I started crying.

"I'm crying because—it is not about the fall. Something wonderful happened."

"Something has deeply moved you. I can see that."

Four years ago my husband Bobby died. The night before he died, a man came to the hospital to visit us. He had never visited us before, and I do not know his name. All I know is that he is a minister who did not measure up to his congregation's requirements. I do not know whether he has been called to another church.

Back to the story: The Sunday night before Bobby died, the minister, dressed neatly in a suit, and carrying his Bible, came to Bobby's hospital room. Holding his Bible, which had pages with verses typed on them pasted inside the covers, he said, "May I read with you?"

He stood on one side of the dying man's bed, and I stood on the other. The churchless pastor read Psalm 23 and other familiar comforting words. We listened intently until Bobby gave me his I'm-tired-that's-enough look.

Continued on p. 210

Stuffed Mushrooms

This recipe can be prepared with mushrooms of various sizes. Use smaller to make a party dish or use large mushrooms to make individual entrées.

Ingredients

Non-stick cooking spray
24 medium large mushrooms (1½" diameter) or 6-8 huge mushrooms
1 tablespoon unsalted butter
1 tablespoon olive oil
⅓ cup chopped mushroom stems
⅓ cup thinly sliced spring green onions
1 cup cooked and peeled shrimp, coarsely chopped
⅓ cup Polish sausage, coarsely chopped
1 teaspoon crushed savory leaves
1 teaspoon dried parsley
1 cup cooked and seasoned collards (without juice)
½ cup breadcrumbs (made from good toast such as crunchy oatmeal bread)
1 tablespoon nuts (such as almonds)
4 ounces cream cheese (not whipped)
2 tablespoons chopped pimientos
⅓ cup light mayonnaise
Creole seasoning (such as Tony Chachere's® or our Swampy Land Seasoning) as desired

Preparation

- Spray a 9 X 13" baking pan. Preheat the oven to 350º.
- Wipe the mushrooms clean with a damp paper towel, and remove the stems. If necessary, use an ice cream scoop to enlarge the mushroom cups.
- Finely chop the stems. You will need ⅓ cup for this recipe.
- Save a few whole shrimp and some pieces of pimiento for garnishes.
- Sauté the chopped mushroom stems, the onions, the shrimp, and the sausage. Add the seasonings and the collards. Continue to cook slowly until the liquid is absorbed. Stir in the breadcrumbs, cream cheese, pimientos, and mayonnaise.
- Grind the toast and nuts in the blender.
- Stir everything together and taste it. You may need to add a little more seasoning.
- Fill the mushroom caps. Garnish with whole shrimp and chopped pimientos.
- Bake for 20 minutes or until the filling is heated throughout.

Equipment/Utensils

9 X 13" baking pan • Cutting board • Sharp knife• Small ice cream scoop with sharp edge •Skillet or sauté pan

Collard and Shrimp Quesadillas

Prepare chili con queso by cooking these ingredients in a saucepan until the cheese melts:

    6 ounces shredded or grated cheddar

    6 ounces cubed Velveeta® cheese product

    1 can Ro*tel® tomatoes and chilies

Have on hand:

    Some well-seasoned cooked collards without liquid

    Cooked medium-sized shrimp

    Burrito-sized flour tortillas

    Non-stick cooking spray

Prepare the quesadillas 1 at time:

    Cover ½ of a tortilla with ¼ cup cooked collards and ¼ cup shrimp.

    Place enough chili con queso over the collards and shrimp to cover them.

    Fold the tortilla in half.

    Spray a skillet with cooking spray.

    Cook each tortilla separately.

Serve with any of the following:

    Guacamole

    Sour cream

    Sliced tomatoes

    Avocados

    Jalapeños

    Fresh cantaloupe

Equipment/Utensils

Saucepan • Skillet

Collard Biscuits

Ingredients

½ cup very finely chopped tender fresh collards
¼ cup very finely chopped green onions including tops
2 teaspoons canola oil
⅛ teaspoon baking soda
Non-stick cooking spray
2 cups all purpose flour
1 tablespoon baking powder
2 teaspoons salt substitute
1 tablespoon Splenda®
1 stick (¼ pound) unsalted butter
1 cup Fat Free Half & Half®
A little more flour
1 egg
1 tablespoon water

Preparation

- Sauté the collards and onions with the baking soda in the canola oil for 1 minute. Set them aside to cool.
- Spray a cookie sheet. Preheat the oven to 400°.
- Mix the dry ingredients.
- Chop the butter finely and work it into the flour mix until the butter is tiny balls the size of peas.
- Add the cream and stir until the dough is mixed.
- Add the cooled collards and onions. Stir until they are distributed throughout the dough.
- Turn the dough onto a flour board. Knead it. (Pat it flat and fold it no more than twice.)

Pat into a flat pile ¾ " thick. Cut it with a small biscuit cutter.

- Place the biscuits on the cookie sheet. Leave some space between the biscuits.
- Combine the egg and the water. Brush the biscuits with the egg wash.
- Bake until the biscuits are golden brown.

Equipment/Utensils

Small skillet • Cookie sheet • Mixing bowl • Pastry cutter • Board for kneading • Pastry brush

Serving Suggestion

Serve hot with small slices of ham or fried sausage. Also include some slices of cheese. Spicy mustard would go well with the biscuits.

Collard-Okra Canapés

Ingredients

Fresh, tender collard leaves
Flour tortillas, fajita size
Neufchatel cheese
Pickled okra
Tiger Sauce®

Preparation

- Heat the collards to wilt them in the microwave 1-2 minutes at a high setting and allow them to cool.
- Spread Neufchatel over the tortillas.
- Remove the stems from the collards and cover the tortillas with single layers of collards. Trim them if necessary.
- Spread another layer of Neufchatel on top of the leaves.
- Place a row of okra near the edge of each tortilla and roll the canapés tightly.
- Cut them into 1" slices.
- Arrange the slices on a plate and serve them with Tiger Sauce® for dipping.

Equipment/Utensils

• Knife • Cutting Board

Angels and Saints (continued)

I looked at the man and said, "Thank you."

"May I pray with you?" he then asked; he prayed and left. After all the other visitors we had enjoyed for five years, that man ministered to us in our time of greatest need.

That night Bobby died. It was, I believe, about 4:00 a.m. Knowing that his time was short, I had tried to stay awake that night, but I did not succeed. Shortly after 4:00, I awakened as I realized a wind was whirling near the window, but the window was closed.

For the first time in years, I realized that Bobby was not in pain. His handsome face was at peace. There was no labored breathing; he was not breathing. I kissed his cheek, which was not yet cold.

Earnie Miles, a nurse who had worked with me in ICU and a long-time friend, was there that night but not as an employee. He came and sat with me until the funeral home personnel arrived. Because of a miscommunication, the funeral home employees were delayed for two hours. Earnie, by sitting and talking with me, ministered to me as he had throughout the years. He would always say simply, "I see what you're going through."

Continued on p. 211

Curried Deviled Eggs

Ingredients

1 dozen eggs
6 tablespoons light mayonnaise
1 tablespoon brown mustard
1 tablespoon lime juice
1 tablespoon Madras curry powder
1 teaspoon ground red pepper
Salt substitute to taste
Black pepper to taste
Red and yellow bell pepper
Baby collard leaves
Small sweet gherkins
Grape tomatoes
Paprika

Preparation

- Boil and peel the eggs. (Place them in cold water, cover the pot, and bring them to a boil. Turn the heat off. Let them sit in the warm water 15 minutes. Peel them in cool water.) Cut them in halves horizontally.
- Remove the yolks and mash them along with the other ingredients. Fill the whites
- Cover a plate or platter with collard leaves. Place the eggs on the leaves. Garnish the eggs with pickles and grape tomatoes. Sprinkle the eggs with paprika.

Saucepan • Mixing bowl

Angels and Saints *(continued)*

While I stood in the hall and the funeral home people loaded him onto their gurney, the day shift arrived to start the day. My friend Rosemary Ficklin said, "He died, didn't he?"

"Yes."

"You know he's better off."

"Yes, he has gone to a better place. I'm sorry I had fallen asleep and wasn't there when he died."

She said, "If God had wanted you to be awake when it was time for Bobby to go and be with Him, you would have been awake, but He let you rest until it was time for you to wake up."

Then everything was good, and I was strong.

Continued on p. 214

Crawfish-Eggplant-Collard Pies

Ingredients

1 very large eggplant
Non-stick cooking spray
2 tablespoons onion flakes
2 tablespoons hot water
½ cup shredded sharp cheddar
1 cup crushed Doritos® Ranchero Tortilla chips (measured after they are rushed)
¼ cup chopped celery
¼ cup lemon juice
1 tablespoon chopped jalapeños
2 teaspoons minced garlic
½ cup frozen chopped collards
2 teaspoons olive oil
½ cup Pace® sweet roasted onion and garlic cooking sauce (or medium salsa)
Crushed red pepper as desired
1 can cream of mushroom soup
12 ounces crawfish tails (cooked)
3 cans refrigerated crescent rolls (8 rolls each)

Preparation

- Peel and chop the eggplant. Microwave or steam it until it is tender.
- Spray a 9 X 13 X 2" baking dish or cookie sheet with non-stick spray.
- Dissolve the onion flakes in hot water.
- Sauté the onion flakes and collards in the olive oil.
- Combine all ingredients except the crawfish and crescent rolls. Stir thoroughly to allow all the flavors to combine. Add the crawfish and toss the mixture.
- Separate the rolls.
- On a flat roll placed on the baking sheet, spoon a dollop of the filling.
- Cover the roll and mixture with another roll. Pinch the sides together by mashing the sides with a fork.
- Spray the tops with non-stick cooking spray.
- Bake in an oven preheated to 450° until golden brown, approximately 20 minutes.

Equipment/Utensils

Steamer or microwave • 9 x 13x 2" baking dish or cookie sheet • Saucepan • Mixing bowl

Notes

- Serve this dish as an appetizer or as party food. Prepare one pie for each guest. Leftover filling may be frozen or used as a stuffing baked in vegetable shells, such as hollowed-out zucchini, eggplants, or potato skins.

- It's sensational in cornbread. Mix a large batch of cornbread according to the mix recipe on the package, but substitute some self-rising flour for ½ the cornmeal. Pour ⅔ the batter into a greased pan. Add the leftover filling mix. Place the remaining layer of cornbread batter on top. Bake as usual.

Crawfish-Eggplant-Crepe Filling

Heat the above mixture in a saucepan until it bubbles. Use it to fill crepes.

Collard Pie Filling

Here's another idea for party pies.

Use crescent rolls as in the above recipe and fill them with the following:

Ingredients

3 tablespoons olive oil
5 cups (16 ounces) frozen chopped collards
12 ounces frozen seasoning blend
⅛ teaspoon baking soda
1 tablespoon Splenda®
⅓ cup balsamic vinegar
Ground red pepper, ground black pepper, and salt substitute to taste
2 cups cottage cheese, drained
2 teaspoons dried dill weed
2 ounces crumbled blue cheese
1 teaspoon Tabasco® or Crystal® hot sauce

Preparation

- Sauté the collards and frozen seasoning blend about 5 minutes.
- Add the baking soda, Splenda®, vinegar, peppers, and salt substitute.
- Stir the ingredients. Cook until all the liquid is absorbed.
- Combine the cheeses, dill weed, and hot sauce. Add this mix to the collards.
- Separate the rolls.
- On a flat roll placed on the baking sheet, spoon a dollop of the filling.
- Cover the roll and mixture with another roll. Pinch the sides together by mashing the sides with a fork.
- Spray the tops with non-stick cooking spray.
- Bake in an oven preheated to 450° until golden brown, approximately 20 minutes.

Equipment/Utensils

9 X 13 X 2" baking dish or cookie sheet • Saucepan • Mixing bowl

Collard Crepes Filling

Use the above mixture to fill crepes.

Artichoke and Collard Dip

Ingredients

1 tablespoon olive oil
1 cup water
1 fresh onion, finely chopped
Salt substitute black pepper, red pepper, and garlic powder
2 tablespoon lemon juice
2 cups finely chopped fresh collards
8 ounces fat free cream cheese
3 ounces grated Parmesan cheese
1 pound shredded Monterey Jack cheese
3 jars (6 ounces each) artichoke hearts, drained and chopped

Preparation

- Place the olive oil and cup of water into a Dutch oven or other sturdy pot.
- Add the onion and cook covered 5 minutes.
- Shake the seasonings into the mixture as desired.
- Add the lemon juice.
- Heat the mixture until it is as hot as possible.
- Add the collards. Cook covered 5 minutes. Remove the cover and continue to cook until the liquid has evaporated.
- Combine all the ingredients and heat in the Crock-Pot® until the cheese is melted. Stir occasionally.
- Serve with spicy nacho chips.

Equipment/Utensils

Dutch oven • Crock-Pot ®

Angels and Saints (concluded)

Back to the tricycle wreck: While I was waiting for Paul to come get me, that same minister, who does not live in my neighborhood to my knowledge and whom I have never seen in this neighborhood, drove by and stopped. "Could I help you?" he said.

"No, thank you. I'm fine."

Mary Lou

Collard Oyster Dip

This cheesy, hot dip is tasty enough to serve as a complete meal, and it is also great to place in a hot dish at a party. A friend, Marie Suares, who grew up in New Orleans, taught me to make this dip with chopped broccoli 40 years ago. I prefer it with collards, which are not lumpy like the broccoli. It's a taste from years gone by I treasure.

Ingredients

1 tablespoon olive oil
2 cups frozen chopped collards
2 cups frozen seasoning mix
⅛ teaspoon baking soda
1 tablespoon red vinegar
½ cup water
8 ounces Velveeta® cheese spread
¼ cup chopped jalapeños
1 can Campbell's® cream of mushroom soup
1 teaspoon Worcestershire sauce
½ teaspoon black pepper
Red pepper to taste
2 teaspoons garlic powder
1 cup fresh oysters

Preparation

- Sauté the collards and seasoning mix in the olive oil. Add the baking soda, red vinegar, and water.
- Cook covered until the collards are tender and all the excess liquid is absorbed.
- Add seasonings and cheese. Stir until melted. Combine with cooked collards.
- Drain, blot dry, and chop the oysters. Add to collard mixture; cook gently for 5 minutes.
- Serve with toast rounds or sturdy chips and optional crushed red pepper.

Notes

- For this recipe do not use the generic brand of soup because it is not as thick as Campbell's®. You will need the dip not to be too thin.
- Also use Velveeta®, which tends to be thicker than the generic brands.
- If you are making the dip for an appetizer at a sit-down meal, you won't need to worry if the dip is slightly thin.
- If, however, you are planning to serve it at a party, you may need to address the fact that it can be slightly thin. You may need to counteract the problem by stirring a bit of cornstarch into a cup of the dip. Then heat that mixture and stir until the cornstarch is dissolved and the dip is smooth. Add a little more if you need it, and then add the dip with the cornstarch to the remainder of the dip and stir as you heat.
- When heating this cheesy dip, be sure to heat it on low.
- We do not recommend eating raw or undercooked oysters. Be sure to cook the oysters until the mixture bubbles and then a few minutes more.

Desserts
Mostly Chocolate And Collards

Apple Collard Raisin Pie

You'll never believe how delicious this pie is until you taste it. Try it with whipped topping. There is enough filling for two pies. You may want to freeze half the filling.

Ingredients

1 tablespoon canola oil
16 ounces (5 cups) frozen chopped
    collards
½ cup water
½ teaspoon ground red pepper
½ teaspoon salt substitute
2 teaspoons cinnamon
½ teaspoon nutmeg
1 teaspoon ginger
1 teaspoon vanilla extract
¼ cup lemon juice
1 cup seedless golden raisins
1 can (14 ounces) sweetened condensed
    milk
1 can (19 ounces) Musselman® Apple
    Pie Filling
2 (9") pie crusts, bottoms and tops

Nutrition Facts

Nutrition Facts
Apple Collard Raisin Pie
per serving ⅛ pie
makes 16 servings

Amount per serving	
Calories	202
Calories from fat	42

	% Daily Value *
Total Fat 4.8g	7%
Saturated Fat 2.6g	13%
Cholesterol 8mg	3%
Sodium 94mg	4%
Total Carbohydrate 36.4g	12%
Dietary Fiber 2.3g	9%
Protein 3.5g	

Percent values are based on a 2,000-calorie per day diet. Your daily values may differ.

Additional Information
20.8% of calories from Fat
72.2% from Carbohydrates
6.9% from Protein

Preparation

- Preheat the oven to 350°F.
- Bake the bottom crust 5 minutes and set aside.
- Sauté the collards in the oil.
- Add the water and all seasonings
- Add the raisins and cook 2 more minutes.
- Stir in the milk and apples.
- Cook until the mix is warm throughout.
- Place half the filling in each piecrust, cover, and bake about 30 minutes or until the piecrust is brown.

Equipment/Utensils

Large cooking pot

Cherry Chocolate Cake

Include collards for a chocolate, chocolate, chocolate cake. A smidgeon of collards liquefied with coffee intensifies the chocolate flavor.

Cake

Ingredients

Non-stick cooking spray
½ cup strong brewed coffee
⅓ cup chopped fresh tender collards
¼ pound unsalted butter
1 teaspoon almond extract
1 teaspoon vanilla extract
3 eggs
¾ cups water
1 (18¼-ounce) chocolate cake mix (Such as Super Moist® Devil's Food)

Preparation

- Spray the cooking pan. Preheat the oven to 350°.
- Blend the warm coffee, collards, and butter in the blender until the collards are liquefied, the coffee is cool, and the butter is melted. Add the eggs and mix them in the blender.
- Combine all the ingredients except the pie filling and mix until smooth.
- Stir the pie filling into the cake batter until it is dispersed throughout the mix.
- Pour the cake batter into the cake pan.
- Bake until the cake pulls away from the sides. Insert a toothpick to check for doneness.

Frosting

Ingredients

1 (15-ounce) container chocolate frosting (Betty Crocker Pour and Frost® or other)
1 cup toasted, finely chopped mixed nuts (such as almonds and pecans)

Preparation

- While the cake is warm, mix approximately ½ cup or frosting with the nuts and spread it over the cake.
- When the cake cools, apply the remaining frosting according to package instructions.

Equipment/Utensils

9 X 13 X 2" glass cake pan • Blender • Mixer • Mixing bowl • Spatula or large flat knife to spread frosting

Christmas Cake

Ingredients

Non-stick cooking spray
½ cup self-rising flour
1 cup grated fresh apples
1 cup grated fresh carrots
1 cup finely chopped frozen collards
2 tablespoons lemon juice
2 cups candied red cherries
1 cup candied green cherries
½ cup chopped candied pineapple
1 yellow cake mix with pudding
3 eggs
⅓ cup cooking oil
½ cup gold rum
1 can coconut pecan frosting

Preparation

- Preheat the oven to 350°F.
- Prepare the cake pan by spraying it and lightly dusting flour on it.
- Pour the lemon juice on the apples, carrots, and collards. Set aside.
- Coat the cherries and pineapple in the remaining flour. Set aside.
- In a large bowl combine the cake mix, eggs, oil, and rum. Beat until smooth.
- Add the apples, carrots, and collards. Continue to stir. Add the candied fruit. Stir lightly.
- Pour the batter into the prepared pan.
- Bake 1 hour or until a knife inserted into the middle of the cake comes out clean and the edges of the cake pull away from the sides of the pan.
- Remove the cake and cool it on a rack in the pan.
- Spread the frosting on top.

Equipment/Utensils

9 X 13 X 2" cake pan • Mixing bowls

Note about Sweetheart Cake on Next Page

One of the most entertaining aspects of developing recipes and experimenting with food ideas is watching people's reactions. Combining foods that are not usually served together often results in pleasurable gastronomic experiences.

When a group of unsuspecting women were served Sweetheart Cake, they ate it with enthusiasm. All but one of the 15 women who tried it ate all of it. One left half on her plate. None of them asked, "What's in this cake?"

Sweetheart Cake

Sweetheart cake is a chocolate cake with exotic inclusions. You will taste the chocolate, the coffee, and the mincemeat. You will not taste the collards. The sharpness of the coffee and the collards balance the sweetness.

Ingredients

Cake
1 Duncan Hines® dark chocolate cake mix
½ cup toasted pecans
1 jar (11 ounces) Fischer and Wieser® mincemeat
1 cup strong brewed black coffee
½ cup frozen chopped collards
¼ pound unsalted butter
1 teaspoon cinnamon
3 large eggs
2 teaspoons vanilla extract

Frosting
1 package prepared Duncan Hines® chocolate fudge frosting
1 cup toasted pecans, finely chopped
⅓ cup candied red cherries

Preparation
- Preheat the oven to 350°. Prepare a pan by spraying it with non-stick cooking spray.
- Place 3 tablespoons of the dry cake mix in a small bowl. Add the toasted pecans and the mincemeat. Set this part aside.
- Add the butter and collards to the hot coffee. When the ingredients are cooled enough to blend, pour them into the blender; blend, and keep blending until the butter is creamed and the collards are liquefied. You don't want anyone to suspect you've added the collards, although you will create a depth of taste to the cake you would not otherwise have.
- Place the cake mix in a large bowl. Stir in the cinnamon. Add the eggs and the contents of the blender. Beat until the cake is very thoroughly mixed. Stir the vanilla into the mix.
- Add the contents of the small bowl. Stir until all the ingredients are moistened and mixed well.
- Pour the ingredients into the cake pan. Be sure that the mix, which will be thick, is spread evenly in the pan.
- Bake until a toothpick inserted in the middle comes out clean and the edges start to pull away from the sides.
- Turn the cake onto a pretty platter and allow it to cool.
- Cover with the frosting. You will have a thick layer. Cover the top with pecans. Slice the cherries in half and scatter them over the top.

Serve the cake in small squares because it is rich.

You Must Taste These Brownies

These are delicious. Here are some comments from those who have eaten them:

You won't know the greens are there, but there is a depth of taste with a little less sweetness than usual.

The collards add a delightful element, which reduces the cloying of the sugar without affecting the chocolate flavor.

Ingredients

Cooking spray
5 tablespoons cool brewed coffee (Some
    leftover coffee will be fine.)
1 stick (4 ounces) margarine
1 cup fresh collard leaves (You need a
    loosely-packed cup of raw greens, not
    too many.)
2 medium eggs
1 package (21.2 ounces) Betty Crocker ®
    Walnut Chocolate Chunk Supreme
    Brownie Mix with Mini Kisses® &
    Walnuts

Preparation

- Preheat oven to 350°F.
- Spray the cooking pan.
- Blend the coffee, margarine, collard leaves, and eggs until the collards are totally smooth.
- Add the blended ingredients to the brownie mix.
- Place in the cooking pan and bake as directed.

Nutrition Facts	
Brownies, Per serving makes 20 servings	
Amount per serving	
Calories	179
Calories from fat	75
	% Daily Value *
Total Fat 8.2g	13%
Saturated Fat 1.5g	8%
Cholesterol 19 mg	6%
Sodium 144 mg	6%
Total Carbohydrate 24.2g	8%
Dietary Fiber 1.1g	4%
Protein 1.7g	

Percent values are based on a 2,000-calorie per day diet. Your daily values may differ.

Additional Information
42% of calories from Fat
54.2% from Carbohydrates
3.8% from Protein

Equipment/Utensils

Cooking pan of choice (See package.) • Blender • Mixing bowl

About Chocolate

Chocolate comes from cocoa beans, which are almond-shaped beans that grow on cacao trees in the tropical areas. The beans are fermented, dried and baked to release their flavor.

Collards for Fun
Dance to the Beat of Your Own Drum

Foxy's Biscotti

Foxy, the standard poodle, is a picky eater, but she loves her new treats. When she hears her biscotti canister being rattled, she runs to me and does all her tricks without being prompted. She has started shaking hands to earn these.

Ingredients

3 cups chopped fresh collards
1 cup nonfat dry milk
1 can (14.75 ounces) salmon including liquid
1 teaspoon baking soda
1 block fish bouillon in 1 cup water
2 eggs
2 tablespoons bacon drippings
1 cup all-purpose flour
2 cups cornmeal mix
1 cup oatmeal
1 teaspoon baking soda
2 teaspoons salt
Non-stick cooking spray

Preparation

- Mix the first 7 ingredients in the blender.
- Mix the next 5 ingredients in a mixing bowl.
- Combine all the ingredients except the spray.
- Drop by tablespoonfuls in sprayed muffin tins. Bake 45 minutes at 300°.
- Remove from the muffin tins and place them on a rack.
- Cut each biscotto in half.
- Place them on a cookie sheet and cook them at 200° until they are dry and hard.

Equipment/Utensils

Blender • Mixing bowl • Muffin tins with small cups • Cooling rack

Notes

- Regarding Foxy's special treats, a cyber friend, wrote, "Won't your pup have 'involuntary' biological imperatives?" So far, Foxy has not had a problem.
- I recommend that you store the biscotti sealed because of the strong odor (delightful to dogs).

Cornbread
The Perfect Complement To Collards

Fresh Corn-Cornbread

Ingredients

3 cups yellow cornmeal
1 cup all purpose flour
6 tablespoons sugar (or Splenda® sweetener)
2 tablespoons baking powder
4 eggs, lightly whisked
1 teaspoon salt

1 cup milk
1 cup non-fat plain yogurt
¼ cup melted butter
¼ cup vegetable oil
2 cups fresh-grated corn kernels plus cream from the corn cobs (see method below)
(Optional) Crisp, Crumbled bacon from 4 strips

Preparation

- Heat oven to 400º. Grease a 14 X 8" baking pan.
- Combine all dry ingredients in one large bowl.
- In another bowl, combine milk, yogurt, melted butter, oil and eggs.
- Add the wet ingredients to the cornmeal mixture until just combined. Do NOT beat.
- Stir in the fresh-cut creamed corn. (See method below.)
- (Optional) Add the crumbled bacon, blend slightly and pour batter into baking pan.
- Bake till golden brown, about 20-25 minutes. Serves 10-12 people.

Method for Creaming Fresh Corn

You will need approximately 8 corncobs.
- Wash corncob well, removing silk. Use a wide, bowl for this step.
- Hold the stalk of the corncob so that it is in a standing position. Hold firmly.
- With a sharp knife, scrape down the sides of the cob, from top edge to bottom all around the stalk or cob, cutting only the outside edge of the kernel, to save the milk.
- After the entire stalk—or cob has been cut this way, then take the knife and scrape hard down the sides from top to bottom, to extract the rich cream.
- Repeat this until you can measure 2 cups of the fresh, creamed corn.

Carolyn Forche`

Carolyn's Quick Cornbread

- For a short-cut version, use 3 cups Aunt Jemima® cornmeal mix.
- Add no other dry ingredients except 3 tablespoons sugar or Splenda®.
- Instead of fresh corn you may elect to use canned cream corn, but don't expect the same flavor or texture.

Carolyn Forche`

Memories of the Mill Cornbread

This recipe is for real cornbread, not that sweet, like-cake cornbread, but REAL CORNBREAD. It is rich, coarse, crunchy, and oh, so satisfying!

- Put 2 tablespoons bacon drippings or shortening in a cast iron skillet in 400° oven.
- Mix 2 cups Prater's Mill Fresh Milled Cornmeal.
- 2 teaspoons baking powder, 1 teaspoon soda, 1 teaspoon salt, 1 tablespoon honey (or a little more if you are like me which is optional), 1 tablespoon wheat germ (to satisfy my health nut cravings in light of the bacon, optional) 1 egg, and enough buttermilk to moisten well, about 1 good cup).
- Batter should be thick. Add the heated shortening you have melted in the iron skillet while preparing the batter, and pour into batter, stirring while it sizzles.
- Put batter into heated skillet and bake in 400° oven 25-35 minutes, or until a crispy golden brown.

Enjoy with lots of REAL butter and more honey, or anything else you like, and if you are really adventurous, dip it into a glass of cold milk!

Jane Galay, Connecting Women and the Arts OnLine 423-478-3072
http://www.NetworkingEveryWoman.com,
Jane@NetworkingEveryWoman.com/PratersMill

Memories of the Mill

Years ago, on the back side of "Hippie Days", I landed in a huge, old, red brick house with nine slat-board rooms and a wrap-around porch. Locals called it then, just as they do now, "The Old Prater's House." You can find it today not far from the absolutely tiny town of Varnell, north of Dalton, just a little ways down on Georgia Highway 2. To my wonder, this charming and historic home became my special place and space for fresh new adventures and warm, fond memories, specially wrapped in New Beginnings.

I was privileged in the early 70's to become the recipient of some good, old "TSH." Should you not know, "Transplant Southern Hospitality" occurs when people are transplanted from the North, or from some of those other states west of the Mississippi, to become radical carriers themselves, of the great warmth found locally in our Southern communities. Astoundingly, these transplants begin opening their homes and inviting even strangers in, sharing their meals in like manner.

We were so graced, my boyfriend and I, when living up in the Detroit area to be invited for Thanksgiving by some folks just transplanted from Michigan. This particular group of old friends, old for us as we were only in our 20's then, together with a few local residents, sported several painters, potters, a printmaker, and some ordinarily gifted others. We were all linked in some fashion to what was known as the Michigan Artrain.

The Michigan Artrain was, and still is as far as I know, an actual six-car train, doubling as a mobile museum; gallery and studio, filled with slide and film presentations. I am sure by now it is updated, having gone digital. As a National Endowment of the Arts tour, it carried breathtaking Art, as in FINE ART, not to be confused with Arts and Crafts, mind you. We opened our Southern tour in Dalton, Georgia, and then had some "down time" weeks later at the Chattanooga Choo Choo, Tennessee.

It was a fantastic experience for one coming from Kansas, as myself. We toured the eight Rocky Mountain States, the state of Michigan, and six of our lovely Southern States, with all expenses paid and an hourly wage. So privileged we were to share our cultural wealth and passion with rural area communities, which otherwise may not have been able to see up close what we lived amid daily. I was the demonstrating potter, the last "exhibit" on the tour, just before the all red, inside and out, famous Caboose. It was a joyful day, reminiscing over turkey!

After eighteen months with the Artrain, long ten-to-twelve hour days and seven-to-ten day stops at a time, we all came to a place of burnout, where we had had enough, and so off we got. Georgia's land, the space, and the beauty had impressed us. Overall though, I think it was the genteel manners and kind, loving treatment we had received from those connected to The Mill, which really drew us back. Well, yes, and the opportunity to turn the Old Mill Store into a studio with living quarters at a more than affordable price. This truly was the incredible plus.

What a Thanksgiving it was! I'll never forget how we took a short walk after ingesting our huge banquet, served on makeshift tables and consumed within ancient walls of the "Old Prater's Store." Just across the bridge covering the Coahulla Creek and down the road was "The Old Prater's House." Little did I know how that short walk would alter my future forever, enriching me in deeper ways than words could ever express.

There we were, our motley crew of long hairs and bell-bottoms, overalls and maybe a long skirt or two, ambling down the highway in a somewhat straight line. We were enjoying full stomachs, sunlight, and our renewed friendships, off to see this unique landmark. "She" was being emptied of her contents, as she had just failed as a restaurant. Welcomed was opportunity to go peruse what we could, excited that we could even get in.

While approaching the house, we had to pass under a great oak tree having survived the last war, the Civil War, which has remained in the front yard to this day. The moment I really saw "her" was just before we turned in to pass under this tree. What I saw was everything lovely to me. I said to myself, "I am going to live there!" Seven weeks later, I did, which is a whole 'nother story.

As I said, my life took a radical change that day. The Old Prater's House became my real home, and it was wonderful living there! My first clay studio filled the pantry, an added-on room in the back. I walked the 500 adjoining acres as best I could, watched beavers slapping their tails on the dark Coahulla Creek water late at night, and got my tongue stung when I almost swallowed a wasp hidden in a Coke can one morning following an all-night kiln firing. I had my first taste of okra and collard greens, and I learned from the locals that all you needed for dinner was milk and cornbread. I fell in love with orange tiger lilies, knew when spring was coming by the spring peepers' croaking. I caught butterflies and lightning bugs, shot firecrackers, and started a field afire. I learned my neighbors' names for once, because they never moved the whole time I lived there. I also saved a chicken that fell off a ConAgra's truck and named her, "Buck-Buck." She finally disappeared into a circle of feathers when a fox got her.

Yes, I had many new adventures, and lots of fun and fond, fond memories, but the best of all came February 4, 1979. That was the most memorable morning I have ever had. At 4:30 am, right there in my bedroom, where I could feel the draft through the wallboards and the heat from my woodstove, I was born again, just like Jesus said I needed to be. Whether you call it being saved, trusting Jesus, God's only Son, meeting your Master or simply inviting Him into your heart to become your own, that is exactly what I did. Surprised, I'd be not, if those old walls could talk and say "I was not the first." From that point forward, reality's Truth has gripped my heart and everything pales in comparison.

From that point forward, only one other beginning stands head and shoulders above all others. It was four months later: I married that boyfriend, becoming his wife by another big tree, our Marriage Tree. This is the one you can still see, standing faithfully by the Coahulla Creek, formed by two trees growing into one. That was our goal, June 3, 1979, so there is where we started, and that's a whole 'nother story, again.

So, what does this have to do with cornbread?

What else, besides wheat, would you grind in a gristmill? Where else would you put a gristmill, but by a free-flowing creek? Where would you want your store to be placed to sell your corn, and where would you like to build your house so it could be close to your gristmill? Last, but not least, what would you bake for breakfast, lunch, or dinner in that house for those you loved?

Your answers are probably just like Benjamin Franklin Prater's and wife, Amanda, after he and his partner, T.H. Pitner, built the gristmill on the Coahulla Creek.

Surprise! Every second weekend in May and October, we would be swamped with people in our front yard, backyard, and side yard, all the way down to the Mill, for the most wonderful, family-friendly jaunt through history. The Mill was becoming one of our nation's most outstanding arts and crafts fairs, now noted in the *National Geographic* as the Prater's Mill Country Fair. All these people were flooding into the Mill for the very same reasons we did—good food and wholesome fellowship. This fair is Southern Hospitality at its best with plenty of quilts, fishing, clogging, fiddlin', funnel cakes, and best of all; the best ever, really good, *cornmeal*, still ground by the old water-powered Mill!

I remember when someone first asked me, "Have you gone to the FIRE yet?" "What fire?" I said. "No, No, the Fire!"

I finally figured out that they were saying, "Fair!"

The Mill celebrated its 150th anniversary in 2005, being first established in 1855 by the Praters. Prater's Mill is now on the National Register of Historic Places, as is my beloved Prater's House. If ever you are in the area during fair time, make sure you buy some of the fresh, ground cornmeal, and *please* make this cornbread! You, too, will have some unforgettable, "Memories of the Mill" Cornbread, so you can say with me, "Taste and see, that the Lord is Good!" Jane Galay, http://www.NetworkingEveryWoman.com

Cheryl's Hot-Water Cornbread

- Place approximately 1 cup of cornmeal and a teaspoon of salt or 1 cup of cornmeal mix into a bowl.
- Pour approximately ½ cup boiling water over the mix. The mix should be firm.
- Stir well.
- Shape by hand. (To avoid burns, wet hands with cool water before picking up batter.)
- Fry in hot oil.
- Turn when one side is a little brown.
- Remove from oil when the other side is brown.

Cheryl Sowers

The following account will clarify any questions about the procedure.

When Cheryl Sowers stopped by to visit, I told her that I was planning to serve collards for supper.

Cheryl asked, "Are you going to make hot water cornbread?"

"No, I don't know how." I hated to admit my ignorance.

"Let me make you some. I'll teach you how to do it."

She poured cooking oil about two inches deep into a big heavy skillet. Then she filled a saucepan with water. "Get the water and the grease real hot. I mean the water has to be boiling."

Cheryl continued, "I usually use white cornmeal with a little salt. If I don't have any cornmeal, I'll use white cornmeal mix."

I asked, "Could you use yellow cornmeal mix? That's all I have."

"Yeah, that'll do. Anything will work." Cheryl poured about one cup of cornmeal mix into a bowl.

"Will that be enough?" (Paul was planning to eat supper with me.)

Cheryl poured another cup of cornmeal mix into the bowl. "Now, turn on the cold water," she said. "I'll need to mix it over here by the sink." She poured hot water into the cornmeal mix. "Pour just enough to make it firm and smooth."

"You don't want it mushy, do you?"

"No, you don't want to let it get soupy," Cheryl said as she stirred quickly.

"My mama makes hers in round patties, but I make long pods," Cheryl said as she wet her hands in cold water and rolled an elliptical mass of cornmeal mix and water in her hands. "Come on. You try it."

I shape my cakes in tubes.

Cheryl dropped the smooth cakes into hot crackling cooking oil. When the bottoms were golden brown, she turned them. "My mother-in-law cooks hers until they are dark brown," she told me. When they were brown on both sides, she placed them on paper towels and blotted them.

"It's time to go pick up my boys at Mama's," Cheryl said, as she rushed away.

Paul said the hot water cornbread was wonderful.

Patricia's Hot-Water Cornbread

Hot water cornbread is a popular north Louisiana food, eaten with Southern style vegetables, such as collards, turnip greens, and field peas. Patricia's instructions are slightly different from Cheryl's.

Ingredients

4 cups water
2 cups cornmeal (yellow or white)
2 teaspoons salt
(Sugar may also be added for sweeter bread.)

Preparation

Boil the water. Then add the cornmeal and salt to the water. Stir until all the lumps are gone. Mold into patties and fry in 1" of hot vegetable oil until brown on both sides.

Patricia Squyres

Equipment/Utensils

Kettle • Bowl • Skillet

Patricia's Note

My mother made the cornbread with her handprint pressed into the patties. As a child, I thought eating the bread with her handprint was such a treat. She served it with macaroni and cheese, pinto beans, and yams.

Radical Revelation

Years ago a lady who was the chief cook for one of the most prominent families in Ruston, Louisiana, told me her secret ingredient in her hot water cornbread. Everyone raves about its lightness!

It's a secret. Don't tell a soul, and don't read *this* aloud.

But since you are reading this book, I'll tell you….

She slips a little baking powder into her hot water cornbread batter! It puffs just a breath of air into it. Imagine that!

Mary Lou

Black-Eyed Pea Cornbread

Ingredients

1 cup cornmeal
½ cup flour
1 teaspoon salt
½ teaspoon baking soda
¾ cup cream-style corn
1 pound ground turkey, cooked and drained
      (You may substitute ground beef or sausage.)
2 eggs
1 cup buttermilk
½ cup oil
1 medium onion, chopped
½ pound grated cheese
1 can drained black-eyed peas with peppers

Preparation

Mix well and bake in a greased 9 X 13" pan at 425° for 40 to 50 minutes until done.

Patricia Squires

Patricia Squires is a member of First Baptist Church of Simsboro, Louisiana. She enjoys cooking for the women's meetings and church functions, as well as for her family.

She has been the director of the church childcare center and preschool since 1989, when she and her husband, Sam, were instrumental in starting the program. She cooks hot meals daily for 45 children. Good nutrition is very important for the growth of the children, ages 6 weeks to 12 years, enrolled in the center.

She enjoys seeing the children eat the food because she knows it will help them grow strong and healthy bodies and minds.

About Black-Eyed Peas

A few black-eyed pea notes:
- Black-eyed peas are a staple in Southern diets.
- Many people eat black-eyed peas on New Year's Day for luck.
- Black-eyed peas are members of the mung bean family.
- Each pea has a small black dot, which remains visible after cooking.
- Black-eyed peas are noted for their full flavor.
- One cup of cooked black-eyed peas has 18 grams fiber.
- In the soup section (p. 158), there is an excellent recipe for Hoppin' John Collard Soup by Dorothy Reinhold, Director of Cut 'n Clean Greens® Test Kitchen.

Holiday Muffins

You can serve these muffins any time of day. Your guests will enjoy these unique multi-grain, fruity, spicy muffins.

Because these muffins are rich and sweet, they will stay moist while they are stored in an airtight container in the refrigerator or freezer.

The yield and cooking time will vary because of the variety of cup sizes of muffin tins.

Ingredients

Non-stick cooking spray
1 (8½-ounce) Jiffy® package corn
   muffin mix
1 cup all purpose flour
1 cup quick-cooking oatmeal
1 teaspoon baking powder
½ teaspoon salt substitute
1 teaspoon cinnamon
½ teaspoon ginger
½ teaspoon nutmeg
⅓ cup chopped English walnuts
½ cup chopped dates
½ cup raisins
1 cup light sour cream
½ cup canola oil
2 tablespoons honey
3 eggs, beaten
¼ cup water

Nutrition Facts	
Holiday Muffin, per serving Makes 18 servings	
Amount per serving	
Calories	231
Calories from fat	91
% Daily Value *	
Total Fat 10.1g	16%
Saturated Fat 2.5g	12%
Cholesterol 40 mg	13%
Sodium 149 mg	6%
Total Carbohydrate 30.3g	10%
Dietary Fiber 1.8g	7%
Protein 4.8g	

Percent values are based on a 2,000-calorie per day diet. Your daily values may differ.

Additional Information
39.3% of calories from Fat
52.4% from Carbohydrates
8.3% from Protein

Preparation

- Spray the muffin tins and preheat the oven to 400°.
- Mix the dry ingredients, including the spices.
- Stir the fruit and nuts into the mix to coat them.
- Add the remaining ingredients and stir until all the mixture is moistened.
- Spoon the mixture into the muffin tins and bake until the muffins are golden brown or until an inserted toothpick comes out clean, about 15-20 minutes.
- Use paper liners if you prefer.
- Allow the muffins to cool a couple of minutes before removing them. If necessary, circle the muffins with a knife before removing them.
- Serve the muffins hot.

Equipment/Utensils

Muffin tins • Bowl • Whisk

Cherry Jalapeño Muffins

Stir up a batch of these colorful muffins, inspired by Terry Chrisman's Christmas Muffin recipe, to serve with barbecue or at a holiday brunch.

The unique blend of sweet and hot flavors with texture contrasts will intrigue your guests.

Also, the presentation is spectacular. The number of muffins will, of course, depend on the size muffin tins you use.

Ingredients

½ cup candied red cherries
½ cup candied green cherries
¾ cup Original Peachtree Schnapps®
½ cup golden raisins
Non-stick cooking spray
1½ cups all-purpose flour
2 eggs
½ cup (2% fat) milk
1 tablespoon lemon juice
1 (8½-ounce) Jiffy® package corn muffin mix
2 teaspoons baking powder
½ teaspoon salt or salt substitute
½ teaspoon cinnamon
½ teaspoon nutmeg
½ teaspoon ginger
½ cup (1 stick) unsalted butter, melted and cooled
A slice of pickled jalapeño for each muffin

Preparation

- Place the cherries in a pint jar and pour the Schnapps® over them. Marinate them covered in the refrigerator overnight.
- Add the raisins 1 hour before cooking time
- Drain the Schnapps® into a mixing bowl. Whisk the eggs, milk, lemon juice and butter with the Schnapps®.
- Dredge the cherries and raisins in ¼ cup flour.
- Preheat the oven to 350°.
- Spray the muffin tins.
- Stir the remaining flour, corn muffin mix, and other dry ingredients together. Add the liquid ingredients and stir until the batter is thoroughly blended.
- Add the cherries.
- Spoon the muffin mix into the cups of the muffin tins.
- Bake about 20 minutes or until the muffins are golden brown and a toothpick inserted comes out clean.

Continued

- Allow the muffins to sit for 2 minutes. Loosen the muffins with a knife and transfer them to a plate.
- Cover the muffins with plastic wrap until serving time.

Equipment/Utensils
Pint jar with lid• Muffin Tins • Bowls • Whisk

Serving Suggestion
Serve these muffins with one of the pretty collard salads or with sweet, spicy barbecue.

Variations
- Use red cherries for Independence Day or Valentine's Day.
- Use green ones for St. Patrick's Day.
- If you prefer, omit the jalapeño slices.
- Try stirring 2 tablespoons chopped candied jalapeños instead of placing peppers on top.
- Terry marinates cherries in wine.

Candied Jalapeños

Candied jalapeños are very easy to prepare. Incidentally, they go well with collards.

- Fill a jar with pickled jalapeño slices, which have been drained.
- Heat equal parts of cider vinegar and white sugar until the sugar dissolves. Stir the vinegar-sugar mixture constantly and do not allow it to boil.
  (Caution: Avoid breathing the fumes of this pungent mixture. It will burn your nostrils.)
- Pour the vinegar and sugar mixture over the pickles.
- After they cool, place a lid on them and leave them in the refrigerator a few days.

Suggestion
Add sweet pineapple chunks or maraschino cherries to the peppers. Place them in a pretty jar and give them to your friends.

Three Reasons to Eat Hot Pepper
- Research shows that capsaicin, the chemical in hot pepper that makes the pepper hot, prevents prostate cancer in rats.
- There's a theory that hot pepper stimulates the digestive system and is therefore helpful, not harmful to digestion.
- Hot foods are more filling than milder ones. Eating something that is spicy and hot requires extra time to eat. Slowing the rate of consuming food satisfies appetites.

The taste for hot pepper is acquired. The more hot pepper you eat the more you'll enjoy it until you reach the amount you like. We all seem to have different tolerance levels for heat in our food.

Macaroni Bread

The first day we talked about writing this book, Paul said, "Try making macaroni bread," I could not believe my ears! I am glad I took his advice. He has a good imagination.

Add the red pepper as you wish.

Ingredients

¼ cup (½ stick) unsalted butter
1 cup chopped red onion
1½ cups extra sharp shredded cheddar cheese
2 cups leftover cold macaroni (prepared according to package instructions)
2 teaspoon lemon juice
1 (8½-ounce) Jiffy® package corn muffin mix
½ teaspoon baking soda
⅛ to ½ teaspoon ground red pepper
2 eggs, beaten
½ cup milk
Non-stick cooking spray

Preparation

- Preheat the oven to 400°.
- Sauté the chopped onions in the butter for about 3 minutes.
- Lightly toss the cheese, macaroni, and lemon juice.
- In another bowl add the baking soda and red pepper to the muffin mix. Stir.
- Stir the eggs and milk into the dry ingredients.
- Spray and preheat he baking pan.
- Add the cheese-macaroni mix to the batter. Stir just enough to mix the ingredients. Do not continue to stir until the ingredients are indistinct.
- Spoon and smooth the mixture into the baking pan, spray the top with cooking spray.
- Bake until a knife, fork, or toothpick inserted in the middle comes out clean, the corners are crusty, and the house smells delightful.

Equipment/Utensils

8" square baking pan • 2 or 3 Mixing bowls • Whisk

Nutrition

If you really want to know about this bread, send me an e-mail. Plan to meet me at the gym.

Halogar Cheese Muffins

All the flavors of garlic, jalapeños, cheddar, corn bread, and biscuits muffined together smell and taste wonderful. Nothing stands out more than anything else. Those who omit ingredients cheat their taste buds.

Ingredients

Non-stick cooking spray
1 package (6 ounces) country biscuit mix
1 package (8½ ounces) Jiffy® corn
  muffin mix
2 tablespoons chopped garlic
2 tablespoons chopped pickled
  jalapeños
1 cup Fat Free Half & Half®
3 eggs
1 cup (4 ounces) sharp cheddar, grated

Preparation

- Preheat oven to 425°F. Spray and preheat the muffin tin. (Don't heat it until it smokes or burns.)
- Reserve ½ cup of the cheese, mix the flour, 1 teaspoon garlic powder, the baking powder, and the baking soda.
- Mix all the ingredients except half the cheese.
- Bake till the muffins are golden.
- Sprinkle the remaining cheese over the muffins.
- Serve hot.

Nutrition Facts	
Halogar Cheese Muffins, Per serving Makes 12 servings	
Amount per serving	
Calories	218
Calories from fat	82
	% Daily Value *
Total Fat 9.2g	14%
Saturated Fat 4.1g	20%
Cholesterol 63 mg	21%
Sodium 502 mg	21%
Total Carbohydrate 27g	9%
Dietary Fiber 0.3g	1%
Protein 7.1g	

Percent values are based on a 2,000-calorie per day diet. Your daily values may differ.

Additional Information
37.5% of calories from Fat
49.5% from Carbohydrates
13% from Protein

Equipment/Utensils

Grater • Muffin tin with 12 medium cups

Note

Jiffy® corn muffin mix is sweeter than some other brands.

Cracklin' Bread

Ingredients

Non-stick cooking spray
2 eggs
⅔ cup Fat Free Half & Half®
2 packages (8½ ounces each) Jiffy® corn muffin mix
2 cups cracklin's

Preparation

- Preheat oven to 400°F.
- Spray and heat the baking pan as the oven heats.
- Whisk the eggs and Half & Half®.
- Add the muffin mix and the cracklin's.
- Pour the mix into the hot pan.
- Bake until an inserted toothpick comes out clean (20-25 minutes).

Equipment/Utensils

8" square baking pan• Mixing bowl • Whisk

About Eggs

Buying and storing eggs:
- Select eggs that are clean and free of shell cracks while in the carton.
- Buy refrigerated eggs.
- Store eggs in the refrigerator.

Good uses of eggs:
- Eggs are valuable in cornbread.
- Eggs go well in collard dishes.
- Collards and eggs are compatible in soufflés.
- Boiled eggs are a good complement to a basic collard dish.

Hominy-Tomato-Collard Cornbread

Topped with extra sauce and cheese, the cornbread becomes a meal.

Ingredients

Non-stick cooking spray
1 thick slice bacon
½ cup finely chopped fresh collard
    leaves
½ cup chopped onions
1 tablespoon lime juice
1 can (15½ ounces) hominy
2 cups Martha White® yellow cornbread
    mix
1 cup all purpose flour
1 teaspoon baking powder
½ teaspoon salt substitute
2 medium eggs
4 tablespoons unsalted butter
3 tablespoons Splenda®
1 cup sun-dried tomato sauce
1 cup (2%) milk
2 ounces grated Monterey Jack cheese

Nutrition Facts

Nutrition Facts	
Hominy –Tomato-Collard Cornbread Per serving Makes 15 servings	
Amount per serving	
Calories	207
Calories from fat	70
% Daily Value *	
Total Fat 7.7g	12%
Saturated Fat 3.5g	18%
Cholesterol 40mg	13%
Sodium 435mg	18%
Total Carbohydrate 28.6g	10%
Dietary Fiber 2.6g	10%
Protein 5.6g	

Percent values are based on a 2,000-calorie per day diet. Your daily values may differ.

Additional Information
33.8% of calories from Fat
55.3% from Carbohydrates
10.8% from Protein

Preparation

- Preheat oven to 375°F.
- Sauté the bacon, chopped collard leaves and onions 5 minutes. Spray the baking dish and place it in the oven.
- In the blender combine half the hominy with its liquid , eggs, butter, sweetener, and tomato sauce. Blend until smooth. Add the collard-onion mixture. Blend until the collards are in small flecks.
- Check on that baking pan!
- Combine the dry ingredients in the mixing bowl. Add the blended ingredients, the hominy, and the cheese. Mix thoroughly. Spoon the batter into the baking pan.
- Bake 25 minutes or until golden brown. Cool slightly; cut into 15 squares.

Equipment/Utensils

- Skillet • 9 X 13 X 2" baking dish • Blender • Mixing bowl

Sour Cream Soft Bread

This simple dish is so good that I shudder when I think about it! As I add this recipe to the book, there's a strong temptation to run into the kitchen, pull the leftover portion out of the refrigerator, and do something I would regret later.

Cook a batch of it for your guests! They'll go out of their orbits.

Ingredients

Non-stick cooking spray
1 pound frozen corn, whole kernels
10 ounces Green Giant® cream-style corn
1 (8½-ounce) Jiffy® package corn muffin mix
2 cups sour cream
½ cup (1 stick) butter, melted
1 cup (4 ounces) shredded cheddar

Preparation

- Spray the cooking pan.
- Melt the butter and thaw the cream-style corn together in the microwave oven.
- In a large bowl, stir together the corn, corn muffin mix, sour cream, and melted butter.
- Pour into the cooking pan. Bake for 45 minutes at 350°F or until golden brown. Remove from oven and top with cheddar.
- Return to oven for 5 minutes or until cheese is melted.
- Serve warm.

Nutrition Facts	
Sour Cream Soft Bread, per serving Makes 18 servings	
Amount per serving	
Calories	174
Calories from fat	120
	% Daily Value *
Total Fat 13.3g	20%
Saturated Fat 8g	40%
Cholesterol 33 mg	11%
Sodium 108 mg	4%
Total Carbohydrate 9.6g	3%
Dietary Fiber 0.6g	2%
Protein 3.8g	
Percent values are based on a 2,000-calorie per day diet. Your daily values may differ.	
Additional Information 69.1% of calories from Fat 22.1% from Carbohydrates 8.8% from Protein	

Equipment/Utensils

3-quart (13 X 9 X 2") Pyrex® baking dish • Mixing bowl • Grater

Trail Mix Muffins

Add a cup of trail mix (chop the large pieces as needed) to dry corn muffin mix and prepare according to package directions.

Fifth Sunday Muffins

Something different, something surprising—that's what these muffins are. The taste may remind you of sausage balls. There's a little spiciness and a little sweetness. These muffins are great with collards, suitable to take to a part after a fifth-Sunday-night sing, delicious with honey.

Ingredients

Non-fat butter-flavored cooking spray
1 can (12 ounces) Treet® lunchmeat
6 ounces Colby cheese
1 cup self-rising flour
1 cup finely chopped walnuts (ground in the blender)
1 cup self-rising flour
2 tablespoons light brown sugar
1 teaspoon cumin
Tiny dash salt
2 or 3 shakes ground red pepper
1 (8½-ounce) Jiffy® package corn muffin mix
1 tablespoon spicy brown prepared mustard
1 tablespoon lemon juice
1 tablespoon minced garlic
3 large eggs
¾ cup evaporated milk
Non-fat butter-flavored cooking spray

Preparation

- Preheat the oven to 350°F and spray the muffin tins.
- Grate the lunchmeat and cheese.
- Place the walnuts in the blender and grind them until they resemble coarse meal. Measure them after they are ground. Place the lunchmeat, cheese, walnuts, flour, sugar, cumin, salt, and red pepper in the mixing bowl. Stir them until the seasonings are dispersed throughout the mix and the ingredients are coated. Add the corn muffin mix.
- Add the remaining ingredients and stir until everything is moistened.
- Spoon the mixture into the muffin tins. Bake until the edges are brown and remove the muffins. You may need to slide a thin knife around the edges.

Yield: 48 muffins

Equipment/Utensils

Muffin tins with small cups • Grater • Mixing bowl • Measuring cups and spoons

Mincemeat Cheese Muffins

Paul and the ladies in my Bible study group raved about these muffin

Ingredients

Non-stick cooking spray
1 (5½-ounce) Bisquick® package All-
    Purpose Baking Mix (or 1⅓ cup)
1 jar (11 ounces) Tiptree® Mincemeat
2 eggs
½ cup (2% fat) milk
1 tablespoon lemon juice
4 ounces (1 cup) extra sharp grated
    Cheddar
1 (8½-ounce) Jiffy® package corn
    muffin mix

Nutrition Facts	
Mincemeat Cheese Muffins, per muffin Makes 36 servings (muffins)	
mount per serving	
Calories	86
Calories from fat	28
% Daily Value *	
Total Fat 3g	5%
Saturated Fat 1.4g	7%
Cholesterol 15 mg	5%
Sodium 136 mg	6%
Total Carbohydrate 12.7g	4%
Dietary Fiber 0g	0%
Protein 1.8g	
Percent values are based on a 2,000-calorie per day diet. Your daily values may differ.	
Additional Information 32.6% of calories from Fat 59.1% from Carbohydrates 8.4% from Protein	

Preparation

- Preheat the oven to 350°.
- Spray the muffin tins.
- Mix the Bisquick® and the mincemeat.
- Whisk the liquid ingredients in a large mixing bowl, and add the remaining ingredients.
- Spoon the muffin mix into the cups of the muffin tins. (Caution: Do not overfill the muffin cups. These muffins will not rise high, and you don't want them to spread too much across the tops.)
- Bake about 20 minutes or until the muffins are golden brown and a toothpick inserted comes out clean.
- Allow the muffins to sit for 2 minutes. Loosen the muffins with a knife and transfer them to a plate.
- Cover the muffins with plastic wrap until serving time.

Equipment/Utensils

Muffin Tins • Bowls • Whisk

More Cornmeal Muffin Ideas

Instead of mincemeat, add combinations of the following:

Pine nuts	Pecan pieces
Slivered almonds	Dried apricot pieces

Cheryl's Cornbread

The secret to the I-need-another-piece taste of Cheryl's cornbread is the skillet. She said, "I don't think bread is bread if it isn't cooked in a cast iron skillet."

Ingredients

2 cups self-rising white cornmeal mix
1 or 2 tablespoons self-rising flour
Pinch of salt
1 egg
¾ cup (approximate) buttermilk
A little oil in the pan

Preparation

- Pour a little oil in the skillet. While the oven is preheating to 375°, heat the skillet.
- Mix the ingredients.
- Pour the excess oil into the bread and stir quickly.
- Pour the batter into the skillet and bake it until it is brown.

Equipment/Utensils

Well-seasoned cast iron skillet • Bowl • Whisk

Cheryl Sowers

Marie's Cornbread

Marie Null says she never cooks, but she does make cornbread.

Marie likes a hint of spicy heat, but not too much. She mixes 2 or 3 packages regular cornbread mix with 1 package Mexican cornbread and follows the directions on the package.

What to Eat with Cornbread

In addition to collards, you may want to try some other foods with cornbread. Pot likker is basic. When I grew up in south Mississippi, my dad would fill an iced tea glass with grumbled cornbread and pour buttermilk or "sweet" milk over the mixture. He would eat it like cereal with a long handled teaspoon.

Some other tasty toppings are honey, syrup, jelly, butter, flavored butter spreads, and apple butter. All these are great on cornbread.

Honey Butter

Place equal parts of unsalted butter and honey in a small bowl. Whisk them until they are light and fluffy. Spread it on your cornbread.

Cheese Cornmeal Muffins

Ingredients

Non-stick cooking spray
1 (8½-ounce) Jiffy® package corn
   muffin mix
½ cup self-rising flour
1 cup (2% fat) milk
¼ cup (½ stick) unsalted butter, melted
1½ cups (6 ounces) grated extra sharp
   cheddar cheese

Preparation

- Preheat the oven to 400°.
- Spray the muffin tin cups.
- Combine the ingredients and mix thoroughly.
- Spoon the mixture into the cups.
- Bake until an inserted toothpick comes out clean and the edges are brown.
- Cool a couple of minutes in the muffin tin.
- Loosen the edges with a knife and transfer the muffins to a plate.
- Cover the muffins with plastic wrap until time to serve them.

Nutrition Facts	
Cheese Cornmeal Muffins Per muffin, 12 muffins Makes 12 servings	
Amount per serving	
Calories	**199**
Calories from fat	101
	% Daily Value *
Total Fat 11.2g	17%
Saturated Fat 6.7g	33%
Cholesterol 27 mg	9%
Sodium 337 mg	14%
Total Carbohydrate 18.7g	6%
Dietary Fiber 0.1g	0%
Protein 5.8g	
Percent values are based on a 2,000-calorie per day diet. Your daily values may differ.	
Additional Information 50.8% of calories from Fat 37.6% from Carbohydrates 11.7% from Protein	

Equipment/Utensils

Muffin Tins • Bowl

Louisiana Corn Cheese Muffins

Make the following changes to the above recipe:

- Reduce the cheese to ½ cup.
- Add 1 cup thawed frozen whole corn kernels.
- Add 1 teaspoon Tabasco® or Crystal® hot sauce.

Zucchini Cornbread

Ingredients

1 medium zucchini
2 eggs
¾ cup unsalted butter
1½ cups self-rising cornmeal mix
1 cup self-rising flour
½ cup granulated sugar
Dash salt
1 teaspoon cinnamon
¼ teaspoon nutmeg
1 tablespoon vanilla extract
1 teaspoon lemon juice
1 cup milk (approximate measure—enough milk to make the dough resemble thick cake batter)
½ cup chopped walnuts

Preparation

- Grate the unpeeled zucchini. Measure 1 cup full for this recipe.
- Preheat oven to 425°.
- Melt the butter in the microwave. Be careful not to overheat it. Pour about ¼ cup butter into the cooking pan.
- In a large bowl beat the eggs.
- Add all the other ingredients except the zucchini and walnuts. Continue to beat until well mixed.
- Add the zucchini and walnuts. Mix thoroughly.
- Bake 30 minutes or until a toothpick inserted in the center comes out clean.

Equipment/Utensils

Grater • 8" square baking pan • Mixing bowl • Small bowl • Whisk

Lemon Poppy Seed Corn Muffins

Lemon Poppy Corn Muffins made from two mixes are effortless to prepare but intriguing to the taste buds.

Ingredients

Non-stick cooking spray
1 package Betty Crocker® Lemon Poppy Seed Muffin Mix
1 package Flavorite® Corn Muffin Mix
½ cup water
1 egg
⅓ cup (2%) milk

Preparation

- Spray a muffin pan.
- Preheat the oven to 400°.
- Stir all the ingredients together until they are thoroughly mixed.
- Pour into the muffin tins and bake 15 to 20 minutes, or until the muffins are light golden brown and the tops spring back when touched.

Note

Flavorite® Corn Muffin Mix was used because it is less sweet than some other brands.

Nutrition Facts	
Lemon Poppy Corn Muffins Per muffin Makes 12 medium muffins	
Amount per serving	
Calories	136
Calories from fat	32
	% Daily Value *
Total Fat 3.5g	5%
Saturated Fat 1g	5%
Cholesterol 19 mg	6%
Sodium 233 mg	10%
Total Carbohydrate 23.4g	8%
Dietary Fiber 0g	0%
Protein 2.7g	
Percent values are based on a 2,000-calorie per day diet. Your daily values may differ.	
Additional Information 23.5% of calories from Fat 68.6% from Carbohydrates 7.9% from Protein	

Equipment/Utensils

Muffin Tins • Bowl

Boston Cornbread

Here's another super-easy, super-tasty cornbread recipe:

- Preheat the oven to 375°. Spray 2 large baking pans with non-stick cooking spray.
- Combine a yellow cake mix and 2 boxes corn muffin mix.
- Add all the liquid ingredients listed on each box.
- Mix with an electric mixer until the batter is smooth.
- Bake in 2 pans until a toothpick inserted in the middle comes out clean.

Asparagus Cornbread

A test group grabbed and gobbled this cornbread. Watching people enjoy food is one of the greatest joys of cooking.

It is one of those cornbreads with a consistency like casserole or firm pudding. Some of us like it that way in Louisiana and Mississippi. Some people in Texas and Tennessee prefer their bread crusty.

Ingredients

2 tablespoons honey
Non-stick cooking spray
1 can (10½ ounces) asparagus cuts and tips, drained and chopped
1 small can (4 ounces) chopped green chilies
1 can (14¾ ounces) cream style corn
8 ounces grated Monterey Jack cheese
2 eggs
1 small box cornmeal mix
¾ cup self-rising flour
1 cup chopped onions
1 stick butter
Shake ground red pepper
Shake Tony Chachere's® Creole seasoning
½ teaspoon salt

Preparation

- Set the honey aside.
- Spray a cooking pan. Heat the oven to 350°.
- Mix all the remaining ingredients.
- Pour the batter into the baking pan. Drizzle honey over the batter.
- Bake approximately 35 minutes or until a toothpick inserted comes out moist.
- Set aside to cool. Transfer to a plate and cut in squares or rectangles.

Equipment/Utensils

9 X 11 X 2" baking pan • Mixing bowl

Note

We use our Smartware® cookware to prepare this bread.

Sweet Potato Cornbread

Our sweet potato bread features pineapple. The subtle flavors combined with a crisp crust make this bread irresistible.

Ingredients

Non-stick cooking spray
¼ cup cooking oil
1½ cups cornmeal mix
1 cup self-rising flour
1 teaspoon baking powder
½ teaspoon salt
1 teaspoon cinnamon
¼ teaspoon nutmeg
½ cup brown sugar
1 cup sweet potatoes
2 cups crushed pineapple in its own juice

Preparation

- Mix the dry ingredients.
- If you are using baked sweet potatoes, peel them. If you are using canned ones, drain them. Mash the potatoes and measure 1 cup full.
- Heat the oven to 450 °. Add the remaining ingredients.
- Bake about 20 minutes or until the bread edges are brown and an inserted knife comes out clean.

Cooking Suggestion

Adding numerous ingredients to a basic recipe often creates a big bowl of cornbread batter. It's fun to make some muffins with the extra and save them for another meal. Since we are all busy these days, it saves time to cook and freeze.

Melody's Oven Bread

Melody's cornbread recipe is unique and intriguing. You'll want to try it. She does not like oil in her cornbread.

Mix

- 3 packages Jiffy® corn muffin mix
- 3 eggs
- Enough milk to make it soupy (but not too soup—about like cake batter
- 2 or 3 teaspoons sugar
- Just a shake of salt
- A good shake of black pepper (not too much though—not enough to make it spicy)
- Pam®

Spray a big black iron skillet with Pam®, put it in the oven, and cook it.

Melody Burch

Melody is taking a short course in phlebotomy at the University of Louisiana at Monroe. Her father taught her to make cornbread this way.

Pepperoni Cornbread

Pepperoni Cornbread is a fun dish that can be served as a snack or as genuine food at a meal.

Ingredients

¼ cup olive oil
2 thinly sliced green onions
2 tablespoons minced garlic
2 teaspoons Tone's® Spicy Spaghetti Seasoning
2 teaspoons basil
¾ cup cornmeal mix
¾ cup biscuit mix
1 large egg
2 tablespoons lemon juice
¼ cup milk or buttermilk (approximate)
4 ounces grated or shredded mozzarella cheese (divided)
1 package (10 ounces) Farm Rich® mozzarella breadsticks with marinara dipping sauce
1 thinly sliced Roma tomato
Thinly sliced pepperoni

Preparation

- Preheat the oven to 400°.
- Sauté the onions, garlic, spaghetti seasoning, and basil in the oil in a large ovenproof skillet.
- Dip the vegetables and seasonings from the oil and set them aside to cool. Save the skillet with the oil in it.
- In a medium bowl combine the cornmeal mix, biscuit mix, egg, lemon juice, milk, vegetables, seasonings, and half the cheese. Add more milk if needed.
- Pour the mix into the skillet. Don't worry about any flecks of seasonings left in the skillet. The bread should be thin.
- Cook the bread 10 minutes. Remove the bread from the oven.
- If the mozzarella breadsticks are frozen, thaw them in the microwave. Cut them into halves horizontally. Place them around the edges.
- Top the bread with the sliced tomato and cheese.
- Drizzle the marinara dipping sauce over the top
- Place a single layer of thin pepperoni on top.
- Return the bread to the oven and cook it until the cheese melts.

Equipment/Utensils

Large ovenproof skillet • Mixing bowls • Knife • Cutting board

Too Good Collard Cornbread

This recipe makes a big skillet full of irresistible cornbread with meat, cheese, vegetables, and hominy. It should be at least enough to feed 8 people.

It is a complete meal, and it tastes too good! It has a gentle hint of Louisiana spice along with the sense of comfort food all at the same time.

This complete meal in a skillet is easy to prepare. Perhaps you would like to serve it with a fruit salad.

Ingredients

Non-stick cooking spray
Oil or solid shortening to grease the skillet
2 tablespoons olive oil
6 ounces seasoning blend* (frozen and chopped onions, celery, peppers, parsley)
8 ounces frozen chopped collard greens*
1 tablespoon minced garlic
2 tablespoons lemon juice
¼ teaspoon ground red pepper
½ teaspoon Madras curry
1 tablespoon brown sugar
¼ teaspoon salt substitute
⅛ teaspoon baking soda
1½ cups Martha White® Self-Rising Cornmeal Mix
1½ cups self-rising flour
4 ounces thinly sliced deli ham, chopped
4 ounces thinly sliced lean Louisiana style sausage, chopped
1 (15½-ounce) can golden hominy, drained
4 ounces (1 cup) grated Monterey Jack cheese
2 eggs
1⅓ cups buttermilk

Preparation

- Heat the oven to 400°.
- Pour the oil into the skillet. Add the seasoning blend, collards, and garlic. Sauté over medium heat until 5-10 minutes or until the collards are tender. Stir occasionally. Add the lemon juice, red pepper, curry, sugar, salt substitute, and baking soda. Remove the mix from the heat and allow it to cool.
- Mix the cornmeal mix and the flour in a large mixing bowl. Add the ham, sausage, hominy, and cheese.
- Beat the eggs. Add them, along with the buttermilk to the bowl. Stir the collard mixture into the batter.
- Wipe skillet clean with a paper towel, and grease the skillet. Pour the batter into the skillet. Spray the top with cooking spray. Bake at 400° F. for 35 to 40 minutes or until golden brown.

Continued

Suggestions

*These measurements are half of the packages of collards and seasoning mix. You can save time by cooking the entire packages and doubling the seasonings and oil. Then you can use the leftover greens mixture in another dish or you can simply eat them as a delicious side.

To expedite cleaning utensils, measure liquids in a large measuring cup that holds at least 2 cups. You can whisk eggs in the same cup.

Equipment/Utensils

10½ " cast iron skillet or large stainless steel skillet (with ovenproof handles) • Cutting board • Sharp knife • Measuring cup • Whisk

Warm Creamy Sauce

Try this sauce with Too Good Collard Cornbread, Crawfish and Shrimp Gumbo Cornbread, or almost anything else in this book.

Ingredients

½ cup creamed corn
1 can (12 ounces) evaporated milk
1 cup water
½ teaspoon (or less) ground red pepper
1 teaspoon rosemary
½ teaspoon Tony Chachere's® Creole seasoning
1 tablespoon brown sugar
2 tablespoons unsalted butter
2 tablespoons self-rising flour
2 ounces cubed or shredded Monterey Jack cheese

Preparation

- Mix the first 7 ingredients thoroughly in a blender.
- Melt the butter in a saucepan, turn off the heat and stir the flour into the butter. Do not brown.
- Pour the liquid into the saucepan. Add the cheese.
- Cook over slow heat and stir until the sauce bubbles and is smooth.

Equipment/Utensils

Blender • Saucepan

Cooking Tip

Always place the lid securely on the blender unless you want to clean the ceiling.

Mayonnaise Cornbread

What a delicious smell! The texture is smooth. This recipe makes cornbread that looks like Mama's with an intriguing slightly sour taste. The sour flavor goes well with honey or jelly. For a special treat, slice some smoked Gouda and serve it over small thin hot pieces of Mayonnaise Cornbread.

Ingredients

2 tablespoons cooking oil for preparing the skillet
1½ cups Martha White® self-rising yellow cornbread mix
1 cup self-rising flour
1½ cups buttermilk
¼ cup sugar
½ cup regular mayonnaise
¼ cup cooking oil

Preparation

- Pour 2 tablespoons cooking oil into the skillet and place it in the oven.
- Preheat the oven to 450°.
- Mix the remaining ingredients in the order listed and spoon them into the skillet.
- Bake until the bread is golden brown around the edges. Place under the broiler a few seconds to brown the top of the bread.
- Insert a dinnerware knife to check for doneness. The bread will be ready after cooking about 15 minutes.
- Loosen the edges with a knife and turn the bread onto a plate.
- Slice into 8 pie-shaped slices.

Equipment/Utensils

Cast iron skillet, 10¼" • Mixing bowl

For the Lord thy God bringeth thee into a good land, a land of brooks of water, of fountains and depths that spring out of valleys and hills; a land of wheat, and barley, and vines, and fig trees, and pomegranates; a land of oil olive, and honey; a land wherein thou shalt eat bread without scarceness. Deuteronomy 8:7-9 KJV

Paula's Bacon Mexican Cornbread Muffins

Thinking about these crisp muffins makes me hungry! They are spicy comfort food with a Mexican flavor.

Ingredients

1 cup yellow self rising cornmeal
2 cups frozen whole kernel corn
1 cup milk
2 eggs
1 onion chopped
½ cup coarsely chopped jalapeño peppers (or to taste)
1 cup shredded mild cheddar cheese
½ teaspoon salt
1 teaspoon baking powder
12 ounce lean bacon cooked very crisp and broken into bits
¼ cup bacon drippings
¼ cup finely chopped red bell pepper for color (optional)

Preparation

- Place frozen corn in colander, rinse with hot water to thaw quickly.
- Place corn in blender; add 1 cup milk and blend until corn is a creamed corn consistency. Pour creamed corn in bowl and add remaining ingredients. Mix well.
- Place in muffin tins sprayed with nonstick spray.
- You can add a little bacon drippings to muffin cups also for added flavor and crispier crust.
- Bake at 375-400 º until golden brown.

Equipment/Utensils

Skillet • Colander • Blender • Mixing bowl • Muffin tins

Paula Howell

Paula's Story

I tell my friend Mary that I am country as cornbread; so I had to make a contribution to her new cookbook. This is my first original cornbread recipe that I actually developed into measurable portions. It was very hard for me because I think cooking should be a free-spirited activity. Measuring and using limited ingredients just isn't something that comes naturally for me. I might even add a little chopped celery or whatever seems right at the time. The meat can be varied too: you may want to use sausage, or a great variation can be hamburger meat browned with Ro*Tel® tomatoes until liquid evaporates. This gives the meat for the cornbread a very Mexican taste.

Mexican cornbread is a great appetizer or snack if cooked in the mini muffin tins. If you aren't in the mood for cornbread, just blend the corn with a little water to make creamed corn, add a stick of butter and salt. Bake until edges brown. This tastes almost like fresh baked corn from the garden.

I don't live in the country any more; so sometimes I make my various cornbread creations to enjoy the taste of home again. I sneak a bite every once in a while just to taste the memories, good times, and love we Southern cooks have been taught to add to everything we cook. I had cornbread almost everyday of my life; so there are lots of memories and warmth that flood through me with every bite. I hope you enjoy this recipe and remember to add your special love, memories, and good times to every batch.

Paula's Helpful Hints and Suggestions

- Bacon stirred into cornbread must be really crisp; otherwise, the cornbread will be soggy.
- If you prefer, you can preheat your 10¼" black skillet with bacon drippings to cook the bread. Muffins will be better for this recipe because there will be more crispy crust.
- Sugar in cornbread? Paula says, "Nah."
- The secret to making good cornbread is cooking it fast in a hot oven.
- To make **Jalapeño Hushpuppies**, add sliced or chopped jalapeños to a hushpuppy mix.

Rye Cornbread

Here's a pan of crusty cornbread with a magnificent taste.

Ingredients

1 tablespoon canola oil
1 cup dark rye flour
1 cup self-rising cornmeal mix
1 cup self-rising flour
1 teaspoon baking powder
1 teaspoon salt or salt substitute
1 tablespoon caraway seeds
1 stick (¼ pound) unsalted butter, melted
3 eggs, beaten
1 cup milk
¼ cup honey

Preparation

- Pour the oil into the skillet and heat it as you heat the oven to 450°.
- Mix the dry ingredients.
- Add the remaining ingredients.
- Pour the batter into the hot skillet.
- Bake about 15 minutes or until the edges of the bread are golden brown.

Equipment/Utensils

Bowl • 10¼" cast iron skillet

Chili Cornbread

Here's another one of those soft cornbreads, which are popular in Louisiana. The taste is lively. Eat it with collards or with taco soup.

Ingredients

3 finely sliced green onions, including tops
3 tablespoons canola oil
⅓ cup canola oil
1½ cups Martha White® yellow cornbread mix
1 cup self-rising flour
½ cup sugar
1 can (15¼ ounces) whole kernel corn, drained
1 can (19 ounces) hot chili without beans
2 cups buttermilk
2 teaspoons cumin
2 teaspoons basil
1 cup (4 ounces) grated or finely diced Mexican Velveeta® cheese
1 cup (4 ounces) grated Monterey Jack Cheese

Preparation

- Place 3 tablespoons cooking oil and the onions in a large cast iron skillet. (You can make one thick pan with the bread up to the brim if you use a 10½" skillet. For thinner bread use a 2 skillets or a large skillet.)
- Preheat the oven to 375°. Cook the onions in the skillet. After approximately 4-5 minutes, remove them from the skillet and set them aside to cool.
- Mix the dry ingredients in a large bowl.
- Whisk the remaining ingredients into the bowl, including the onions.
- Pour the batter into the hot skillet.
- Bake until the cornbread is slightly moist in the middle. Test it with a toothpick or knife. One thick pan of bread will need to cook about 50 minutes. Shorten the time for thinner pans.

Equipment/Utensils

1 or 2 large skillets (See preparations notes above.) • Grater • Cutting board • Sharp knife Large mixing bowl • Small mixing bowl

About Iron

Because some people have too much iron and because cooking in iron is one more way to obtain iron, we try not to use it often. Nothing works as well, though, as a seasoned iron skillet to make cornbread.

Cheryl's Mexican Cornbread

This Mexican cornbread is crusty with a soft center. It tastes so good that you will need to allow two pieces for every person who tries it.

Cheryl said, "My stepfather makes Mexican cornbread with ground beef. That's really good too."

Ingredients

1 pound bulk sausage
2 cups diced onions
1 tablespoon minced garlic
¼ cup pickled Jalapeño slices
1 can Ro*Tel® tomatoes and green chilies
1 pound cheddar cheese, grated
1½ cups self-rising cornmeal mix
½ cup self-rising flour
1 teaspoon cumin
3 eggs
1 stick butter (unsalted)
16 ounces creamed cheese
Cooking oil
Milk, approximately ½ cup (buttermilk preferred)

Preparation

- Preheat the oven to 375°.
- Brown the sausage, onions, and garlic. Add the Jalapeño slices and Ro*Tel®; continue to cook until the liquid evaporates.
- Remove the sausage mixture from the skillet, set it aside to cool.
- Prepare the skillet by wiping it with a paper towel. Pour enough cooking oil into the pan to coat it well. Heat it in the oven.
- Mix the cheese, cornbread mix, cumin, eggs, butter, and corn. Add enough milk to give the mixture the consistency of thick cake batter.
- Pour half the batter into the pan. Spread the sausage mixture over the batter. Cover with the remaining batter, and top it off with half the cheese. Since this recipe makes more than a skillet full, follow the same procedure with the muffins.
- Bake for 1 hour.

The recipe makes a large amount—a 10¼" skillet full plus 12 medium muffins.

Equipment/Utensils
10¼" cast iron skillet • Muffin tin • Mixing bowls • Grater

Louisiana Polenta

Enjoy Louisiana Polenta beside collards or on top of collards.

Ingredients

Non-stick cooking spray
1 stick (½ cup) unsalted butter
1 tablespoon minced garlic
½ teaspoon ground red pepper
½ teaspoon ground black pepper
2 tablespoons Tone's® spicy spaghetti seasoning mix
2 teaspoons salt substitute
3 cups chicken stock
1 quart milk
2 cups stone ground cornmeal (Finely ground cornmeal tends to lump.)
All purpose flour
Extra virgin olive oil

Preparation

- Spray a 9 X 13 X 2" glass baking pan generously.
- Heat the butter, garlic, peppers, salt substitute, stock, vinegar, lemon juice, and milk to boiling in a large heavy saucepan or Dutch oven. Stir often.
- Turn the heat off and sprinkle the cornmeal slowly into the liquid. Whisk constantly. Don't stop stirring.
- When all the cornmeal is added and the mixture is smooth, return it to low heat. Continue to stir as you cook it over very low heat until it thickens. (It should resemble thick grits.)
- Pour it into the baking pan and spread it smoothly.
- Refrigerate the polenta until it is thick.
- Just before serving, cut the polenta in desired shapes—squares, strips, or triangles—and dredge in flour.
- Deep-fry it in canola oil.
- Serve immediately.

Serving Suggestion

- We like to cut these in strips and serve them with sliced Asiago cheese and individual bowls of marinara sauce.
- Sometimes we simply cut it in squares, heat it in the microwave, and dig in with our forks.

Equipment/Utensils

9 X 13 X 2" baking pan • Large heavy saucepan or Dutch oven • Whisk • Knife • Skillet

Crawfish and Shrimp Gumbo Cornbread

Gumbo cornbread has the great flavor of okra without the gooey texture. Personally, we love gooey gumbo textures, but if you don't you can make this cornbread to enjoy the flavor without being bothered by the okra.

Ingredients

1 tablespoon canola oil
2 cup frozen breaded okra
1 package (10-12 ounces) frozen Creole seasoning mix (chopped onions, pepper, celery)
1 stick unsalted butter
12 ounces crawfish tails with fat
1 cup small frozen shrimp, cooked and peeled
1 can (10 ounces) Ro*Tel® tomatoes with green chilies
2 tablespoons lemon juice
2 cups Martha White® yellow cornbread mix
1½ cups self-rising flour
½ teaspoon baking soda
2 tablespoons brown sugar
1 teaspoon salt free Tony Chachere's®
½ teaspoon ground red pepper
3 eggs
2 cups buttermilk (approximate)

Preparation

- Preheat skillets with canola oil in it. Heat oven to 400°.
- Brown the okra, in the butter. Add the seasoning mix, crawfish and shrimp. Sauté. Add the Ro*Tel® and lemon juice. Sauté 3 minutes and turn off the heat.
- Mix together the cornbread mix, flour, baking soda, sugar, Tony Chachere's®, and red pepper.
- Beat the eggs and add them to the dry ingredients. Add 1½ cups buttermilk. Stir until the dry ingredients are moistened. Add the crawfish, shrimp, and vegetable mixture.
- It is impossible to predict the amount of moisture you will have from the Ro*Tel and the crawfish. Add enough buttermilk to make the batter like thick cake batter.
- Pour into 2 heated skillets pan and bake for 25 minutes or until toothpick comes out clean when inserted into middle.
- If your oven allows, place the bread under the broiler for a few seconds to brown it. Watch it carefully so you won't burn it.
- Allow the bread to cool 5 minutes. Slice it into generous servings. Run an egg-turner spatula under the pieces to prevent leaving the yummy crust in the skillets.

Equipment/Utensils

2 Skillets, 10¼" • Skillet or Dutch oven • Small mixing bowl • Medium mixing bowl

Variation of Crawfish and Shrimp Gumbo Cornbread

For moister bread, add 4 ounces grated Monterey Jack cheese.

Taste Testers' Comments

It was so good! I'll be your taste tester any time!

> Danon Roberts
> Peachtree Dental
> Ruston, Louisiana

I liked it. Maybe it needs to be a little hotter. Add some jalapeños. I liked it better with cheese.

> Patti Hancock
> Monroe, Louisiana

Butter Pecan Cornbread

One regret about this recipe: my mother did not know about it when I was a little girl!

Ingredients

1 stick (¼ pound) unsalted butter
1 cup chopped pecans
1 tablespoon canola oil
1½ cups self-rising cornmeal mix
1 cup self-rising flour
½ teaspoon baking powder
1 cup milk
3 eggs, beaten
2 tablespoons honey

Preparation

- In a small saucepan melt the butter with the pecans in it. Don't burn the butter, but let the pecans cook slightly. Allow them to cool.
- Heat the oven to 450°. Heat the skillet with the oil in it.
- Combine the dry ingredients.
- Add the remaining ingredients.
- Spoon the batter into the hot skillet.
- Bake 10-12 minutes.

Equipment/Utensils

Small saucepan • Medium and small mixing bowls • 10¼" skillet

If thou shalt confess with thy mouth the Lord Jesus, and shalt believe in thine heart that God hath raised him from the dead, thou shalt be saved. Romans 10:9 KJV

La Pièce de Résistance

Crawfish Cornbread

When I was a little girl taking piano lessons, the teacher always placed the best performer at the end of the recital programs. Here is the last recipe in the book. Need I say more?

I don't want you to think about the calories until you've tasted it. Write me, and I'll share the nutritional analysis.

Ingredients

1 pound crawfish with fat
2 cups cheddar cheese, grated
1 box Jiffy® Cornbread Mix
3 eggs
1 stick butter (unsalted)
1 can cream style corn
1 teaspoon Tony Chachere's®
1 teaspoon red pepper
2 jalapeños, seeded and chopped
1 teaspoon baking soda
½ cup red bell pepper, chopped
½ cup onion, chopped
1 bunch green onions, chopped

Preparation

- Sauté onions and peppers in butter until tender. Add crawfish to vegetables and cook for 5 minutes. Set aside.
- Mix together cheese, cornbread mix, eggs, corn, seasoning, jalapeños, and baking soda. Add crawfish and vegetables to mixture. Pour into greased 9 X 13 " pan and bake at 350° for 45 minutes or until toothpick comes out clean when inserted into middle.   Cathy George

About Crawfish Cornbread

Crawfish Cornbread is indescribably delicious! Each bite is memorable!

However, a description is desperately essential for the sake of all those who follow after.

The delicate blending of flavors and textures is indeed masterful. The spices deliciously complement the unique flavor of the crawfish tails. As a dedicated spicemouth™. I must say the delicate lacing of herbs, green onions, red bell peppers, and jalapeño peppers is masterful.

The moist texture of the cornbread mixed with the smoothing texture of the sharp cheddar cheese, catapults this truly extraordinary dish into a category all its own. Each bite renders itself memorable, as it bathes the diner's mouth with textures and flavors uniquely broad, delicate, and delicious.

Though there may be other dishes that are its equal, it is difficult to think of any.   Paul

We had a friend visiting from New York. The poor fellow had never tasted crawfish!
For him Crawfish Cornbread was love at first bite.

Cathy George

Cathy is a beautiful, intelligent woman who loves the Lord, her husband, her children, all her family, and her friends. She works as a pharmacist.

Having lived *Down South*—that's south Louisiana—she is an experienced crawfish cornbread baker. Cathy lived near Lafayette, Louisiana, in the region where the inhabitants have an ingrained and abiding knowledge of how to cook crawfish.

About her marvelous Crawfish Cornbread recipe that she learned from her mother, she said, "It's good at room temperature. We used to eat it when we went tailgating."

Many of the people who have lived and cooked in south Louisiana have a rich food heritage. Some of those recipes are spreading throughout the world. Wherever we go, we visit the local restaurants. More often than not we pick up menus, and our eyes are drawn while the waiters point to south Louisiana food.

Since the dispersion of the New Orleans populace, Cajun and Creole food is extending even farther than before. Ironically New Orleans is being resurrected everywhere while the physical construction of the city lags woefully.

Some of the south Louisiana cooks will tell you exactly how to make your food taste that wonderful south Louisiana way. Cathy is such a person.

And, oh yes, here is a useful tip about Cathy's cooking in general. I heard her telling somebody after church one Sunday one of her best secrets.

Here it is:
    She said, "I use a lot of rosemary in my cooking."

And He will love thee, and bless thee, and multiply thee…. He will also bless the fruit of thy womb, and the fruit of thy land, thy corn, and thy wine, and thine oil. Deuteronomy 7:13 KJV

Growing Up In Collard Country
When Life Was Green

The stories in this section are contributed by Paul Elliott, who insists they are true.

Growing Up in Collard Country

Memoirs by Paul Elliott

I grew up in north central Texas south of Fort Worth. I didn't know anything about collards at the time, because, to my knowledge, they weren't grown in our "parts." At least I never heard of them. What I didn't recognize was that they would grow there; you just had to plant them. I suspect folks in "them parts" still don't realize what they're missing.

But you can't educate all the people at once, I suppose. Nevertheless, I'll keep trying.

Saturday Entertainment

In the early spring of my sixth grade year, my parents moved with their three sons from Fort Worth south to a small house on a farm. The two-bedroom, one-bath house was on two acres. Of course two acres hardly qualified as a farm. Our saving grace was that the owner of the remaining thirty-eight of the forty-acre parcel invited us to use them as long as we wished by paying the annual taxes. What a bargain at about $40 per year! Now, we could be "real" farmers.

Neither my father, a Presbyterian minister, nor my mother, a high school English teacher, had grown up in the country; so learning to farm was a challenge for all of us. It fell my responsibility, as the oldest of the three, to shoulder most of the farming activities with my father.

Did we ever mess up! Too often, neither brilliance, logic, nor intuition works in the farming operation. In fact, those qualities are frequently exactly counterproductive.

We soon learned that Saturday was the day farmers went to town. So, we went to town on Saturday. For us, as with fellow farmers, "town" was the feed store—Fincher's Feed Store, in our case.

The serious farmers could always be found there by 9 a.m. to purchase all the things a feed store carries: feed, seed, tools, some heavier equipment, gloves, calf nursing buckets, halters, ropes, fencing, chicks, ducklings, and turkey poults, along with a myriad of other stuff—all fascinating things to an eleven-year-old boy. Of course, having my father along, who still knew everything, because I was only eleven, allowed me to affect a certain swagger of importance, whose affectation was visible only to the swaggerer. Nevertheless, it was a heady experience for this almost-12-year-old.

To our delight, when we shared some of our struggles and failures as farmers, the experienced farmers would chuckle good-naturedly at our dilemmas, then tell us how to recover or to do it "right" next time.

Initially, my impression was that the feed store was roomy with a very congenial atmosphere among "us farmers." That changed almost imperceptibly on a weekly basis. Soon, though the congenial atmosphere remained, Fincher's seemed distinctly crowded. The large room with the potbellied stove, cash register, and barrels of nails now seemed definitely overcrowded.

My father, Big John, a very intelligent, well-educated man with an abiding sense of humor and the ability to laugh at himself, had made a sage observation. On our arrival one Saturday morning, the crowd was overflowing. The packed room had spilled out onto the large loading dock, down the broad wooden steps, and out onto the huge graveled parking lot. My heart sank: I knew we didn't have time to fight the crowd of burly farmers to purchase our meager list of supplies. Understanding people as he did, he had made a very cogent observation.

Big John said, "Paul, watch what happens when we walk up to the crowd."

What's going to happen, I thought, was that we would eventually have to return home without our purchases.

Was I wrong!

As we approached the crowded steps, a path through the crowed materialized. Well enough, but now we were on the large loading dock packed with farmers. Again, a pathway to Fincher's front door materialized. The door was held for us, and a path to the cash register in the middle of the large room miraculously appeared!

By now in life, I was well aware that being a minister was one thing, but parting the Red Sea was quite another. This miracle was only slightly less impressive.

As with all fabricated "miracles," the performer has some secret knowledge not available to other observers. What Big John had figured out was that the weekly enlarging crowd was of our own inadvertent doing.

Those of you with small town experience understand the speed with which information travels in such an environment. Word of our farming escapades had spread like wildfire through the local farming community, and farmers came from far and wide.

We had become the Saturday entertainment! Our farming errors had become legendary! Lifelong farmers, who had learned farming from their fathers and grandfathers, had never supposed one could mess up the ways we were messing up!

Word of the Elliotts' Farming Escapades had spread throughout three counties to my knowledge. I'm sure there was the sound of a mighty rushing wind as farmers left other area feed stores for Fincher's every Saturday.

Big John pointed out to me that Mr. Fincher had become much more friendly and accommodating with successive Saturdays. By this time he was downright solicitous. We, after all, had produced a windfall of business for him.

Family farmers, being the wonderful bunch they are, would thoroughly enjoy our mistakes, then tell us how to avoid or fix them. Occasionally, one or more of them would volunteer to do the work for us when we didn't have the necessary tools or equipment.

The farming experience was as wonderful as the farming people in our area, yet it taught me I didn't want to choose farming as an occupation. But more about that later.

For the wages of sin is death; but the gift of God is eternal life through Jesus Christ our Lord. Romans 6:23 KJV

The Flight of the Bumblebee

Rarely does a farm boy allow something of interest to go unexplored. At age fourteen, I was no exception, nor was Gingham, our dog. Gingham, a fifty-pound Johnsonian mix, had located an area of interest over to the side of the hay bales. If you are forty-something or older you remember that kind of bale. You know, the small rectangular ones baled with two strands of baling wire or twine. The rectangular ones of yesteryear, largely supplanted by the huge round ones left in the fields nowadays, could be managed with a hay hook and stacked neatly in the barn for winter feeding.

Oh, yeah, "Johnsonian?"

That was a mixture of whatever canine genes were passing through Johnson County, Texas, at the time. In Gingham's case, it appeared to be a combination of German Shepherd and Alaskan Malamute (Husky) among other less identifiable things.

Twice each day at milking time, Gingham would go to that area of interest and scratch halfheartedly next to the corrugated metal wall before going to the corresponding area outside the barn and digging more earnestly in the dirt at the base of the wall. Our experience with the dog in question suggested that there was a quarry of some interest hidden under the hay in that position.

My examination of the site suggested it would be more productive for us to reach Gingham's quarry by removing the hay bales from the inside rather than digging in the dirt on the outside of the barn. Being the oldest of the three boys, I took charge and began rearranging the bales for easier access.

Suddenly better access was had!

Now visualize the gate to our hay barn.

It had originally had a regular wooden frame gate covered with sheep wire. However, an overly energetic yearling calf with horns enjoyed exercising them on this gate. After several repairs of the gate, I gave up and simply foiled said yearling by nailing three pieces of 2 X 4 to each post with the top piece being about chest high. When we needed to feed hay, we would simply climb over the 2 X 4's like a ladder and toss the hay over the fence into the hay trough outside the fence.

Oh, yeah, the "better access?"

It revealed a hive of now-swarming bumblebees, each one intent on inflicting retribution on *me!* My brothers, not yet targeted, wisely retreated to another corner of the hay barn. I never even considered climbing the 2 X 4 gate, but vaulted it in one swift move leading the bumblebee swarm to the barnyard. Dodging and circling, I managed to shed myself of most of the swarm. The leader, however, still had me in his cross hairs.

Stopping to look back was my only mistake!

The lead bee hit the middle of my forehead just above the bridge of my nose stinger first. Every time I swiped at him, my hand hit my glasses and glanced away from the avenger. Meanwhile he busied himself injecting copious quantities of venom. Finally, a swipe knocked off my glasses with the next one ridding me of his presence. He no sooner hit the ground than my large booted foot environmentalized him.

Shortly my rounded face exhibited two small slits, above two smaller holes atop one large, horizontal slice. The swelling took several days to subside and left a small crater which I wear to this day where his stinger was applied.

The Gingham Dog and the Calico Cat

Gingham, the dog, actually arrived shortly after Calico, the cat. Calico was one of Prissy's fifty-five plus offspring. Her name was obvious because of her coat. Once we had a Calico cat, the puppy arriving shortly thereafter from a neighbor's litter had to be given the name Gingham.

Gingham grew up with Calico and her littermates. He learned to bite tails thereby avoiding the worst of the claws. Neither wisdom nor good judgment was his strong suit. He had a habit of placing his open mouth down over a cat's back and gently closing his jaws slightly as though measuring him or her for lunch. When these "measurements" were a little too snug, the measuree would whirl sinking a handful of claws in Gingham's upper lip. His yelps signaled his loss of interest in further measurement activity.

Calico developed the added technique of hanging onto his lip as he released and rolling out from under him while still holding her purchase. Gingham, remaining as motionless as possible, would issue a plaintive whimper that quickly turned into whines as Calico continued her discipline. Her mercy returned gradually, and she would release him. It appeared to have no lasting benefit or effect. Gingham was not the brightest bulb in the string. His memory wasn't very good either. Before long, he was back at his testing and measurements.

Prissy

The reigning queen of cathood as well as most everything else at our place was Prissy. To our certain knowledge she gave birth to over fifty-five kittens. She had about three litters of four to five kittens annually. She was a wonderful mother teaching them to be very effective mousers, ratters, and bird hunters. On a farm in those days, we had never heard of commercial cat or dog food. Everyone fended for him or herself growing fat and sleek in the process.

A trick Prissy quickly learned and just as quickly passed on to her current litter of kittens was to drink a stream of milk we would direct while milking. The cats would pace impatiently in an arc about four to six feet away, and we would oblige them in order.

As you might imagine, Prissy had little sense of humor when it came to youthful dogs. Who would with that many kittens to raise? She did, however, have her own twist of macabre humor. The size of the canine mattered only in how she would intimidate him—not whether. For Gingham, she had a sky-jacking maneuver.

As I mentioned, Gingham was not the smartest canine and his memory resembled that of one in his senility to boot. He never appeared to learn anything from this repeated "training" at Prissy's "hands" except that she was not a cat with which one should trifle.

In spite of her pressing schedule, Prissy had learned the value of patience. The large wooden staved holding tank for our windmill's water sat atop a scaffolding about twenty feet in the air. The lowest level of welded pipe horizontal braces was about four feet above the ground. Prissy found this to be conveniently high to be out of sight of both kittens and large dogs.

Prissy would sit patiently on this horizontal brace until said dog, completely unaware of her presence, carelessly strolled beneath. She would deftly step off the brace onto the middle of Gingham's back. Accelerating to his maximum straight-line speed punctuated by yelps borne as much of the stunned terror as the pain of Prissy's twenty claws imbedded in the hide of his back, Gingham tore across our acre-sized back yard. His relief came only when Prissy grew tired of the ride and dismounted her steed in the garden. Gingham never seemed to learn what caused these Prissy attacks, nor did Prissy appear to tire of his training.

A Horn Ache

One of my 4-H projects was a Jersey heifer named Lassie. She was more adventuresome than was customary for her species. She had a streak of mischievousness but always held her horned head erect with both ears high unless she wanted to play. In that case, she would lower head, snort, and wag her head as though preparing for a mock goring, something she never tried.

The summer of her second year of life we had a bumper crop of peaches in our small orchard. As snacks, I fed her the ones which had fallen to the ground some of which were green and others which were partially rotten. It seemed the more rotten the peach, the better she liked it. Soon she would refuse the green ones in favor of the rotten ones. The connection eluded me until I returned home one afternoon to find my juvenile bovine had broken through the fence into the orchard.

Hurrying into the orchard to capture my vagrant project, I noticed how pristine was the under-tree area of each of the twenty-odd peach trees—seeds only remained. The closer I drew to Lassie the more I realized something was clearly wrong with her! Somehow she just didn't look right. Injury from the fence-break? Barbed wire laceration? As I got closer, I realized her slightly lowered head tilted to the left but her neck veered to the right. Her usually erect ears were askew about half-mast with one flying a little lower than the other, and her weight was borne more on her left legs than her right—very unusual for cattle.

What neurological mishap had my heifer suffered?

As I got closer, I called her name. She responded with noticeable disco-ordination which continued erratically!

Lassie was drunk! Yes, drunk! She had been in the orchard long enough to clean up every fermented peach in the orchard.

My besotted, subdued 4-H project was mostly better the next day. But have you ever had such a bad hangover your head hurt all the way out into your horns?

"Sirs, what must I do to be saved?"
"Believe on the Lord Jesus Christ, and thou shalt be saved, and thy house."
Acts 16: 30-31 KJV

Raising Turkeys

Wild turkeys are among the smartest, shrewdest, most cautious birds on the planet. Their excellent attributes led Benjamin Franklin to propose, with good reason, that the wild turkey be our national bird.

White domestic turkeys are the polar opposite. They take every opportunity to wound or kill themselves. We learned this lesson the hard way.

Since turkey poults weren't pigs, my father's only prohibition, we got a dozen at Fincher's when they arrived one spring. We broke out the chick incubator we found in the barn and installed it in the garage whose concrete floor seemed suitable after first laying down a layer of newspaper as one would do for hatchling chickens.

Before the turkey poults were under the incubator a whole day, some were squatted down or lying on their sides seemingly unable to stand. The healthy ones were pecking at them. Even though each poult had been "debeaked"—a process of cutting off the front half of the upper beaks of chicks and turkey poults to prevent pecking one another to death—the healthy turkeys could still stab the "downed" ones. However, the question remained as to the injury or disease causing the "downed" birds.

Another phenomenon presented itself. The turkeys would jump at the light bulb in the center of the incubator designed to keep them warm. There was a wire frame around the light bulb to protect the baby birds from heat injury. Well enough, but the turkeys were jumping at the light trying to peck the bulb. Occasionally one would hang his leg in the wire protector and die hanging thereby. Turning off the light did not work either. Some would die in the cold at night.

To stop the carnage, a Saturday consultation was in order! There were two diagnoses. "You never put turkey poults on paper, they'll get spraddled." Spraddled is a condition where each of their long legs slips laterally in opposite directions tearing their pectoral muscles. They go down and can't get up. OK, our ignorance of "turkey farming."

The second diagnosis? "Turkeys are just stupid." OK, I guess that was also our ignorance of turkey farming. Mr. Fincher gave us a special deal on another dozen turkey poults. There were more casualties and we got six more poults on "special" from Mr. Fincher. I think he may have felt sorry for us for having embarked on this project so abjectly ignorant of proper turkey farming knowledge. On the other hand, our farming ignorance had brought Fincher's Feed Store a windfall profit every Saturday for quite a while.

Those turkeys were, indeed, the most stupid birds we had ever supposed existed. A schoolmate of ours occasionally stumbled to school sleepless from rescuing turkeys all night at his family's commercial turkey farm. The most common reason was from wind. The wind would blow leaves and debris airborne spooking the turkeys, which would run into fences and piling on until newcomers to the crowd would simply run over their comrades' bodies and over the fences. Ronald would spend the night capturing the escapees and unpiling the windrowed bodies, as he tried to save lives.

Thirty baby turkeys later we had six that were half grown and were looking forward to sharing Thanksgiving turkey with friends. It was early September, and school had started; so I put these six in a wire cage four feet wide by three feet high by six feet long. Knowing that turkeys had to be kept out of the rain lest they put their beaks in the air allowing the rain to run down into their nostrils drowning them, I covered two-thirds of the cage with lengths of asphalt roofing material—all I had.

You guessed it! Returning home on the school bus one afternoon after a rain, I found four dead turkeys. Why only four? Four was the maximum number of turkeys that could fit in the two feet of uncovered cage and drown. The two remaining had not been able to get out from under the covering to drown themselves.

We finally got two turkeys to the Thanksgiving table. We didn't think a 6.7% yield on turkeys was worth trying it a second year.

As I think about it, I have known some people suffering severe risk of TPDS, pronounced tepids, for Turkey Poult Drowning Syndrome. The characteristic? Noses so high in the air rain would flood their lungs.

Mephitis mephitis, Young and Old

One afternoon while in our back field, Gingham had spooked a family of skunks. The mother had run off with several young ones, but Gingham had managed to bark one of the babies to a standoff. With the young one's attention fixed on the dog, I was able to slip up behind him and grab him by his tail.

I knew I dared not turn loose of his tail unless I wanted to risk a "perfuming." I arrived home still holding the baby skunk by the tail where I was joined by my brothers. They alerted our mother, poor, long-suffering woman, who obliged by calling our vet to see if we could have the skunk descented so we could make him a pet. The message was relayed to me that if the nose-to-tail length was more than six inches, the skunk was likely too old to make a good pet even though he could do the surgery.

My problem now was how to measure the nose-to-tail length on a baby skunk wanting loose while being held by the tail. Somehow the measurements were made and determined to be longer than six inches.

My next and more pressing problem was how to return him to the wild without suffering a very unpleasant remembrance. Consultation with my brothers concluded we should release him in the field close to his mother and siblings where there had been some metal garbage dumped some years before our arrival. In the collection of rods and cans, there was a gallon paint bucket on its side. Standing behind the can, I hung the skunk in front of it and released him. He scampered into it, and I scampered away.

Success!

"No one can make you feel inferior without your consent." Eleanor Roosevelt

. . . and Old

The aforementioned dog, Gingham, our constant companion for all activities great and small, accompanied us on every venture from his station at the back door of the house. This included the daily milking and feeding chores. In the aforementioned hay barn, Gingham developed an interest in a section of bales several feet from the one with the now vacant bumblebee hive.

Over several weeks, Gingham became more and more insistent in his digging efforts between some bales close to the corrugated metal siding at the back of the hay supply. One day we realized he was going to dig his way to whatever prey he had located; having had the bumblebee experience, however, we were appropriately cautious. None of us, especially *moi* intended to be stung or stung again. Once stung, twice . . . uh . . . oh, . . . twice whatever it was. Anyway, we intently watched Gingham's progressively more frantic plowing down between a particular pair of bales, but at a safe distance.

Gingham's digging went from insistent to more frantically determined. Hay flew in the air as he dug down between the bales. He got so deep only his hind quarters remained visible with his tail signaling a semaphore pattern suggesting he was close to the quarry. He lunged, then recoiled, then lunged again. Suddenly, midst the lunges and retreats, we heard muffled barks—muffled, but clearly his most ferocious and threatening. Surely, he was about to seize his prey!

Indeed, he was!

Suddenly, Gingham began a silent, but determined retreat. My brother, Steve, closest to the assault, peered briefly into the hole left by Gingham's hasty departure. Pausing ever so briefly, he shouted, "Skunk!" Drew, the youngest, vaulted the 2 X 4's across the gate closely followed by Steve. Being the oldest and most scientifically inclined, I pressed forward to verify what appeared to be Steve's overly hasty conclusion. As I peered into the hole, I found myself nose to nose with two beady black eyes.

"Nose to nose" was an inadequate description! Never in my life, before or since, have I smelled such a completely revolting odor! To call it nauseating is wholly inadequate. It was far worse! I felt my stomach involuntarily convulsing in my upper abdomen. Why I didn't vomit remains a mystery. The churning continued as I vaulted the 2 X 4 fence/gate. I confirmed the black and white stripes on Gingham's "quarry" as I cleared the hay barn looking for the rest of "the force."

I found Gingham lying down licking and pawing his face which contained several splotches of a yellowish oily substance. Steve and Drew watched Gingham in his misery from a respectful distance. As I arrived, my stomach convulsions diminished; but when I got too close to Gingham's downwind zone, the churning resumed.

After several cans of tomatoes, the application of which the Saturday consultants assured us would neutralize the skunk odor, we finally gave up. We couldn't stand any close association with Gingham for about three weeks. He seemed to understand he was *persona non grata.*

During the several days before any of the four of us dared to go near the hay barn, the skunk family departed unmolested. When we got down to the hay bales defining the skunk den, we simply dragged them into the back field with hay hooks, all my budding scientific interest having been long before satisfied.

Alligator Snapping Turtles

About half way from the barn to the back of our property was a small creek. Until the break of the Texas mid-fifties drought in 1957, we had seen no water in the creek. Suddenly the creek was flowing about 200 yards wide. When it returned to its banks it had a good supply of fish, frogs, and turtles. Most of the turtles were the usual smooth backed type.

However, one afternoon I was walking along the bank when I spotted the largest turtle I had ever seen swimming in the shallows. He seemed about three feet in diameter with a head that protruded on a two-foot neck! The turtle, once captured, measured about half that—still an impressive animal.

His moss-covered shell had a jagged ridge from fore to aft suggesting a prehistoric origin. There were even several leeches on his shell from one-quarter to one and one-half inches long. The leeches got agitated when I pulled the turtle out of the water. His mouth with its hooked beak would periodically issue a loud, threatening hiss. Needless to say, my brothers and I saw no reason to get close enough to test his strike range.

We carefully handled him with hoes and shovels and moved him to a steel barrel close to our house for further study. In that process we discovered that he would expertly snap a half-inch wooden dowel in two. He sometimes had to take a second snap to bisect a three-fourths inch dowel. We tried different sized sticks, but neither their sizes nor hardness were sufficiently uniform as to represent any scientific validity. Nevertheless, we were intrigued by his ability to trim things waved in front of his beak.

We tired of said study after a few days and, to our mother's great relief, retaining all our fingers, toes, ears, and noses moved him back to the creek.

Later we learned there were such things as alligator snapping turtles and that ours was only a medium-sized one! Our mother retained her distaste for anything headed by a beak.

A Lapful of Cow

Angie was our bovine matriarch inherited from the previous owner. She was a Holstein/Angus mix who gave a reasonable amount of milk twice a day. My father would do the morning milking, and I and my brothers would do the evening chores including the milking.

We soon learned that you had to keep your head in Angie's flank just forward of her thigh to keep her from lifting her hoof and placing it in the milk bucket. Of course, the cats and Gingham were delighted with such an event. They would drink so much they could scarcely waddle away to sleep it off. The rats and mice, too, were relieved for hours by no cat pressure.

One Saturday morning at Fincher's, my father complained to the consultants that Angie was raising the hoof on the leg he was bracing to block her from stepping into the bucket. He thought she was just poised to step into the bucket any moment he might move his blocking head. He also noted his neck was beginning to give him trouble. "Why, John, she's just leaning on you. Next time she does that, just jerk back suddenly and see what happens," a farming consultant brayed.

The next morning my father had scarcely begun milking in his customary stance when Angie lifted her hoof. My father jerked his head back unexpectedly and Angie nearly fell in his lap! The milk bucket flew, my father fell backward off his three-legged stool, and Angie stumbled and staggered to regain her hoofing! When the dust settled, my father quickly learned to position himself so as to block the hoof without serving as Angie's leaning post. He passed his technique on saving the rest of us such an ignominious unseating.

Smoky, The Racehorse

Smoky cost twenty-five dollars. He was a retired cow pony who had become rope shy we were told. Our veterinarian peered in his mouth and pronounced him about twenty years old. He further opined Smoky's smaller size and conformation suggested he was a quarter horse. We nodded with understanding.

He was a reasonably tolerant horse, but took full advantage of our underestimation of his intelligence and experience. Our first saddle was slightly small for us, but its stirrups could be let out farther than for most saddles its size. Nevertheless, we managed. On my second ride, the saddle seemed too loose so that it began to slip around Smoky's trunk. I dismounted and tightened the cinches fore and aft. Again it seemed to loosen excessively with scarcely any riding

The problem became critical when I spun around Smoky's trunk dismounting unceremoniously completely lacking decorum as the saddle swung loosely to and fro in a pendular motion under his chest.

How to cinch the saddle tightly was clearly a problem for the Saturday morning consultants.

The disappointment this Saturday was in not being allowed to complete my tale before the laughter broke out around Fincher's Feed Store. "Boy, he's just holding his breath on you," one consultant brayed between guffaws, "Just knee him hard in the ribs, then tighten the cinches."

Smoky? Holding his breath just to keep the cinches loose? Well, it did make sense.

I had to perfect my saddling technique that very afternoon. Listening carefully for any suggestion of an inhalation, I threw the saddle onto Smoky's back. Nothing. I threaded the cinch strap through the girth ring. Preparing to tighten down, I drew my leg way back and thoroughly kneed Smoky's ribs.

The grunting explosion through Smoky's mouth and nose blew green-tinged horse slobber a full eight feet forward of the horse! The simultaneous explosion from his other end was no less impressive, though less green!

His chest was suddenly half its previous diameter. Before he could reinflate, I quickly tightened the cinch. Never again did the saddle loosen. I don't recall Smoky even trying his "puffed up" attitude again. Green-tinged horse slobber? It was probably grass but could have been collards.

Getting Smoky in from the field was a daily challenge. As we drove him in with the cattle, he would walk and trot toward the barnyard gate. Never seeming to find the gate, he would run between us and the fence back out into the field. After about three futile passes, he would finally "find" the gate and "allow" us to feed him. While not really a problem for the Saturday morning consultants, the subject did come up one week.

After comments on how well Smoky had trained us, the consensus was "ice cream salt." Yep, ice cream salt. "You got a shotgun, boy?"

"Yes sir, a 20-gauge pump," I proudly announced.

"Open a couple of your shells and replace the lead shot with ice cream salt. When he starts to 'miss' the gate, pepper his rump from about twenty-five to thirty yards away."

It worked! Never again did I have to "show" Smoky how wide that gate was or its location. All I had to do was carry my shotgun to the field. Even a broom handle filled the bill. I am thankful Smoky never challenged me to discharge my broomstick.

Smoky's talents unfolded gradually as we grew to know him. Put a child on him, and he would walk as though he were on eggs. With his teenaged owners he was not so charitable. He would walk too close to heavy gateposts rolling our legs painfully between them and his body. He persistently found a way to use the lowest limb of any close tree to attempt scraping us off. At his choosing he would suddenly race to the barnyard gate to end the ride irrespective of the rider's wishes.

Oh, yes, the Saturday morning consultants had a solution: "Pull one rein around hard. He can't run in a straight line with his head pulled to one side. If he gets too close to a post or tree, pull his head around hard with one rein and hit his nose with your fist." That worked! As a matter of fact, it improved virtually all of Smoky's "ignorant" behavior. It turned out neither ignorance nor lack of understanding was Smoky's problem—stubbornness was. Must have had some mule in him.

Was Smoky ever born to race! He loved it and had an astonishingly competitive spirit. When several of us in the neighborhood were riding, Smoky would keep prancing trying to start a race until we finally came to a large field without fences. We would let the horses run! Smoky would leap to a start and quickly gain the lead, which he would never relinquish. The race was over when Smoky decided it was—not any of the rest of us, boys or horses. I suppose had he ever engaged a faster steed; he would have died trying to win the race, because he never lost.

Two Birds with One Stone

I enjoyed dove hunting and did so annually nearly every day of the season. We had many volunteer sunflowers in some of our fields mainly along the creek and around the stock tank. The doves loved this food source.

Customarily, I would take my 20-gauge pump shotgun when I went out each afternoon to round up the cattle. After several days of bagging several birds each, there needed to be more challenge. Leaving the rest of the shells at home, I would go out with the maximum gun load of three shells. My goal was to return with three birds. This became easier to do as the season wore on.

The new challenge was to return with more birds than the number of shells fired. This is possible if there are two birds flying in close formation. The trick is to wait until the two reach an angle with respect to the hunter where they are both in the pattern of the shot as it reaches them. Of course, if the hunter is to be sure to return with more birds than shells fired, he must try to get two birds with each shot, especially the first. I got pretty good at that trick and had a freezer full by season's end.

There was a side benefit of rounding up the cattle with shotgun in hand—Smoky remembered where the gate was.

"Always do more than is required of you." General George S. Patton

Riding Cowback

Angie, our main cow, was a faithful animal. Though she was never disinclined to test the alliances and limits, she was, for the most part, rather docile. When I drove the cattle in from the field each afternoon, it occurred to me that I might return from the field on Angie's back.

Convinced I shouldn't make my first mounting of the bovine steed in the open, I tried that in the barnyard hoping not to duplicate the annual Spanish "running of the bulls." To my delighted surprise, Angie tolerated my "cow breaking" event with amazing equanimity. I soon learned she was more tolerant of my riding atop her hips as one would ride a burro as opposed to riding behind her shoulders as one would ride a horse. That was fine with me. Comfortable transportation was my goal.

I learned it mattered not to Angie whether I sat astride her back or sat on her back at right angles with legs draped to the right or to the left. I also found that dove hunting from the variety of positions was easier. Angie was never disturbed by the fire of my shotgun. I could dismount to retrieve birds and catch up to Angie, who would continue her amble toward the barn.

I am thankful Angie never broke into the peach orchard consuming the fermented peaches leaving me with the hazardous choice of riding with a drunken bovine driver. Friends don't let friends drive drunk (en bovines).

Dexter the Hunt Cat

Dexter was a most unusual cat by cat standards. He came to us as a two-thirds grown animal from some person in our acquaintance. It did not take long for us to figure out why Dexter had been offered the country life at our place. He rarely did a simple meow. Instead Dexter had the most raucous caterwaul we had ever heard.

One of his favorite tricks was to leap onto a screen by my parent's bedroom with a reverberating twang letting out his most obnoxious yell—at two a.m. Only impassioned intervention by us three boys preserved Dexter's life and limb.

Dexter was a hunter not only in the sense of most felines, but he accompanied us to the pasture looking for adventure. He was a swimmer and seemed to like the water much as tigers do. Approaching the creek, rather than selecting a narrow part across which he could jump, he would simply jump as far as possible swimming the remainder of the distance across. Climbing out on the far side he would give himself one thorough shake and proceed with his hunting.

Dexter and Gingham worked the hunt together in a cooperative fashion. Field rats were Dexter's favorite prey, though anything running in the fencerow was at risk. Gingham would dine on anything warm-blooded.

In our part of the country, the wild grasses and shorter weeds grew about eighteen inches tall. This allowed them to overlap the lowest strand of the barbed wire fences as they died forming a tent over the fencing under which the wildlife developed a runway. These were wildlife superhighways. Rats, mice, rabbits, and other fauna would run relatively concealed for long distances with excellent forward visibility except where each fence post produced a zigzag.

On the trip out into the pasture, Dexter would periodically issue a hunting call with a sound resembling "wowmp." About two-thirds of the way out on our trip to round up the cattle each afternoon, he would suddenly become silent and disappear from view as he took up a vigil in the superhighway. Gingham would go into the far field and begin his return with a crisscrossing pattern across the fencerow to drive the prey in Dexter's direction.

The only evidence of Dexter's presence was a periodic rustle in the fencerow as the scurrying prey charged into his waiting mouth. He would dispatch each scurrier, step forward over the body, and reload for the next victim. One afternoon I counted the bodies of ten field rats, two mice, and one cottontail. Before departing the field, he and Gingham would eat their fills and return home to sleep off the meal.

Horse Apple Grenades

The old style cherry bomb was a gratifying firework—dangerous but gratifying. Not only was its fuse more reliable than those of the standard firecracker, the explosion was much more powerful. Put one under an overturned number ten tin can, and it would convert the can into pieces—the circular bottom and the unwrapped, flattened rectangular sidewall.

Another attractive feature of the cherry bomb's fuse was that it would continue to burn when thrown into the stock tank. A stock tank, for those of you not from collard country, is a man-made pond to provide water for the farm or ranch stock, usually cattle. They make good swimming holes and fishing ponds.

A word of caution about swimming in stock tanks. Most of the time they are rather muddy. Swimming in your underwear leaves them stained red and giving away your likely forbidden foray. You have to either get back home and wash them surreptitiously to cover your sins or simply swim naked, our usual choice, since high banks made our forays safe from prying parental and neighbor eyes. Oh, yes, there was a third solution. You could swim with all your clothes on or dip them in the tank water before leaving and issue a bald-faced lie to your parents about "falling in." Our upbringing precluded this blatant a sin.

But back to explosives. Throwing a lighted cherry bomb into the stock tank or creek produced a decent result, but it had a tendency to float reducing the "show." Young, inquiring minds cast about for "enhancers." The cherry bombs inserted into mud balls were satisfactory, but hazardous. If the "artillery officer" misfigured and launched too soon, the grenade would sink too deeply in the water producing a muffled effect. Launching too late produced an airburst sending everyone for cover to avoid the shrapnel—somewhat unsettling even for fearless teenaged boys.

A less lethal solution was needed. Eureka, the fruit of the Bois d'arc tree filled the bill. Commonly called "horse apples" the pithy, softball-sized inedible fruit fit the hand well, and a cherry-bomb-sized hole could be easily and quickly drilled with a Barlow knife. When the horse apple grenade hit the water, it would sink only briefly and little. The resulting explosion was not muffled. In the event the "artillery officer" misjudged and an airburst resulted, the pithy "shrapnel" was essentially harmless. What a delightful result! The battles raged!

Tarzan and the Windmill

Our well water was pumped by a windmill. For the most part this worked fine and reliably. Occasionally, though, we would need some sort of well service. Perhaps it was to put new "leathers" on the bottom part of the sucker rod that made the seal against the well casing.

Our "well man," Dee Thurman, had the usual truck with a wench attached. He would back it up to the windmill tower, take the cable with a block (pulley) attached, hang the block beneath the fan and lower the cable to earth where the sucker sections could be pulled and successively unscrewed until the valve mechanism on the bottom of the sucker rod was accessible for service.

Well service is a physically demanding occupation. All the equipment is heavy, and much of it is awkward in size or shape. Thus, physical strength is a distinct benefit in the well service business. Usually the man who serviced our well worked by himself; however, for several visits he had a helper.

This man amazed all onlookers. The muscles in his arms, chest, shoulders, and back bulged. He could grab an overhead cross member of the windmill tower with either hand and do a single-handed chin-up. We immediately nicknamed him Tarzan. Every time we needed well work, the word would filter into the neighborhood producing an admiring group of our friends. We three and other onlookers would line up to see whether Tarzan would be helping. Of course, before any work could commence, we insisted Tarzan do his pull-ups first with one arm, then with the other.

On his arrival, Tarzan once astounded all onlookers by doing ten pull-ups with one arm, then the other! Were we impressed! He forthwith declared the entertainment over and proceeded to the work at hand. This was probably the result of a conspiracy between my father and the well man to shorten the entertainment segment of the service call.

I have wondered in years since, what the hourly rate was for our entertainment by Tarzan. The well man did not complain—why should he, he was being paid—nor did our father, who probably counted the additional cost well worth our enjoyment—one of the many dimensions of fatherhood.

Rocks from the Sky

Once we switched over to caged layers restricted to the chicken house, the chicken yard was taken over by ragweed. The ragweed in our area grew to about five feet by the time school started each fall. We would arrive home on the school bus about two hours before our parents. Our parents had encouraged us to do our homework during that time, but preferring to leave homework until the very last minute, we mostly did "other things."

At fifteen, twelve, and ten years of age, three boys can think of countless "other things" to do, especially on a farm. On this particular early fall afternoon, we were using the watering hose for some purpose likely other than watering any plant life. As the oldest, I had sternly admonished the other two not to spray me, "...or else." I hadn't decided what the "or else" would be, but I hoped neither would dare to find out. Such was not the case.

Drew, the ten-year-old, took it upon himself to unceremoniously spray his imminence! Drew, cackling with delight, dropped the hose and ran through the chicken yard gate and into the high ragweed plants hoping to hide. This dripping insult demanded redress!

As Drew's bobbing head and shoulders appeared tracing his flight through the ragweed, I picked up several flat driveway stones each about the weight of two golf balls. I planned a very high throw so the stones launched in sequence would land close causing a disturbing swishing sound as they landed close to my fleeing brother.

It did not turn out according to plan.

My very first stone flew in a high, arching trajectory landing squarely on top of Drew's head with a sickening thud! It could not have been more perfect had I been trying to hit him! Suddenly disappearing into the ragweed, Drew fell silent in mid-cackle!

I had *killed* my little brother! How *would* I explain to my parents who were scheduled to arrive home in about an hour?

I sprinted through the ragweed to the place of his disappearance. He was still alive! Praise the Lord! But he was crouched where he had fallen holding his copiously bleeding scalp moaning softly.

Oh, no! I feared he would soon die of blood loss! I had never seen so much blood in my life! *How* would I explain to my parents? Even if I could successfully dispose of his body, how could I silence my other brother who would be only too delighted to blackmail me for the rest of my natural life? Besides that, my parents would probably miss Drew within several days, I reasoned.

Life can be so complicated.

Noting that the blood was still flowing rather freely, I summoned my Boy Scout training to apply pressure. After about an eternity, this worked quite well. "What are we going to do with all this blood?" asked the middle boy, Steve. Whew! That "we" was unbelievably welcome and reassuring! It indicated he was accepting some of the blame.

With that reassurance, I assumed my proper role of "leader" to recover from the mess "we" had created. "Get the hose," I ordered as I helped the now limping Drew back to the driveway. As Drew kept pressure on his scalp wound, Steve and I washed him at arm's length as one would a skunked dog. Steve ran for a change of clothes. We squirreled away Drew's bloody ones in the garage to surreptitiously wash them at a later time. By now the wound no longer required the pressure; so I carefully combed Drew's hair to cover the defect.

With the renewed confidence that Drew would not soon die, I apologized. Drew indicated he would not soon forget this little episode. Not wishing to encourage this thinking, I issued some veiled threat should he ever divulge the afternoon's events.

It must have worked. I don't think my parents ever learned of the day rocks falling from the sky nearly took the life of their youngest son.

Jed, the Prickly Pear King

Jed (the names have been changed to protect both guilty and innocent) was a neighborhood friend. He was in our horseback riding group and scout troop. Anytime we went camping with or without the scout troop, it was Jed's habit of throwing rocks, twigs, and anything else at hand into the creek, fire, or center of the circle of scouts.

At first it was a surprise when he picked up a prickly pear cactus leaf or fruit impaling himself with the fine, hair-like needles. On subsequent occasions the mood went from a hoped-for lack of impalement to an anticipated one with a hoped-for minimal injury.

It was so predictable that Jed would grasp some part of a cactus plant one would have believed he had done it on purpose were it not for the pain he suffered with the grasping as well as the treatment to remove the needles.

The rest of us pleaded, to little avail, that he look at what he grasped or where he laid his hand before doing so. We came to anticipate the injury and carried extra, readily accessible adhesive tape to apply to the patch of bristles on his person to remove them by traction. A pair of tweezers and magnifier completed the essentials.

Our scoutmaster became so concerned he came as close as one can come in the nonmilitary setting of ordering Jed not to get himself stuck by cactus needles. My recollection is that it stopped only when we got old enough to quit camping and developed other interests.

The Primal Scream of a Lost Soul

In late August of 1957 about ten seasoned Boy Scouts in our middle teens went on a weeklong wilderness camp to Possum Kingdom Lake. The "wilderness" area of that time is now a full-blown scout camp, I understand. However, at the time there were no roads into the area, and it was in an area of the lake with little activity. We launched our canoes, lashed in the equipment, and paddled the six hours necessary to reach the camp area.

After a wonderful week of camping, sailing, canoeing, and campfires disrupted only by some well-fed raccoons, we struck camp and canoed about half the way back. Our plan was to simply pull our canoes up on the beach and spread out our sleeping bags to sleep without pitching any tents. The next morning we would finish paddling to the launching ramp for the drive back home.

The dry area where we spread our sleeping bags was still well out of the forested region about 200 feet to our rear. The nearly full harvest yellow moon shone eerily through the high thin scattered layer of clouds. By 9:30 we were sound asleep.

To this day, I don't know what time it was that I was suddenly awake! I don't even remember that I felt as though something had awakened me—I was simply suddenly wide awake with a sense of fear and a pounding heart. All I could hear was the gentle lapping sound of the lake water striking the shore fifty feet away. My heart slowed and drowsiness returned. I almost fell asleep again, when I suddenly realized what had awakened me initially!

The most bloodcurdling, spine-chilling scream I had ever heard or even imagined happened again! My heart raced and pounded harder than it had ever done. I was truly petrified! That sound made me want to be so still and silent I tried to stop breathing. I was convinced that it was hopeless to try to outrun or outswim whatever "it" was that had made that sound!

After what seemed like an eternity, my heart slowed somewhat and my air hunger forced me to resume breathing. I contemplated the best manner of escape. I finally concluded I could sprint to the beach, push a canoe straight into the lake, and ride it like a surfboard until I could grab a paddle and make good my escape. As I wondered how I could get my fellow scouts to join me in this desperate attempt at survival, the scream like that of a lost soul happened again!

Again, my heart jumped pounding into my throat and my breathing stopped! Suddenly, our scoutmaster laughed!

Laughed!

How could he?

"Don't you guys know what that is?" he queried. Frankly we didn't, nor had we any wish to know, much less meet "it!"

He had realized that each of us was more terrified than the other lying very wide-awake desperately trying not to breathe.

"It's an owl," he said. To a man, the rest of us remained to be convinced. He continued, "The owls make that scream to startle the little animals so they will jump." What about us big animals?

"He will then spot them and fly down to capture them," he concluded.

Grabbing our flashlights we all began talking at once, as much to relieve fear as to exchange information. Our scoutmaster picked up several rocks, walked closer to the edge of the trees, and threw them into the forest to frighten off the owl. To our great relief, it worked.

We wakened shortly after daylight, the worse for wear with injured pride, and finished our expedition without incident.

Useful Information for Cooking Collards And Cornbread

Here's a short collection of assorted facts.

Equivalents

Measurements
> 3 teaspoons = 1 tablespoon
> 16 tablespoons = 1 cup
> 2 cups = 1 pint
> 4 quarts = 1 gallon
> 8 fluid ounces = 1 cup
> 16 ounces = 1 pound

Butter
> 1 pound = 2 cups
> 1 stick = ¼ pound = ½ cup = 8 tablespoons

Buttermilk
> 1 tablespoon vinegar plus milk to make 1 cup = substitute for 1 cup buttermilk

Cream Cheese
> 3 ounces = ⅓ cup

Cheese
> 1 cup = 4 ounces grated cheese

Garlic
> ⅛ teaspoon garlic powder = 1 clove garlic
> ½ teaspoon minced garlic = approximately 1 clove garlic

Eggs
> 1 egg = ¼ cup
> 1 egg white = 3 tablespoons
> 1 egg yolk = 1 tablespoon

Herbs
> 1 tablespoon fresh herbs = 1 teaspoon dried herbs

Lemon Juice
> Juice of 1 lemon = 2 or 3 tablespoons

Onions
> 1 medium onion = ½ cup chopped

Potatoes
> 1 medium potato = 1 cup diced or cubed

Recipe Index

About the Authors

Paul Elliott is a marketing consultant, living in Dallas and Louisiana. He has a son and a daughter in college. He specializes in the psychology of the target customer and teaches his clients to think like their customers. He is dedicated to the practice of testing everything. One of his fortes is copywriting. He designs marketing programs for online and offline businesses. Clients frequently seek his advice about website designs, marketing dilemmas, and business development. He has written a valuable book, *88 Marketing Tips That Will Change Your Life!*™, which can be obtained by visiting http://www.FractalMarketing.net.

Mary Cheatham has had careers as a high school English teacher and a registered nurse. Since childhood she has had a passion for writing. Using the penname, Jane Riley, she has published a novel, *Solomon's Porch,* available at http://www.Amazon.com and another story cookbook, *Flavored with Love,* now in its third edition. She has a variety of interests that she pursues with enthusiasm, such as spending time with her dogs, appearing on television cooking shows, and writing song lyrics. She enjoys marketing, editing, and cooking. She lives in Louisiana at her home for more than thirty years, and in Wisconsin near her daughter, a dairy nutritionist, and her son-in-law, a veterinarian.

If you do not own this book, go ahead and buy yourself a copy.

If you have purchased this book, congratulations! We know you will enjoy using it as much as we enjoyed preparing it.

Visit us at: http://www.FlavoredWithLove.com/cpgift and http://www.CollardLovers.com/cpgift to receive a bonus we have prepared for you.

We are joyful to share recipes from some incredibly talented cooks. For example . . .

- Dorothy Reinhold, who runs the test kitchen for Cut n Clean Greens, has been featured in *Sunset Magazine* and other food publications. We are delighted that this prize-winning food authority has shared some of her greatest collard recipes with us to publish in *The Collard Patch*.

- Jim Rooker; an outstanding south Louisiana chef, has contributed recipes by John Martin Terranova, his mentor, who is now deceased. John was lauded for his work as the executive chef of the Castle, an exquisite restaurant located in the old stables of historic Dunleith Plantation, Natchez, Mississippi.

- Carolyn Forche`, a well-known author, lecturer, editor, and writing coach, wrote the popular, highly acclaimed, and prize-winning children's book, *Colors Come From God ... Just Like Me!* She is sharing her favorite collard greens recipe and her favorite cornbread recipe.

We are excited about all the recipes shared with us in this cookbook. Like you, our families will treasure it for generations.

Many of the finest culinary artists we know consider collards a distinctive food—a medium with the properties needed to allow them to express their creativity.

If you like spinach, you will love collards! Spinach enjoys popularity as a food that is good alone or as the star of healthy and tasty dishes. Collard greens are gaining in popularity and are being used in a variety of ways. It is possible to use collards in most recipes the way you use spinach if you make minor changes in the preparation. Collards, which are more versatile than spinach, can be used in ways that spinach cannot.

The Collard Patch with its section "Growing Up in Collard Country" provides the perfect reading for your relaxation and entertainment at the end of a stressful day. The anecdotes about an innocent albeit impish childhood can be read individually; but since they are chronological events in Paul's life, they have continuity. You'll want to read and reread them.

Read these stories and go inside the mind of a boy becoming a man as he faces all manner of hilarious hardships, such as being sprayed by a skunk, dealing with his drunk cow, and being frightened by a screeching owl on a Boy Scout campout.

Also you will be inspired and blessed as you read all we are sharing with you. Even if you don't ever cook, you'll enjoy *The Collard Patch*.

This book features the most popular collard greens recipe in the world! Heart Health Recipes, 288 Big Pages, 214 Remarkable Recipes!

YES, Mary! (Cut out this order form and mail it.)
Please send me:

☐ *The Collard Patch* (newly released story/cookbook)

☐ *Flavored with Love, Mary Lou's Family and Friends Can Cook, Third Edition* (revised and expanded story/cookbook)

Name: (First)_____ (Last)_____

Mailing address:(Street)_____

(City)_____ (State)_____ (Zip)_____

Phone Number (if needed to check order):_____

I am enclosing:

☐ a check

☐ a money order

(To pay with a credit card, go to http://www.CollardLovers.com or http://www.FlavoredWithLove.com and make your purchase.)

Send the cookbook to:

☐ the address listed above **(We promise not to share your personal information with anyone.)**

OR (for gifts) to ☐ Name:

(First)_____ (Last)_____

Mailing address:(Street)_____

(City)_____ (State)_____ (Zip)_____

Here's my e-mail address so I can receive future special offers and announcements:_____

Order several! They make GREAT GIFTS
for friends, relatives, and special occasions!

The Collard Patch	$22.97	X __ (number of books)	$
Flavored with Love, Third Edition	$22.97	X __ (number of books)	$
U. S. Shipping and Handling	4.00	X __ (number of books)	$
Gift Wrapping + Gift Card	4.00	X __ (number of books)	$
Sales Tax (Louisiana Residents 8.5%)	1.95	X __ (number of books)	$
TOTAL	XX	XXXXX	$ _____

Mail order to: Blue Moon Books—Louisiana

207 N. Service Rd. E. #213

Ruston, LA 71270 Call us at 318-548-1716, if you have any questions.

Write Paul@CollardLovers.com or Mary@CollardLovers.com to receive a free gift you're sure to love.

285

Super Bargain!

Buy any 2 cookbooks for only $35.00 plus shipping and handling of $8.00 (and Louisiana tax, if you live in Louisiana).
This is a savings of $14.94!

—*The Collard Patch* (newly released story/cookbook) is all about collard greens—growing, cooking, and eating—and stories about growing up in Collard Country. **If you think you don't like collards, you haven't tasted *our* collards!**

—*Flavored with Love, Mary Lou's Family and Friends Can Cook, Third Edition* (revised and expanded story/cookbook) is a wonderful experience with recipes for some of the best food you'll ever put in your mouth and wonderful stories of life in the South. Imagine the delightful aromas wafting through your house as you enjoy the stories. **The earlier editions are completely sold out, and this one has many more recipes and wonderful stories!**

Order several! They make GREAT GIFTS
for friends, relatives, and special occasions!

☐ Mary, I can hardly wait for the delicious food and delightful stories! My check for $43.00 ($46.66 for Louisiana residents) is enclosed. **Please rush my order!**
BE SURE to put your address on the other side of this page.

Any Special Instructions?

For a **special free gift** visit us at: http://www.FlavoredWithLove.com/cpgift   and
http://www.CollardLovers.com/cpgift

(Give your friends a copy of this form.)

YES, Mary! (Cut out this order form and mail it.)

Please send me:

☐ *The Collard Patch* (newly released story/cookbook)

☐ *Flavored with Love, Mary Lou's Family and Friends Can Cook, Third Edition*
(revised and expanded story/cookbook)

Name: (First)_____ (Last)_____

Mailing address:(Street)_____

(City)_____ (State)_____ (Zip)_____

Phone Number (if needed to check order):_____

I am enclosing:

☐ a check

☐ a money order

(To pay with a credit card, go to http://www.CollardLovers.com or
http://www.FlavoredWithLove.com and make your purchase.)

Send the cookbook to:

☐ the address listed above   (We promise not to share your personal information with anyone.)

OR (for gifts) to ☐ Name:_____

(First)_____ (Last)_____

Mailing address:(Street)_____

(City)_____ (State)_____ (Zip)_____

**Here's my e-mail address so I can receive future special offers and
announcements:**_____

Order several! They make GREAT GIFTS
for friends, relatives, and special occasions!

The Collard Patch	$22.97	X ___ (number of books)	$
Flavored with Love, Third Edition	$22.97	X ___ (number of books)	$
U. S. Shipping and Handling	4.00	X ___ (number of books)	$
Gift Wrapping + Gift Card	4.00	X ___ (number of books)	$
Sales Tax (Louisiana Residents 8.5%)	1.95	X ___ (number of books)	$
TOTAL	XX	XXXXX	$ _____

Mail order to: Blue Moon Books—Louisiana

207 N. Service Rd. E. #213

Ruston, LA 71270 Call us at 318-548-1716, if you have any questions.

Write Paul@CollardLovers.com or Mary@CollardLovers.com to receive a free gift you're sure to love.

287

Super Bargain!

Buy any 2 cookbooks for only $35.00 plus shipping and handling of $8.00 (and Louisiana tax, if you live in Louisiana).

This is a savings of $14.94!

—*The Collard Patch* (newly released story/cookbook) is all about collard greens—growing, cooking, and eating—and stories about growing up in Collard Country. **If you think you don't like collards, you haven't tasted *our* collards!**

—*Flavored with Love, Mary Lou's Family and Friends Can Cook, Third Edition* (revised and expanded story/cookbook) is a wonderful experience with recipes for some of the best food you'll ever put in your mouth and wonderful stories of life in the South. Imagine the delightful aromas wafting through your house as you enjoy the stories. **The earlier editions are completely sold out, and this one has many more recipes and wonderful stories!**

Order several! They make GREAT GIFTS
for friends, relatives, and special occasions!

☐ Mary, I can hardly wait for the delicious food and delightful stories! My check for $43.00 ($46.66 for Louisiana residents) is enclosed. **Please rush my order!**

BE SURE to put your address on the other side of this page.

Any Special Instructions?

For a **special free gift** visit us at: http://www.FlavoredWithLove.com/cpgift and
http://www.CollardLovers.com/cpgif

olivia rodrigo
SOUR

ISBN 978-1-70514-577-7

Visit Hal Leonard Online at
www.halleonard.com

Contact us:
Hal Leonard
7777 West Bluemound Road
Milwaukee, WI 53213
Email: info@halleonard.com

In Europe, contact:
Hal Leonard Europe Limited
42 Wigmore Street
Marylebone, London, W1U 2RN
Email: info@halleonardeurope.com

In Australia, contact:
Hal Leonard Australia Pty. Ltd.
4 Lentara Court
Cheltenham, Victoria, 3192 Australia
Email: info@halleonard.com.au

contents

BRUTAL

Words and Music by OLIVIA RODRIGO
and DANIEL NIGRO

Sweetly

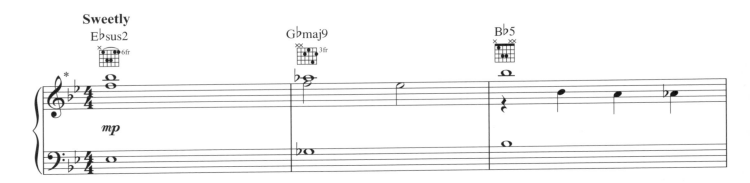

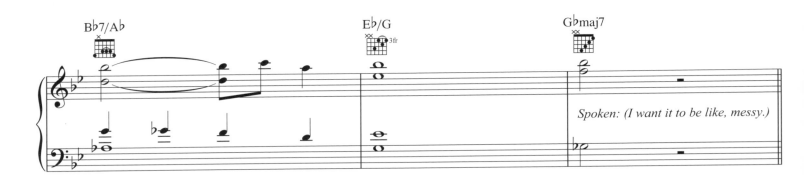

Spoken: (I want it to be like, messy.)

Moderate Rock

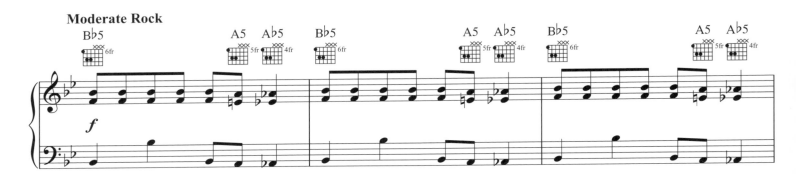

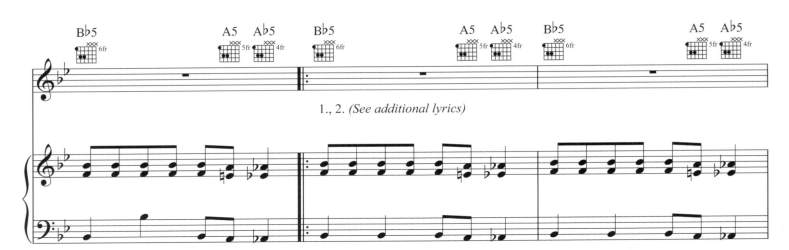

1., 2. (See additional lyrics)

* *Recorded a half step higher.*

E - go crush is so se - vere. God, it's bru-tal out here.

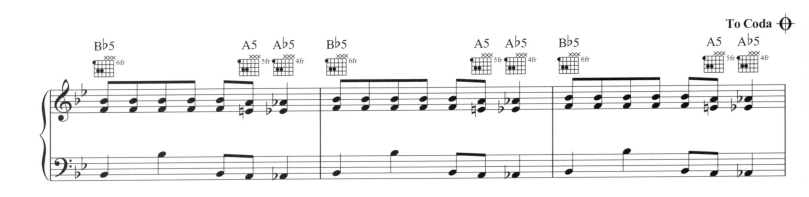

To Coda ⊕

3. *(See additional lyrics)*

D.S. al Coda

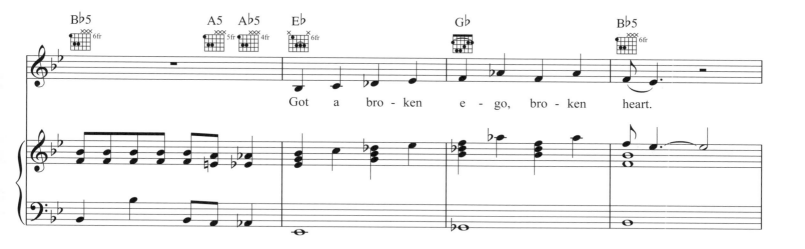

Got a bro-ken e - go, bro-ken heart.

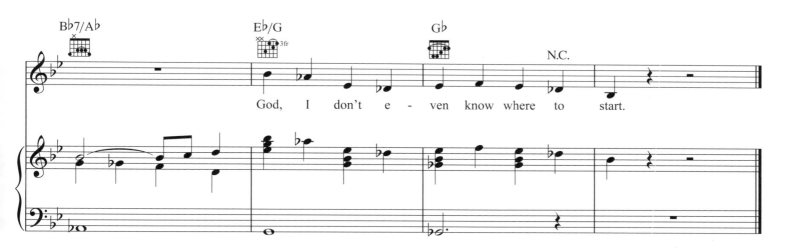

God, I don't e - ven know where to start.

Additional Lyrics

1. I'm so insecure, I think that I'll die before I drink.
   And I'm so caught up in the news of who likes me and who hates you.
   And I'm so tired that I might quit my job, start a new life.
   And they'd all be so disappointed 'cause who am I, if not exploited?

2. And I'm so sick of seventeen. Where's my fuckin' teenage dream?
   If someone tells me one more time, "Enjoy your youth," I'm gonna cry.
   And I don't stick up for myself, I'm anxious and nothing can help.
   And I wish I'd done this before. And I wish people liked me more.

3. I feel like no one wants me and I hate the way I'm perceived.
   I only have two real friends and lately, I'm a nervous wreck
   'Cause I love people I don't like. And I hate every song I write.
   And I'm not cool and I'm not smart and I can't even parallel park.

TRAITOR

Words and Music by OLIVIA RODRIGO
and DANIEL NIGRO

Moderate Waltz

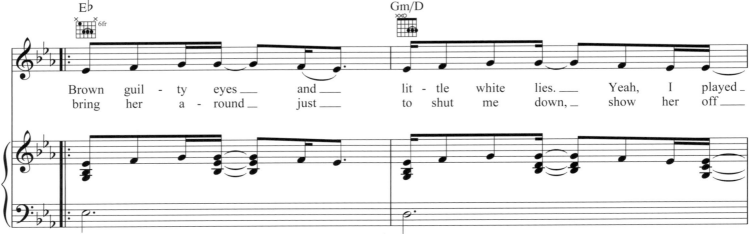

1 STEP FORWARD, 3 STEPS BACK

Words and Music by OLIVIA RODRIGO,
JACK ANTONOFF and TAYLOR SWIFT

Piano Ballad, freely

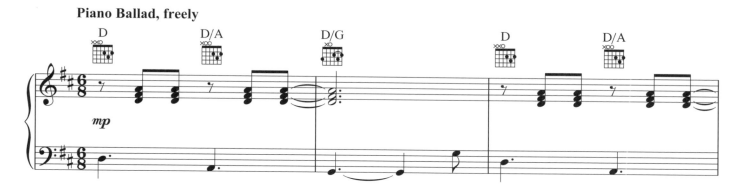

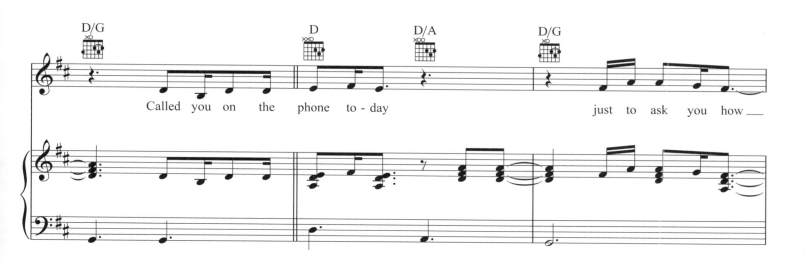

Called you on the phone to-day just to ask you how ___ you were.

___ you were. All I did was speak nor-mal-ly,

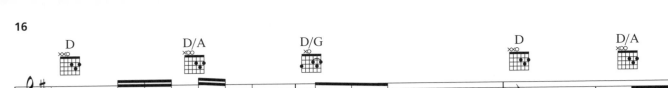

DRIVERS LICENSE

Words and Music by OLIVIA RODRIGO
and DANIEL NIGRO

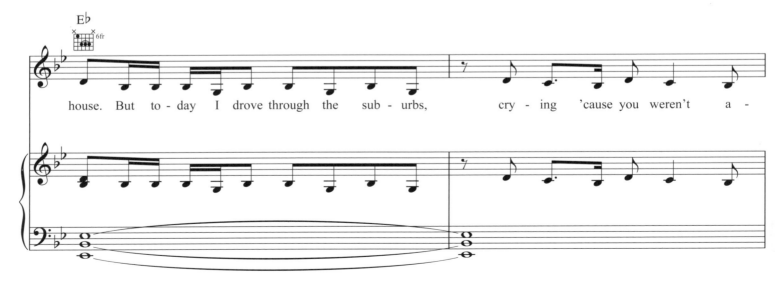

DEJA VU

Words and Music by OLIVIA RODRIGO
and DANIEL NIGRO

Car rides ___ to Mal-i-bu, ___ straw-ber-ry ice cream, one spoon for two, ___ and trad-ing jack- ets, laugh-ing 'bout how small it looks on you.

GOOD 4 U

Words and Music by OLIVIA RODRIGO
and DANIEL NIGRO

To Coda ⊕

CODA

Ah. _____

Ah. _____

Ah. _____

May - be I'm too e - mo - tion - al, ___ but your ap - a - thy's like a wound ___

floor of my __ bath-room. __ But you're so un-af-fect __-ed, I real-ly don't

get it, but I guess good for you. ___

Well, good for you, I guess you moved on real-ly eas-i-ly.

ENOUGH FOR YOU

Words and Music by
OLIVIA RODRIGO

JEALOUSY, JEALOUSY

Words and Music by OLIVIA RODRIGO,
DANIEL NIGRO and CASEY CATHLEEN SMITH

Recorded a half step lower.

FAVORITE CRIME

Words and Music by OLIVIA RODRIGO
and DANIEL NIGRO

HOPE UR OK

Words and Music by OLIVIA RODRIGO
and DANIEL NIGRO

Gentle Ballad

Knew a boy _ once when I was small, _ a tow-head blond with eyes _ of salt. _
My mid-dle school friend _ grew up a-lone, _ she raised her broth-ers on _ her own. _

_ He played the drum _ in the march-ing band. _
_ Her par-ents hat-ed who _ she loved. _

and I hope that you're _ o - kay. ___

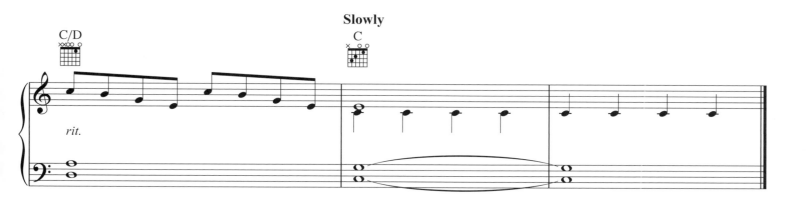

HAPPIER

Words and Music by
OLIVIA RODRIGO

Recorded a half step lower.